Business Ethics

Business Ethics

New Challenges for Business Schools and Corporate Leaders

Edited by

Robert A. Peterson
and O.C. Ferrell

M.E.Sharpe
Armonk, New York
London, England

Library of Congress Cataloging-in-Publication Data

Business ethics : new challenges for business schools and corporate leaders / edited by
Robert A. Peterson and O.C. Ferrell.
    p. cm.
Includes bibliographical references and index.
ISBN 0-7656-1458-8 (cloth : alk. paper)
   1. Business ethics—Congresses. I. Peterson, Robert A. (Robert Allen), 1944–
II. Ferrell, O.C.

HF5387.B8725 2004
174´.4—dc22   2004005153

Printed in the United States of America

The paper used in this publication meets the minimum requirements of
American National Standard for Information Sciences
Permanence of Paper for Printed Library Materials,
ANSI Z 39.48-1984.

BM (c) 10   9   8   7   6   5   4   3   2

To our families

Contents

Figures, Tables, and Appendix

Preface

Business Ethics: New Challenges for Business Schools and Corporate Leaders is the result of a unique symposium held in Denver, Colorado, in the fall of 2003. The symposium was unusual in several distinct ways. It represented a first-time collaborative effort by the School of Business at Colorado State University and the McCombs School of Business at The University of Texas at Austin. Moreover, it brought together, for the first time, internationally recognized business leaders, outstanding leaders of nonprofit organizations, and distinguished academics, including business professors, philosophers, and university administrators.

The symposium was also unique in that it addressed a wide variety of topics relating to ethics in the contexts of business practice and business education. The topics were approached from diverse and sometimes conflicting perspectives during two days of spirited panel discussions, individual presentations, and informal interactions.

Analogous to the symposium, this volume is unusual in that it is a compact resource containing new insights for leaders in business and educational organizations. As such, its purpose is to serve as a catalyst to stimulate thinking and research on ethical leadership and business ethics initiatives. More specifically, the volume captures and communicates the essence and excitement of the symposium. Consequently, the volume should be read at least twice, the first time for breadth and the second time for depth, to fully appreciate the scope and nuances of the contributions.

The thirteen chapters in the volume develop different perspectives for creating ethical leadership and establishing organizational ethics initiatives. Each chapter was specifically written for this volume and reflects critical feedback that was received from symposium participants. Consequently, each chapter has been "well-honed" to maximize its value. Most of the chapters pose issues and questions related to ethical decision making at individual, organizational, regulatory, and societal levels. Several of the authors crafted their contributions to be provocative and highlight perceived deficiencies in corporate America, business education, and even society. Such critical evaluations, whether focused on business or educational organizations, are constructive in that they force readers to confront the nature and importance of business ethics and provide challenges for future ethics leadership initiatives. Collectively, the contributions in this volume should provide business and educational organizations and their key stakeholders with new insights with which to develop and implement ethics leadership initiatives.

Acknowledgments

As with any endeavor, appreciation is due to a number of organizations and individuals. The symposium would not have taken place without the support and guidance of Colorado State University, The University of Texas at Austin, and the sponsors providing financial and logistical support. These sponsors include:

> *Business Ethics* magazine
> Cutco/Vector Marketing Corporation
> Deloitte and Touche
> Direct Selling Education Foundation
> EthicsPoint
> Houghton Mifflin Company
> IC² Institute (The University of Texas at Austin)
> Newmont Mining
> PricewaterhouseCoopers
> The Madhuri and Jagdish N. Sheth Foundation

Thanks are also due to the staff of the Center for Business Ethics and Social Issues at Colorado State University, particularly to Liza Hunn and Jan Morgan, and to Galen Bollinger and Dorothy Brady of the McCombs School of Business at The University of Texas at Austin. To all of the above—organizations, sponsors, and individuals alike—we express our heartfelt thanks.

Robert A. Peterson   O.C. Ferrell
McCombs School of Business   School of Business
The University of Texas at Austin   Colorado State University

Business Ethics

1

A Framework for Understanding Organizational Ethics

O.C. Ferrell

Organizational ethics is one of the most important, yet perhaps one of the most overlooked and misunderstood concepts in corporate America and schools of business. Organizational ethics initiatives have not been effectively implemented by many corporations, and there is still much debate concerning the usefulness of such initiatives in preventing ethical and legal misconduct. Simultaneously, business schools are attempting to teach courses and integrate organizational ethics into their curricula without general agreement about what should be taught or how it should be taught.

Societal norms require that businesses assume responsibility to ensure that ethical standards are properly implemented on a daily basis. Such a requirement is not without controversy. Some business leaders believe that personal moral development and character are all that is needed for effective organizational ethics. These business leaders are supported by certain business educators who believe that ethics initiatives should arise inherently from corporate culture and that hiring ethical employees will limit unethical behavior within the organization. A contrary position, and the one espoused here, is that effective organizational ethics can be achieved only when proactive leadership provides employees from diverse backgrounds with a common understanding of what is defined as ethical behavior through formal training, thus creating an ethical organizational climate. In addition, changes are needed in the regulatory system, in the organizational ethics initiatives of business schools, and in societal approaches to the development and implementation of organizational ethics in corporate America.

According to Richard L. Schmalensee, dean of the Sloan School of Management at Massachusetts Institute of Technology, the question is, "How can we produce graduates who are more conscious of their potential . . . and their obligation as professionals to make a positive contribution to society?" He states that business schools should be held partly responsible for a cadre of managers more focused on short-term gains to beat the market rather than on building lasting value for shareholders and society (Schmalensee 2003).

This introductory chapter provides an overview of the ethical decision-making process. It begins with a discussion of how ethical decisions are made in general and then offers a framework for understanding organizational ethics that is consistent with research, best practices, and regulatory developments. Using this framework, the chapter then discusses how ethical decisions are made in the context of an organization and poses some illustrative ethical issues that need to be addressed in organizational ethics.

Defining Organizational Ethics

Ethics has been termed the study and philosophy of human conduct, with an emphasis on the determination of right and wrong. For managers, ethics in the workplace refers to rules (standards, principles) governing the conduct of organization members. Most definitions of ethics relate rules to what is right or wrong in specific situations. For present purposes, and in simple terms, organizational ethics refers to generally accepted standards that guide behavior in business and other organizational contexts (LeClair, Ferrell, and Fraedrich 1998).[1]

One difference between an ordinary decision and an ethical one is that in an ethical decision accepted rules may not apply and the decision maker must weigh values in a situation that he or she may not have faced before. Another difference is the amount of emphasis placed on a person's values when making an ethical decision. Whether a specific behavior is judged right or wrong, ethical or unethical, is often determined by the mass media, interest groups, the legal system, and individuals' personal morals. While these groups are not necessarily "right," their judgments influence society's acceptance or rejection of an organization and its activities. Consequently, values and judgments play a critical role in ethical decision making, and society may institutionalize them through legislation and social sanctions or approval.

Individual versus Organization

Most people would agree that high ethical standards require both organizations and individuals to conform to sound moral principles. However, special factors must be considered when applying ethics to business organizations. First, to survive, businesses must obviously make a profit. Second, businesses must balance their desire for profits against the needs and desires of society. Maintaining this balance often requires compromises or trade-offs. To address these unique aspects of organizational ethics, society has developed rules—both explicit (legal) and implicit—to guide owners, managers, and employees in their efforts to earn profits in ways that do not harm individuals or society as a whole. Addressing organizational ethics must acknowledge its existence in a complex system that includes many stakeholders that cooperate, provide resources, often demand changes to encourage or discourage certain ethical conduct, and frequently question the balancing of business and social interests. Unfortunately, the ethical standards learned at home, in school, through religion, and in the community are not always adequate preparation for ethical pressures found in the workplace.

Organizational practices and policies often create pressures, opportunities, and incentives that may sway employees to make unethical decisions. We have all seen news articles describing some decent, hardworking family person who engaged in illegal or unethical activities. The *Wall Street Journal* (Pullman 2003) reported that Betty Vinson, a midlevel accountant for WorldCom Inc., was asked by her superiors to make false accounting entries. Vinson balked a number of times but then caved in to management and made illegal entries to bolster WorldCom's profits. At the end of eighteen months she had helped falsify at least $3.7 billion in profits. When an employee's livelihood is on the line, it is difficult to say no to a powerful boss. At the time this chapter was written, Vinson was awaiting sentencing on conspiracy and securities fraud and preparing her twelve-year-old daughter for the possibility that she will be incarcerated.

Importance of Understanding Organizational Ethics

Understanding organizational ethics is important in developing ethical leadership. An individual's personal values and moral philosophies are but one factor in decision-making processes involving potential legal and ethical problems. True, moral rules can be related to a variety of situations in life, and some people do not distinguish everyday ethical issues from those that occur on the job. Of concern, however, is the application of rules in a work environment.

Just being a good person and, in your own view, having sound personal ethics may not be sufficient to handle the ethical issues that arise in the workplace. It is important to recognize the relationship between legal and ethical decisions. While abstract virtues such as honesty, fairness, and openness are often assumed to be self-evident and accepted by all employees, a high level of personal, moral development may not prevent an individual from violating the law in an organizational context, where even experienced lawyers debate the exact meaning of the law. Some organizational ethics perspectives assume that ethics training is for people who have unacceptable personal moral development, but that is not necessarily the case. Because organizations consist of diverse individuals whose personal values should be respected, agreement regarding workplace ethics is as vital as other managerial decisions. For example, would an organization expect to achieve its strategic mission without communicating the mission to employees? Would a firm expect to implement a customer relationship management system without educating every employee on his or her role in the system? Workplace ethics needs to be treated similarly—with clear expectations as to what constitutes legal and ethical conduct.

Employees with only limited work experience sometimes find themselves making decisions about product quality, advertising, pricing, hiring practices, and pollution control. The values that they bring to the organization may not provide specific guidelines for these complex decisions, especially when the realities of work objectives, group decision making, and legal issues come into play. Many ethics decisions are close calls. Years of experience in a particular industry may be required to know what is acceptable and what is not acceptable.

Even experienced managers need formal training about workplace ethics to help them identify legal and ethical issues. Changing regulatory requirements and ethical concerns, such as workplace privacy issues, make the ethical decision-making process very dynamic. With the establishment of values and training, a manager will be in a better position to assist employees and provide ethical leadership.

Understanding Ethical Decision Making

It is helpful to consider the question of why and how people make ethical decisions. Typically it is assumed that people make difficult decisions within an organization in the same way they resolve difficult issues in their personal lives. Within the context of organizations, however, few managers or employees have the freedom to decide ethical issues independently of workplace pressures. Philosophers, social scientists, and various academics have attempted to explain the ethical decision-making process in organizations by examining pressures such as the influence of coworkers and organizational culture, and individual-level factors such as personal moral philosophy.

Figure 1.1 presents a model of decision making. This model synthesizes current knowledge of ethical decision making in the workplace within a frame-

Figure 1.1 **A Framework for Understanding Ethical Decision Making in the Workplace**

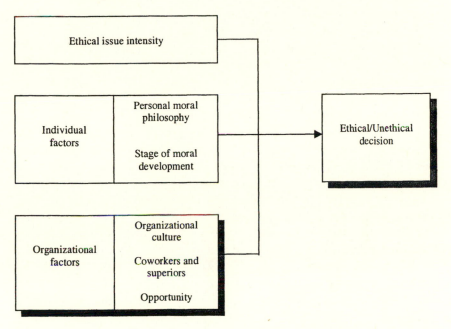

work that has strong support in the literature (e.g., Ferrell and Gresham 1985; Ferrell, Gresham, and Fraedrich 1989; Hunt and Vitell 1986; Jones 1991; Trevino 1986). The model shows that the perceived intensity of ethical and legal issues, individual factors (e.g., moral development and personal moral philosophy), and organizational factors (e.g., organizational culture and coworkers) collectively influence whether a person will make an unethical decision at work. While it is impossible to describe precisely how or why an individual or work group might make such a decision, it is possible to generalize about average or typical behavior patterns within organizations. Each of the model's components is briefly described below; note that the model is practical because it describes the elements of the decision-making process over which organizations have some control.

Ethical Issue Intensity

One of the first factors to influence the decision-making process is how important or relevant a decision maker perceives an issue to be—that is, the intensity of the issue (Jones 1991). The intensity of a particular issue is likely to vary over time and among individuals and is influenced by the values,

beliefs, needs, and perceptions of the decision maker, the special characteristics of the situation, and the personal pressures weighing on the decision.
All of the factors explored in this chapter, including personal moral development and philosophy, organizational culture, and coworkers, determine why
different people perceive issues with varying intensity (Robin, Reidenbach,
and Forrest 1996). Unless individuals in an organization share some common concerns about specific ethical issues, the stage is set for conflict. Ethical issue intensity, which reflects the sensitivity of the individual, work group,
or organization, triggers the ethical decision-making process.

Management can influence ethical issue intensity through rewards and
punishments, codes of conduct, and organizational values. In other words,
managers can affect the perceived importance of ethical issues through positive and negative incentives (Robin, Reidenbach, and Forrest 1996). If management fails to identify and educate employees about problem areas, these
issues may not reach the critical awareness level of some employees. New
employees who lack experience in a particular industry, for example, may
have trouble identifying both ethical and legal issues. Employees therefore
need to be trained as to how the organization wants specific ethical issues
handled. Identifying ethical issues that employees might encounter is a significant step in developing employees' ability to make decisions that enhance organizational ethics.

New federal regulations that hold both organizations and their employees
responsible for misconduct require organizations to assess areas of ethical and
legal risk. Based on both the 2002 Sarbanes-Oxley Act and the United States
Sentencing Commission guidelines, these strong directives encourage ethical
leadership. If ethical leadership fails, especially in corporate governance, there
are significant penalties. When organizations communicate to employees that
certain issues are important, the intensity of the issues is elevated. The more
employees appreciate the importance of an issue, the less likely they are to
engage in questionable behavior associated with the issue. Therefore, ethical
issue intensity should be considered a key factor in the decision-making process because there are many opportunities for an organization to influence
and educate employees on the importance of high-risk issues.

Under the Sarbanes-Oxley Act, boards of directors are required to provide
oversight for all auditing activities and are responsible for developing ethical
leadership. In addition, court decisions related to the Federal Sentencing
Guidelines for Organizations hold board members responsible for the ethical
and legal compliance programs of the firms they oversee. New rules and
regulations associated with Sarbanes-Oxley require that boards include members who are knowledgeable and qualified to oversee accounting and other
types of audits to ensure that these reports are accurate and include all infor-

mation material to ethics issues. A board's financial audit committee is required to implement codes of ethics for top financial officers. Many of the codes relate to corporate governance, such as compensation, stock options, and conflicts of interest.

Individual Factors

One of the greatest challenges facing the study of organizational ethics involves the role of individuals and their values. Although most of us would like to place the primary responsibility for decisions with individuals, years of research point to the primacy of organizational factors in determining ethics at work (e.g., Ferrell and Gresham 1985). However, individual factors are obviously important in the evaluation and resolution of ethical issues. Two significant factors in workplace integrity are an individual's personal moral philosophy and stage of moral development.

Personal Moral Philosophy

Ethical conflict occurs when people encounter situations that they cannot easily control or resolve. In such situations, people tend to base their decisions on their own principles of right or wrong and act accordingly in their daily lives. Moral philosophies—the principles or rules that individuals use to decide what is right or wrong—are often cited to justify decisions or explain behavior. People learn these principles and rules through socialization by family members, social groups, religion, and formal education.

There is no universal agreement on the correct moral philosophy to use in resolving ethical and legal issues in the workplace. Moreover, research suggests that employees may apply different moral philosophies in different decision situations (Fraedrich and Ferrell 1992); and, depending on the situation, people may even change their value structure or moral philosophy when making decisions. Individuals make decisions under pressure and may later feel their decisions were less than acceptable, but they may not be able to change the consequences of their decisions.

Stage of Moral Development

One reason people may change their moral philosophy has been proposed by Lawrence Kohlberg, who suggested that people progress through stages in their development of moral reasoning. Kohlberg contended that different people make different decisions when confronted with similar ethical situations because they are at different stages of what he termed cognitive moral development (Kohlberg 1969). He believed that people progress through the following three stages:

- The preconventional stage of moral development, in which individuals focus on their own needs and desires;
- The conventional stage of moral development, in which individuals focus on group-centered values and conforming to expectations;
- The principled stage of moral development, in which individuals are concerned with upholding the basic rights, values, and rules of society.

Obviously there is some overlap among these stages, so cognitive moral development should probably be viewed as a continuum rather than a series of discrete stages. Although Kohlberg did not specifically apply his theory of cognitive moral development to organizations, its application helps in explaining how employees may reason when confronted with an ethical dilemma. Kohlberg's theory suggests that people may change their moral beliefs and behavior as they gain education and experience in resolving conflicts, which in turn accelerates their moral development.

Can moral philosophy and moral development predict ethical behavior in businesses and other organizations? Fraedrich and Ferrell (1992) found that only 15 percent of a sample of businesspersons maintained the same moral philosophy across both work and nonwork ethical decision-making situations. One explanation may be that cognitive moral development issues that relate to a person's nonwork (e.g., home, family) experiences are not the most significant factors in resolving ethical issues within an organization. The ethics and values of an individual's immediate work group, rather than his or her moral development, may be the most important consideration in determining ethical conduct in organizations.

Nevertheless, most experts agree that a person's stage of moral development and personal moral philosophy play a role in how values and actions are shaped in the workplace. This may be especially true for top managers, who usually set the formal values of an organization. However, the informal use of these values and expectations plays a major role in the daily decisions that employees make. Many of these informal rules contribute to the organization's ethical climate.

Former Tyco International CEO Dennis Kozlowski, who set the leadership tone at his company, stood trial for allegedly taking $600 million in unauthorized bonuses, loans, stock sales, and other payments from the company. During his trial, the court wanted to know what the board of directors was doing while Kozlowski furnished his luxury Manhattan duplex with millions of dollars in rugs, china, and bookcases and spent $1 million for his wife's birthday party—all billed to the company. Kozlowski's personal ethics were on trial, but his ethical leadership influenced everyone in the organization (McCoy 2003).

Organizational Factors

Although individuals must make ethical and legal decisions at work, they often make these decisions in committees and group meetings and through discussions with colleagues. Decisions in the workplace are guided by an organization's culture and the influence of others—coworkers, supervisors, and subordinates.

Organizational Culture

Organizations, like societies, have cultures that include a shared set of values, beliefs, goals, norms, and ways to solve problems. As time passes, an organization comes to be seen as a living organism, with a mind and will of its own. Although most organizational cultures reinforce ethics, some organizations, like Tyco, create a culture that supports unethical decisions. If a company derives most of its profits from unethical or illegal activities, individuals who join this organization will have a difficult time surviving unless they too participate in these activities.

For example, even though Enron had a code of ethics and was a member of the Better Business Bureau, the company was devastated by unethical activities and corporate scandal. According to Lynn Brewer, former Enron executive and coauthor of *House of Cards: Confessions of an Enron Executive,* (Brewer and Hanson 2002), many Enron managers and employees knew the company was involved in illegal and unethical activities. Many executives and board members at Enron did not understand how organizational ethical decisions are made and how to develop an ethical corporate climate. They did not realize that top executives and boards of directors must provide ethical leadership and a system to resolve ethical issues. In the case of Enron, managers eventually paid for these ethical lapses through fines and imprisonment.

The ethical climate of an organization is a significant element of organizational culture. Whereas an organization's overall culture establishes ideals that guide a wide range of member behaviors, the ethical climate focuses specifically on issues of right and wrong. The ethical climate of an organization is its character or conscience. Codes of conduct and ethics policies, top management's actions on ethical issues, the values and moral development and personal moral philosophies of coworkers, and the opportunity for misconduct all contribute to an organization's ethical climate. In fact, the ethical climate actually determines whether certain issues and decisions are perceived as having an ethical component.

Organizations can manage their culture and ethical climate by trying to hire employees whose values match their own. Some organizations even measure potential employees' values during the hiring process and strive to hire individuals who fit within the ethical climate rather than those whose beliefs and values differ significantly.

As previously mentioned, some business leaders believe that hiring or promoting ethical managers will automatically produce an ethical organizational climate. However, individuals may have limited opportunity to apply their own personal ethics to management systems and decision making that occurs in the organization. Ethical leadership requires understanding best practices for organizational ethical compliance and a commitment to build an ethical climate. Over time, an organization's failure to monitor or manage its culture may foster questionable behavior. Sometimes entire industries develop a culture of preferential treatment and self-centered greed. The once conservative mutual fund industry found itself in a major scandal in 2003 after allowing large customers to engage in short-term and after-hours trading, in violation of their own organizations' rules. The mutual fund organizations gave hedge fund customers the right to make frequent trades in and out of funds, a practice not accorded ordinary investors. Firms such as Janus, Alliance Capital, and Pilgrim violated their own rules and now face legal actions. Another example of an unethical industry culture is reflected in New York attorney general Eliot Spitzer's settlement in which ten major Wall Street firms were collectively fined a total of $1.4 billion because their investment bankers had exerted undue influence on securities research to enhance relationships with their investment banking customers (*Business Week* 2004). Small investors were the victims of these unethical and illegal cultures of preferential relationships with certain customers.

The Influence of Coworkers and Supervisors

Just as employees look for certain types of employers, they are also particular about the people with whom they work. Managers and coworkers within an organization help people deal with unfamiliar tasks and provide advice and information daily in both formal and informal contexts. Managers provide direction regarding workplace activities to be performed. Coworkers offer help in the form of discussions over lunch or when a supervisor is absent. In fact, one often hears new or younger employees expressing fear about approaching "the boss" on a tough ethical issue. Thus, the role of informal culture cannot be underestimated. Numerous studies (e.g., Ferrell and

Gresham 1985) confirm that coworkers and supervisors have more impact on an employee's daily decisions than any other factor.

In a work group environment, employees may be subject to the phenomenon of groupthink, going along with group decisions even when those decisions run counter to their own values. They may take refuge in the notion of "safety in numbers," when everyone else appears to back a particular decision. Indeed, coworker peers can even change a person's original value system. This value change, whether temporary or permanent, is likely to be greater when a coworker is a supervisor, especially if the decision maker is new to the organization. Employees may also resolve workplace issues by unquestionably following a supervisor's instructions even when the instructions conflict with the employee's personal values.

Supervisors can also have a negative effect on conduct by setting a bad example or failing to supervise subordinates. ClearOne Communications Inc. relieved its CEO and CFO of their respective responsibilities after they were named as defendants in a complaint by the Securities and Exchange Commission (Wetzel 2003). A civil complaint alleged that they directed sales personnel to push extra products to customers beyond their orders to inflate sales and earnings. Eliminating such unethical managers within an organization can improve its overall ethical conduct. In this case, it was alleged that the CEO and CFO not only directed unethical actions but also contributed to an unethical corporate climate.

Finally, it should be mentioned in passing that individuals also learn ethical or unethical conduct from close colleagues and others with whom they interact regularly. Consequently, a decision maker who associates with others who behave unethically will be more likely to behave unethically as well.

Opportunity

Together, organizational culture and the influence of coworkers may foster conditions that limit or permit misconduct. When these conditions provide rewards of financial gain, recognition, promotion, or simply the good feeling from a job well done, the opportunity for unethical conduct may be encouraged or discouraged. For example, a company policy that does not provide for punishment of employees who violate a rule (e.g., not to accept large gifts from clients) provides an opportunity for unethical behavior.

Bellizzi and Hasty (2003) found a general tendency to discipline top sales performers more leniently than poor sales performers for engaging in identical forms of unethical selling behavior. Neither a company policy stating that the behavior in question was unacceptable nor a repeated pattern of unethical behavior offset the general tendency to favor the top sales performers. A superior sales record appears to induce more lenient forms of discipline despite managerial actions that are specifically instituted to produce more equal forms of discipline. Based on their research, Bellizzi and Hasty concluded that an opportunity exists for top sales performers to be more unethical than poor sales performers.

Opportunity usually relates to employees' immediate work situation— where they work, with whom they work, and the nature of the work. The specific work situation includes the motivational carrots and sticks that supervisors can use to influence employee behavior. Organizations can improve the likelihood of compliance with ethics policies by eliminating opportunities to engage in misconduct through the establishment and aggressive enforcement of formal codes and rules. Clearly, in the top sales performer example, the codes and rules were not adequately implemented.

One important conclusion that should be drawn from the framework presented here is that ethical decision making within an organization does not depend solely on individuals' personal values and moral philosophies. Employees do not operate in a vacuum, and their decisions are strongly affected by the culture and ethical climate of the organization in which they work— the pressures to perform their jobs, the examples set by their supervisors and peers, and the opportunities created by the presence or absence of ethics-related policies. As organizations take on an ethical climate of their own, they have a significant influence on ethics among employees and within their industry and community.

Ethical Issues

This section briefly describes three highly visible ethical issues facing corporate America. These issues have been associated with the major ethical scandals of the early twenty-first century.[2] The issues are presented to provide concrete examples of the types of misconduct that should be identified and prevented through organizational ethics programs and ethical leadership. An ethical decision is a problem situation requiring an organization or individual to choose among several actions that must be evaluated as right or wrong, ethical or unethical.

Conflict of Interest

A conflict of interest exists when individuals must choose whether to advance their own interests, the interests of their organization, or the interests of some other group or individual. An illustrative alleged conflict of interest occurred when Citigroup made a $1 million donation to the 92nd Street YMCA nursery school in Manhattan as an alleged quid pro quo so that financial analyst Jack Grubman's children could attend the exclusive school. Grubman, an analyst for Salomon Smith Barney, supposedly upgraded his rating for AT&T stock to help Sanford Weill, CEO of Citigroup, the parent company of Salomon Smith Barney, in a power struggle. Weill subsequently agreed to use his influence with the nursery school to gain admission for Grubman's children. Although Grubman denied elevating his rating for AT&T to gain his children's admission, they were in fact enrolled (Nelson and Cohen 2002). To avoid conflicts of interest, employees must be able to separate their private interests from their business dealings.

Likewise, organizations must avoid conflicts of interest when providing goods and services. Arthur Andersen served as the outside auditor for Waste Management Inc. while simultaneously providing consulting services to the firm. This led the Securities and Exchange Commission to investigate charges that the consulting fees obtained by Andersen may have compromised the independence of its financial audits. Andersen eventually paid $7 million to settle the charges. It later paid $100 million to settle a lawsuit brought by Waste Management shareholders. Within a year, Andersen found itself stuck in a pattern, paying out millions of dollars to settle similar federal charges and shareholder lawsuits relating to accounting irregularities at Sunbeam, Qwest Communications, WorldCom, Enron, Global Crossing, and many other organizations (Byrne 2002b).

In most developed countries, it is generally recognized that employees should not accept bribes, personal payments, gifts, or special favors from people or organizations that hope to influence the outcome of a decision. However, bribery is an accepted way of doing business in many countries. Summerour (2000) estimated that $80 billion is paid out worldwide in bribes or other payoffs every year. It has been estimated that four out of ten companies lost business in the last five years because a competitor paid a bribe. American companies were ranked fifth, behind Canada, Germany, Netherlands, and the United Kingdom in complying with anticorruption laws (Miller 2002). Bribes also have been associated with the downfall of many managers, legislators, and government officials.

Fraud

When individuals engage in deceptive practices to advance their own interests over those of their organization or some other group, charges of fraud may result. In general, fraud is any false communication that deceives, manipulates, or conceals facts to create a false impression. Fraud is considered a crime, and conviction may result in fines, imprisonment, or both. According to Neese, Ferrell, and Ferrell (forthcoming), fraud costs U.S. organizations more than $600 billion per year; the average company loses about 6 percent of total revenue to fraud and abuses committed by its own employees. The most common fraudulent activities reported by employees about their coworkers are stealing office supplies and shoplifting, claiming to have worked extra hours, and stealing money or products.

The accounting profession has changed dramatically over the last decade. The profession used to have a clublike mentality, and people who became certified public accountants (CPAs) were not concerned about competition. Until 2002 the profession regulated itself. At that time the Sarbanes-Oxley Act placed regulation of public accounting firms under the Securities and Exchange Commission. In recent years, consolidation in the industry increased competition and put pressures on accountants to increase the billable time spent with clients, reduce client fees, and surcome to client requests for altered opinions concerning financial conditions or lower tax payments.

Accounting firms have a responsibility to report a true and accurate picture of the financial condition of their clients. Failure to do so may result in charges and fines for both the accounting firm and the client. Scrutiny of financial reporting increased dramatically in the wake of the accounting scandals in the first years of the twenty-first century. As a result of the negative publicity surrounding the allegations of accounting fraud at a number of companies, many firms were forced to take a second look at their financial documents. In 2002, a record 330 companies chose to restate their earnings to avoid being drawn into the scandal.

Communications that are false or misleading can destroy stakeholders' trust in an organization and may at times even be considered fraudulent. False and misleading advertising is increasingly a key issue in organizational communications. Abuses in advertising can range from exaggerated claims and concealed facts to outright lying. Such abuses range from the unethical, which they clearly are, to the illegal.

Discrimination

Another important organizational ethics issue is discrimination. Once dominated by white males, the U.S. workforce currently includes significantly more females, African-Americans, Hispanics, and other minorities, as well as disabled and older workers. Within the next fifty years, Hispanics will make up 24 percent of the population, whereas African-Americans will make up 15 percent and Asians and Pacific Islanders 9 percent. These groups have traditionally faced discrimination and high unemployment rates and have been denied opportunities to assume leadership roles in corporate America.

Despite nearly forty years of legislation to outlaw it, discrimination remains a significant ethical issue in organizations. The most important legislation is Title VII of the Civil Rights Act of 1964, which prohibits employment discrimination on the basis of race, national origin, color, religion, or gender. This legislation is fundamental to employees' rights to join and advance in an organization according to merit alone.

Need to Discover Ethical Issues

Pressure for ethics audits to discover ethical issues should come from top managers who are looking for ways to track and improve ethical performance. Additionally, under the Sarbanes-Oxley Act, CEOs and CFOs may be criminally prosecuted if they knowingly certify misleading financial statements. Thus, they may request an ethics audit as a tool to improve their confidence in their firm's reporting processes. Some companies have established a high-level ethics office in conjunction with an ethics program, and the ethics officer may campaign for an ethics audit as a way to measure the effectiveness of the firm's ethics program. Regardless of where the impetus for an audit comes from, its success hinges on the full support of top management, particularly the CEO and the board of directors. Without this support, ethical leadership will not be a part of the corporate culture. Hopefully, the framework presented here will, among other things, provide insights and guidelines for establishing and maintaining this ethical leadership.

Notes

1. Some of the material in this section has been adapted from LeClair, Ferrell, and Fraedrich (1998), with the permission of O'Collins Corporation.
2. These ethical issues were adapted from McAlister, Ferrell, and Ferrell (forthcoming).

2

Personal Moral Codes and the Hunt-Vitell Theory of Ethics

Why Do People's Ethical Judgments Differ?

Shelby D. Hunt and Scott J. Vitell

People's ethical judgments differ. Why? Examples can be found in realms as diverse as the accounting profession, intellectual property rights, advertising, personal selling, and university admissions. Why did some partners at PricewaterhouseCoopers believe it was ethically *right* to charge clients the gross ticket price on travel expenses, thus pocketing "back end" travel rebates, while other partners believed it *wrong* to do so (Weil 2003, C1)? Why do some people believe it is ethically *right* to download copyrighted music, while others believe it is *wrong*? Why do some people believe it is *right* to advertise products targeting children, while others believe it is *wrong*? Why do some people believe that providing gifts to purchasing agents is *right*, while others believe it is *wrong*? Why do some people believe it is *right* to consider race and ethnicity in university admissions policies, while others believe it is *wrong*?

The simple answer to these questions is that people's ethical judgments differ because of differing personal moral codes. However, this answer prompts one to ask: What are the components of personal moral codes, and why do such codes differ? As a contribution to our knowledge of ethical decision making, this chapter uses a particular theory of ethics, the Hunt-Vitell theory of ethics, to model the process of ethical decision making, explicate the construct of "personal moral code," and, therefore, provide a framework for answering the "why" questions in the first paragraph.

The chapter is structured as follows. First, we provide a brief overview of the theory underlying the Hunt-Vitell model. Next, we discuss empirical tests of the theory. The theory is then used to show how "why" questions in ethics can be understood. We conclude by examining the utility maximization concept in neoclassical economics and showing how the Hunt-Vitell model can contribute to our understanding of this concept.

Overview of the Hunt-Vitell Model

The purpose of the original *Journal of Macromarketing* article that developed the Hunt-Vitell (hereafter, H-V) theory was to provide a general model of ethical decision making that would draw on both the deontological and teleological ethical traditions in moral philosophy (Hunt and Vitell 1986). Deontologists believe that "certain features of the act itself other than the *value* it brings into existence" make an action or rule *right* (Frankena 1963, 14). Teleologists, on the other hand, "believe that there is one and only one basic or ultimate right-making characteristic, namely, the comparative value (nonmoral) of what is, probably will be, or is intended to be brought into being" (Frankena 1963, 14). Since its original development, the H-V model has undergone extensive empirical testing by numerous scholars. As a result of the testing, as well as the comments of various scholars on the theory, the model underwent a modest revision in 1993 (Hunt and Vitell 1993). The discussion here follows the analysis in the revised model.

The H-V model, displayed in Figure 2.1, addresses the situation wherein an individual confronts a problem perceived as having ethical content. This perception of an ethical problem situation triggers the process depicted by the model. If the individual does not perceive some ethical content in a problem situation, subsequent elements of the model do not come into play.

Given that an individual perceives a situation as having ethical content, the next step is the perception of various possible alternatives or actions that might be followed to resolve the ethical problem. It is unlikely that an individual will recognize the complete set of possible alternatives. Therefore, the evoked set of alternatives will be less than the universe. Indeed, ultimate differences in behaviors among individuals in situations that have ethical content may be traced, in part, to differences in their sets of perceived alternatives.

Once the individual perceives the evoked set of alternatives, two kinds of evaluations will take place, a deontological evaluation and a teleological evaluation. In the deontological evaluation, the individual evaluates the inherent rightness or wrongness of the behaviors implied by each alternative. The process involves comparing each alternative's behaviors with a set of predetermined deontological norms. These norms represent personal values or rules of moral behavior. They range from general beliefs about such things as

Figure 2.1   **Hunt-Vitell Theory of Ethics**

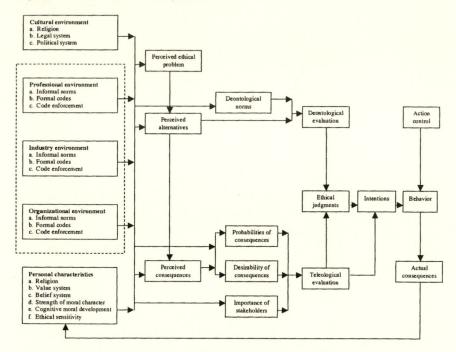

Source: Hunt and Vitell (1986, 1993). Copyright © 1991 by Shelby D. Hunt and Scott J. Vitell.

Note: The portion of the model outside the dashed lines constitutes the general theory. The portion inside the dashed lines individuates the general model for professional and managerial contexts.

honesty, stealing, cheating, and treating people fairly to issue-specific beliefs about such things as deceptive advertising, product safety, sales kickbacks, confidentiality of data, respondent anonymity, and interviewer dishonesty. The norms take the form of beliefs of the following kinds: "It is always right to . . ."; "it is generally or usually right to . . ."; "it is always wrong to . . ."; and "it is generally or usually wrong to. . . ."

In the teleological evaluation process, four constructs are paramount: (1) the perceived consequences of each alternative for various stakeholder groups, (2) the probability that each consequence will occur to each stakeholder group, (3) the desirability or undesirability of each consequence, and (4) the importance of each stakeholder group. Both the identity and importance of the stakeholder groups will vary across individuals and situations. For example, the stakeholders may (or may not) include one's self, family, friends, customers, stockholders, suppliers, or employees.

Although the H-V model proposes that the desirability and probability of consequences, as well as the importance of stakeholders, influence the teleological evaluation process, no specific information-processing rule (such as a lexicographic process) is postulated. Indeed, the model proposes that the information-processing rules will differ across different people's personal moral codes. The overall result of the teleological evaluation will be beliefs about the relative goodness versus badness brought about by each alternative, as perceived by the decision maker. One interpretation of the teleological evaluation (TE) process for an alternative K, with regard to stakeholders $1, 2, 3, \ldots m$, who have differing importance weights (IW), is:

$$TE_K = \sum_{n=1}^{n=m} [IW_1 \times \text{PosCon}_1 \times P_{\text{Pos}}] - [IW_1 \times \text{NegCon}_1 \times P_{\text{Neg}}]$$
$$+ [IW_2 \times \text{PosCon}_2 \times P_{\text{Pos}}] - [IW_2 \times \text{NegCon}_2 \times P_{\text{Neg}}] + \ldots$$

In this formula,

$$
\begin{aligned}
IW_1 &= \text{importance of stakeholder 1} \\
\text{PosCon}_1 &= \text{positive consequences on stakeholder 1} \\
\text{NegCon}_1 &= \text{negative consequences on stakeholder 1} \\
P_{\text{Pos}} &= \text{probability of positive consequences occurring} \\
P_{\text{Neg}} &= \text{probability of negative consequences occurring}
\end{aligned}
$$

The core of the model comes next. The H-V model posits that an individual's ethical judgments (for example, the belief that a particular alternative is the most ethical alternative) are a function of the individual's deontological evaluation (i.e., applying norms of behavior to each of the alternatives) and the individual's teleological evaluation (i.e., an evaluation of the sum total of goodness versus badness likely to be provided by each alternative for all relevant stakeholders). That is, $EJ = f(DE, TE)$, where EJ is ethical judgments, DE is deontological evaluation, and TE is teleological evaluation. It is possible that *some* individuals in *some* situations will be strict (e.g., "Kantian") deontologists and, therefore, will completely ignore the consequences of alternative actions (i.e., $TE = $ zero). However, the theory maintains that it is unlikely that such a result would be found across many individuals for many different situations. Similarly, although it is possible that some individuals in some situations might be strict (e.g., "utilitarian") teleologists (i.e., $DE = $ zero), such a situation is unlikely across many individuals for many situations.

Consistent with general theories in consumer behavior (e.g., Engel,

Blackwell, and Kollat 1978; Howard and Sheth 1969) and the Fishbein and Ajzen (1975) model, the H-V model posits that ethical judgments impact behavior through the intervening variable of intentions. Like Petty and Cacioppo (1986), the H-V model proposes that both ethical judgments and intentions should be better predictors of behavior in situations where the ethical issues are central rather than peripheral. Supporting this view, research by Newstrom and Ruch (1975) found the ethical beliefs of a group of managers to be highly congruent with their claimed frequency of behavior.

The H-V model proposes that ethical judgments will sometimes differ from intentions because *TE* also independently affects intentions. That is, although an individual may perceive a particular alternative as the most ethical alternative, he or she may intend to choose another alternative because of certain preferred consequences (e.g., there might be significant positive consequences to oneself as a result of choosing the less ethical alternative). The theory suggests that when behavior and intentions are inconsistent with ethical judgments, one of the consequences will be feelings of guilt. Therefore, two individuals, *A* and *B*, may engage in the same behavior, but only *A* may feel guilty because *B*'s behavior was consistent with his or her ethical beliefs.

What is called "action control" in the model is the extent to which an individual actually exerts control in the enactment of an intention in a particular situation (Ajzen 1985; Tubbs and Ekeberg 1991). That is, situational constraints may result in behaviors that are inconsistent with intentions and ethical judgments. One such situational constraint may be the opportunity to adopt a particular alternative. Zey-Ferrell, Weaver, and Ferrell (1979) empirically documented the influence of opportunity on behavior in situations having ethical content. Similarly, Mayer (1970) identified opportunity as one of the three conditions impinging on ethical behavior.

Following behavior, there will be an evaluation of the actual consequences of the alternative selected. This is the major learning construct in the model. These actual consequences provide feedback to the construct labeled "personal characteristics." Hegarty and Sims (1978) examined whether a system of perceived rewards and punishments could change behaviors in a situation involving ethical content. They concluded that "the results lend support to the notion that many individuals can be conditioned (i.e., can 'learn') to behave unethically under appropriate contingencies" (456).

The H-V model identifies several personal characteristics that might influence the decision-making process. Unquestionably, an individual's personal religion influences ethical decision making. A priori, one might suspect that highly religious people, compared with nonreligious people, would have more clearly defined deontological norms and that such norms would play a stronger role in ethical judgments. Wilkes, Burnett, and Howell (1986) explored the meaning and measurement of "religiosity" in consumer research. The measures of religiosity that they developed would seem to be appropriate for exploring the extent to which strength of religious belief per se results in different decision processes. However, religiosity is a complex variable, and multidimensional scales (e.g., Allport and Ross 1967) may more appropriately measure the various facets of this construct.

An individual's value system would also unquestionably affect the decision process. In general, we urge researchers to explore many different values and the impact that these values have on ethical decision making. Consider, for example, "organizational commitment" as one such value. Hunt, Wood, and Chonko (1989) found that corporations that have high ethical values will, subsequently, have employees who are extremely committed to the organization's welfare. This is an apparently positive outcome. However, is it possible that individuals exhibiting high organizational commitment (even due to the organization's high ethical values) will then engage in questionable behavior if such behavior were thought to be beneficial to the organization? Only research can answer this question fully. A recent four-country study (Vitell and Paolillo 2003) does, however, indicate a link between organizational commitment and the decision maker's perception that ethics should be a long-term, top priority of the organization.

"Belief systems" focus on the individual's set of beliefs about the world. For example, one might consider Machiavellianism as a belief system, as has been explored by Singhapakdi and Vitell (1991). More generally, the kinds of beliefs we have in mind are those that reflect how the individual believes the world "works." To what extent does an individual believe that all people are motivated solely by self-interest? In moral philosophy terms, to what extent does a person believe all others are guided by ethical egoism? The H-V model suggests that, to the extent that an individual believes this is how the world actually works, this belief will guide the individual's behavior by influencing the perceived consequences of alternatives and their probabilities.

Williams and Murphy (1990) suggest that strength of moral character is an important moderator of the relationship between intentions and behavior. Drawing on Aristotle's virtue ethics, Williams and Murphy emphasize, among other things, the important function of role models in developing a virtuous moral character (i.e., one demonstrating such virtues as perseverance, courage, integrity, compassion, candor, fidelity, prudence, justice, public-spiritedness, and humility). Thus, individuals with high moral character would have the strength of will to behave in a manner consistent with their ethical judgments.

The subject of cognitive moral development (Kohlberg 1984; Rest 1986; Trevino 1986) has received much attention in the ethics literature. A study by Goolsby and Hunt (1992) found that marketing practitioners compare favorably with other social groups in their level of cognitive moral development. Moreover, Goolsby and Hunt found that marketers scoring high on cognitive moral development tend to be female, highly educated, and high in social responsibility. Because a higher stage of cognitive moral development implies a greater capacity to reason through complex ethical situations, it would seem that individuals high in cognitive moral development would, among other things, bring in more deontological norms in any situation and would also consider the interests of more stakeholders in their decision making. Using a sample of 323 purchasing agents, Cole, Sirgy, and Bird (2000) explored whether cognitive moral development moderates the relationship between the desirability of consequences to self-versus-others and *TE*. They found, contrary to their hypothesis, no moderating relationship.

As a final personal characteristic, some people are, quite simply, less ethically sensitive than others. That is, when placed in a decision-making situation having an ethical component, some people never recognize that there is an ethical issue involved at all. Recall that the model starts with the perception that there is, indeed, some ethical problem involved in the situation. The systematic study of ethical sensitivity has begun in the areas of dentistry (Bebeau, Rest, and Yamoor 1985), professional counseling (Volker 1979), and accounting (Shaub 1989). In marketing, Sparks and Hunt (1998) explored the ethical sensitivity of marketing researchers and found, among other things, that the sample of practitioners was more ethically sensitive to research ethics issues than a sample composed of marketing students. Sparks and Hunt concluded that "the greater ethical sensitivity exhibited by marketing research practitioners can be attributed to their socialization into the marketing research profession, that is, by their learning the ethical norms of marketing research" (105).

Like Shaub (1989), Sparks and Hunt (1998) found a negative relationship between relativism and ethical sensitivity. Two factors, they proposed, may account for this negative finding. First, the disbelief in moral absolutes may reduce the likelihood of ethical violations standing out among other issues. In a world where all issues are relativistic shades of gray, ethical issues may just blend in with everything else. As a second explanatory factor, relativists may consider ethical issues in general to be less important than nonrelativists.

Sparks and Hunt (1998) also found a significant, negative relationship between ethical sensitivity and formal training in ethics received by respondents. One potential explanation for this surprising finding is that, rather than strengthening beliefs in the existence of morally right and wrong behavior, existing ethics education programs may be serving only to strengthen relativistic views. Nucci and Pascarella (1987) note that a historical goal of U.S. colleges and universities was to develop moral responsibility and students' character by teaching ethical thought and action. However, McNeel (1994) points out that ethics training in higher education has become, increasingly, "value free."

Since the work of Bartels (1967), marketing has stressed the role of culture in influencing ethics. Likewise, the H-V model stresses the importance of "cultural environment" in influencing the process of ethical decision making. As components of culture, the H-V model suggests that researchers focus attention on religion, legal systems, and political systems.

The boxes in the model (Figure 2.1) labeled "industry environment," "professional environment," and "organizational environment" specifically orient the model toward ethical situations for people in business and the professions. The H-V model proposes that all industries, professional associations, and organizations have complex sets of norms, some of which are formalized in codes, but most of which are informal. These norms, therefore, form a framework by which individuals are socialized into their respective organizations, professions, and industries. Much work needs to be done in identifying the extant informal norms across different industries and professional associations. For example, to what extent do the norms related to personal selling in the steel industry differ from those in the chemical industry or in advertising? It would seem that these differing sets of informal norms would play prominent roles in influencing which deontological norms an individual would consider as governing moral reasoning in specific decision contexts.

To close our overview, we stress that the H-V theory is a positive, not a normative, theory of ethics. That is, its objective is to increase our understanding of ethical decision making by means of a process theory that explains and predicts phenomena in situations having ethical content. Its purpose is not to provide normative guidance for making decisions that are more ethical. This distinction seems often to get lost in critiques of the model. For example, Laczniak and Murphy (1993) reviewed the H-V theory and concluded, "One of the essential problems of the reasoned action model [i.e., the H-V model] approach is that it never clearly specifies whether the [deontological and teleological] evaluations are made from the standpoint of the self-interest of the individual, the manager as representing the shareholders of the organization, or the manager taking into account all the various stakeholders (i.e., consumers, employees, etc.). . . . Perhaps the greatest shortcoming of such models is that they are basically *descriptive*" (48; italics in original). Three points about this critique are worth noting. First, as a positive theory of ethics, the H-V model provides a framework for explor-

ing the issue of whose standpoint decision makers actually use in their ethical evaluations. The theory does not (and should not) prescribe whose standpoint individuals should use. Therefore, the absence of such a prescription
is not, as Laczniak and Murphy allege, an "essential problem" of the theory.
Second, because the H-V model is clearly identified as a positive model, it
is not a shortcoming that it is descriptive; rather, its very purpose is to be
descriptive. Third, both positive and normative theories have value in research on ethical decision making. Indeed, both kinds of theories can, and
should, inform each other.

Empirical Tests of the Theory

Scores of studies have used the H-V model as a theoretical foundation for
empirical investigation and theoretical analysis. Our research design for the
first test of the theory explored how some 200 sales and marketing managers
responded to a bribery scenario detailed in our 1986 paper (Vitell and Hunt
1990). Briefly, the results showed that managers did tend to depend on both
deontological and teleological factors when making ethical judgments and
that managers also tended to form their intentions for behaviors by relying
both on their ethical judgments and teleological considerations. Moreover,
we were able to conclude, "If one wants to foster more ethical behavior on
the part of one's subordinates, the results of this study indicate that it would
be better to reward ethical behavior than to punish unethical behavior" (Vitell
and Hunt 1990, 262). However, the results also revealed a major shortcoming of the research design, to wit, many respondents simply did not see the
bribery scenario as a true ethical dilemma (respondents seemed to clearly
favor the alternative of issuing an order to the salespeople to stop giving
excessive gifts, but not reducing their compensation). Therefore, we urged
future researchers to create scenarios for testing the model that involve "true
ethical dilemmas" (261).

In another test, Mayo and Marks (1990) explored how 100 marketing researchers would handle a marketing research ethical problem that centered
on a research report that had questionable validity and reliability. Focusing
on the "core" relationships of the model, Mayo and Marks concluded, "The
results provide substantial support for the relationships proposed in this part
of the model, . . . ethical judgments to resolve dilemmas are found to be
jointly determined by deontological and teleological evaluations, . . . [and]
the relationship between judgments and intentions to adopt an ethical alternative is attenuated when its implementation does not result in a preferred
consequence" (163). However, as Mayo and Marks pointed out, their measures of several of the model's constructs were problematical (170). In a

commentary on the Mayo and Marks study, Hunt (1990, 175) also questioned the validity of several of their measures and asked, "In the process of coming to a summary ethical judgment in a situation, do people first come to an intermediate 'stopping point,' which may be referred to as 'deontological evaluation,' then combine this belief with their teleological evaluation?" Viewing deontological evaluation and teleological evaluation as "processes" not "constructs," Hunt concluded that the best answer to this question was no. Therefore, direct measures of deontological evaluation and teleological evaluation are probably inappropriate. Instead of direct measures, empirical research should use "inferred" ones (Hunt 1990, 175).

A study by Singhapakdi and Vitell (1991) explored the relationship between several background variables, including "Machiavellianism" and "locus of control," and the deontological norms of 529 members of the American Marketing Association. Machiavellianism is a personality trait associated with a manipulative, unethical leadership style (Hunt and Chonko 1984), and people who have a high "internal locus of control" believe that events that happen to them occur because of their own behavior or their own personal characteristics (Rotter 1966). Using the marketers' agreement or disagreement with seven items drawn from codes of ethics of the American Marketing Association as a measure of "deontological norms," Singhapakdi and Vitell found that those marketers scoring low on the Machiavellianism scale and those exhibiting a high "internal locus of control" had higher deontological norms.

Using the same American Marketing Association sample, Singhapakdi and Vitell (1990) also explored the relationships between various background factors and both "perceived ethical problems" and "perceived alternatives." They found that marketers scoring high on the Machiavellianism scale perceived ethical problems as less serious and were unlikely to view punishment of unethical behavior as a viable alternative. On the other hand, marketers in organizations enforcing a code of ethics perceived ethical problems as more serious and were more likely to view punishment of unethical behavior as an acceptable course of action.

Unlike most ethics studies, which use cross-sectional research designs, the study by Hunt and Vasquez-Parraga (1993) used an experimental design to explore how 747 sales and marketing managers would handle ethical problems relating to salespeople lying to their customers about plant capacity in order to negotiate better prices with purchasing agents, and recommending expensive products in their product lines even though less expensive products would better fit customer needs. This study represents the strongest test yet of the H-V model, because it employed an experimental design, overcame some of the measurement problems associated with previous tests, and used structural equation modeling techniques.

The results showed that goodness-of-fit indices were extremely high (0.999 and 0.994), the squared multiple correlations for "ethical judgments" and "intervention" were large (0.691 and 0.657, respectively), the total coefficient of determination for the structural equations was impressive (0.717), the signs of all the parameters were in the expected direction, and all hypothesized paths were statistically significant. In short, the study found that the model fit the data very well. Equally important, the researchers found that, at least in the situations they investigated, marketers relied primarily on deontological factors and only secondarily on teleological factors in forming both their ethical judgments and their intentions to act. The study also found that female marketers (compared with males) seemed to rely more heavily on deontological considerations in forming their ethical judgments and less heavily on teleological considerations in determining their intentions to act. Finally, marketers who worked for companies that "strongly enforced" their codes of ethics (compared with those that did not) were more influenced by deontological considerations in forming their intentions to intervene and were less influenced by teleological considerations.

Using a sample of 450 Turkish sales managers, Menguc (1997) replicated the Hunt and Vasquez-Parraga (1993) study. He found that "Turkish sales managers rely primarily on deontological evaluations in determining whether a salesperson's behavior is ethical or unethical, but teleological evaluations also play a role" (Menguc 1997, 346). He also found that Turkish sales managers score considerably higher in their intentions to intervene through discipline (i.e., punishment), when compared with U.S. managers. Overall, he concluded that the "findings provide support for the 'core' of the Hunt-Vitell theory of ethics" (346).

Burns and Kiecker (1995) also used the experimental design of the Hunt and Vasquez-Parraga (1993) study, but with a sample of 418 certified public accountants (CPAs) and scenarios that involved a CPA making recommendations on clients' tax returns. Burns and Kiecker extended the research design by specifically measuring the deontological orientations (DO) and teleological orientations (TO) of respondents. That is, they measured respondents' stated predispositions toward treating ethical issues deontologically and teleologically. In the replication phase of their research, their findings confirm those of Hunt and Vasquez-Parraga. That is, the CPAs relied on both deontological and teleological evaluations in forming ethical judgments. Also, they found in the extension phase of their study that the paths from ethical judgments to intentions and from the teleological evaluation to intentions in the H-V model are much higher for the TO subsample than the DO subsample. Therefore, "taken collectively, the results show strong support for the H-V model" (Burns and Kiecker 1995, 42).

Understanding Ethical Judgments

We return now to addressing ethical judgments, in general, and the "why" questions raised in the first paragraph, in particular. The H-V model provides a framework for explicating the "personal moral code" and why people's ethical judgments differ. That is, people's ethical judgments differ because they have different personal moral codes, and the differences in moral codes result from differences in:

- the rules for combining the deontological and teleological evaluations;
- the deontological norms held by people;
- the relative importance of particular norms;
- the rules for resolving conflicts among norms;
- the rules for interpreting the applicability of norms in particular situations;
- the importance weights assigned to particular stakeholders;
- the positive consequences for particular (e.g., very important) stakeholders;
- the negative consequences for particular (e.g., very unimportant) stakeholders;
- the probabilities of positive and negative consequences for particular stakeholders.

Consider, for example, the issue of universities' admissions policies. Those who argue that the use of race and ethnicity as factors in admissions policies is wrong often focus on the deontological evaluation. That is, they argue first that it is (deontologically) wrong to discriminate on the basis of race and ethnicity. Second, they argue that when universities use race and ethnicity in admissions policies to favor particular races or ethnicities over others, such policies constitute racial and ethic discrimination. Therefore, they reason, the use of race and ethnicity in universities' admissions policies is wrong.

In contrast, those who argue that the use of race and ethnicity in admissions policies is right often focus on the teleological evaluation. They argue that, because of past and present injustices, the importance weights given to certain classes of stakeholders (e.g., African-Americans and Hispanics) in the teleological evaluation formula should be higher than those given to other stakeholders (e.g., non-Hispanic whites and Asians). Furthermore, the use of racial and ethnic preferences in admissions policies results, with high likelihood, in highly favorable consequences falling on individuals in the most important classes of stakeholders and the undesirable consequences falling on individuals in the less important classes. Therefore, the use of race and ethnicity in university admissions policies is right.

Now consider the issue of copyrighted music and intellectual property rights. Those who argue that it is wrong to download copyrighted music tend to focus on a deontological evaluation. They argue that the downloading is inherently wrong because it is stealing and because it violates the intellectual property rights of those who created the music. However, it is also possible to argue against downloading music from a teleological perspective. A teleological argument would be that several stakeholders suffer significant monetary harm, including those who create the music, produce the music, and work for the individuals or companies involved in the creation and production. Therefore, downloading copyrighted music is wrong deontologically (because it is theft) and teleologically (because numerous stakeholders suffer harmful consequences).

On the other hand, those who argue that it is acceptable to download music customarily argue from a teleological (either an egoistic or perhaps even utilitarian) perspective that maintains, first, that no one is really harmed by this behavior. They might muse that the companies actually publishing the music are not harmed very much, if at all, while the individuals doing the downloading (and perhaps their friends) benefit significantly from the use of the materials at little or no cost. Therefore, there are large positive consequences for important stakeholders (i.e., the users) and minimal negative consequences for unimportant stakeholders (i.e., artists and publishers). Furthermore, according to this argument, the actual performer of the music is aided by the wider dissemination of the music and increased popularity, which perhaps even lead to greater monetary rewards for the artist and publisher. In summary, differences in a deontological versus teleological perspective, as well as differences in perceived consequences and/or the desirability of consequences, may be used to explain differences in ethical judgments regarding the issue of downloading copyrighted music.

With respect to providing gifts to purchasing agents, those who believe that this is wrong often argue from a deontological perspective. They hold that the giving of any gift, no matter what the size, constitutes attempted bribery, smacks of impropriety, and creates a potential conflict of interest for the purchasing agent. Those who view gifts as wrongful behavior also argue from a teleological perspective that the giving of gifts causes harm because such gifts are likely to unfairly influence the purchasing agent's behavior. Thus, gifts potentially cause harm to the purchasing agent's firm (perhaps because the firm purchases a lesser quality product) and/or to the competitors of the selling firm (because of potential lost sales).

In contrast, those who argue that the giving of gifts (at least small ones) is not wrong tend to focus exclusively on teleological issues. That is, they argue that no one is harmed by this practice because the size of the gift is not likely to be enough to influence a purchasing agent's decision. Thus, part of the difference in ethical judgments regarding the giving of gifts might be due to differences in a deontological versus teleological evaluation and/or differences in one's perception of the probability of particular consequences.

Of course, defenders and opponents might use numerous other arguments to argue for the rightness or wrongness of the various ethical issues described above. The point to be made here is that the H-V model contributes to understanding all such arguments. All such arguments, we maintain, can be categorized and further explicated by means of the constructs in the model.

Understanding Utility Maximization

Perfect competition theory in neoclassical economics assumes that the personal moral codes of all people can be described as utility maximization. But what does utility maximization mean? How does utility maximization differ (if it differs) from utilitarianism? Because utility maximization is so ubiquitous in economics, business, and marketing, this section uses the H-V model to understand it. We begin our analysis by reviewing how "utility" and "utility maximization" have evolved in the neoclassical economics research tradition.

Consider the ontology of "utility" and "utility maximization" in the neoclassical tradition. Concepts in science are ontologically substantive, to use Etzioni's (1988) terminology, when they have, or are posited to have, existence in the real world. For example, "money," "land," and "capital" are labels (note the use of quotation marks) in English that identify concepts that refer to money, land, and capital (note the absence of quotation marks). Because substantive concepts are posited to refer, they figure prominently in assertions that are true or false empirically. In contrast, consider the ontology of the purely formal concepts "or," "not," "6," and "B." These are labels in English (and certain other languages) for concepts that have no empirical content. Although assertions containing only formal concepts may be true or false logically, mathematically, or by linguistic convention, such assertions have no observational or empirical truth content. Therefore, is "utility" substantive or formal in neoclassical theory?

As discussed in Hunt (2000, Section 2.2), the concept of marginal utility enabled William Stanley Jevons (1835–1882) and Leon Walras (1834–1910) to import differential calculus into economics. For them, utility was a continuous function and marginal utility was its first derivative, that is, $MUX = dU/dx$. But what is the entity being maximized when one sets the first derivative of the utility function to zero? To what, if anything, does utility refer? Jevons and Walras interpreted their equations as representing a "calculus of pleasure and pain," consistent with the English philosopher Jeremy Bentham's (1748–1832) "hedonic calculus." Bentham (1789) had proposed that utility is the property in any object that produced pleasure or happiness, rather than pain or unhappiness. He then argued that legislation is moral if it produces the greatest happiness (or utility) for the greatest number of people. Therefore, for Jevons, Walras, and Bentham, utility was a substantive concept that referred to one's self-interest in pleasure or happiness. The substantive concept of self-interest and the hedonic view of utility accorded well with Adam Smith's theory that marketplace transactions result in good consequences, even without altruism on the part of participants. Thus, Smith's (1776/1937, 14) famous lines state, "It is not from the benevolence of the butcher, the brewer or the baker that we expect our dinner, but from their regard to their own interest. We address ourselves not to their humanity but to their self-love, and never talk to them of our own necessities but of their advantages."

The neoclassical tradition often defines utility as a substantive concept that is consistent with Bentham's hedonic view of self-interest, as the following four examples illustrate. "The members of a household will seek to maximize their total utility. This is just another way of saying that the members of households try to make themselves as well off as they possibly can in the circumstances in which they find themselves" (Lipsey and Steiner 1975, 142). "People consume goods and services because their wants, or preferences, are served by doing so: they derive satisfaction from consumption. . . . Utility is simply a subjective measure of the usefulness, or want satisfaction, that results from consumption" (Browning and Browning 1983, 56). "Utility . . . [is] the total satisfaction derived from the consumption of goods and services" (Samuelson and Nordhaus 1995, 764). "Utility . . . [is] a measure of happiness or satisfaction" (Mankiw 1998, 781).

Etzioni (1988) used "P-utility" as a label for the self-interest, hedonic interpretation of utility. He then defended it as a substantive concept: "P-utility has longstanding philosophical and psychological foundations, it provides a major explanatory concept and generates testable hypotheses. . . . to the extent that it is hypothesized that the pursuit of P-utility is a major explanatory factor, the hypothesis is clearly valid. . . . to argue that people are pleasure-driven . . . surely explains a good part of human behavior" (28, 34).

Interpreting utility in the self-interest, hedonic manner poses a serious problem for the neoclassical tradition in which maximizing self-interest is empirically false. Indeed, Etzioni (1988, 51–66) cited scores of studies that indicate that many people do act unselfishly on many occasions. He also noted that empirical works on economic decisions related to public goods, free riders, the cooperative behaviors in prisoner's dilemma experiments, and the voting behaviors of citizens also contradict the self-interest maximizing thesis. For example, he discussed the findings of Marwell and Ames (1981): "A large number of experiments, under different conditions, most of them highly unfavorable to civility, show that people do not take free rides, but pay voluntarily as much as 40 percent to 60 percent of what economists figured is due to the public till if the person was not to free ride at all. The main reason: the subjects consider it the 'right' or 'fair' thing to do" (Etzioni 1988, 59).

The empirical falsity of the substantive interpretation of utility maximization that Etzioni documented has been acknowledged in the neoclassical tradition. Three responses are common. First, some argue that utility and utility maximization are not substantive. Instead, utility is a formal concept, an empty abstraction. As Samuelson (1947/1983, 9) put it, utility is an "empty convention" and "meaningless in any operational sense." Similarly, utility "is now simply a name for the ranking of options in accord with any individual's preferences" (Alchian and Allen 1977, 40). Likewise, "what modern economists call 'utility' is nothing more than the rank ordering of preference" (Hirshleifer 1980, 85). Indeed, the concept of utility "need not refer to anything" (Little 1957, 20).

The advantages for the neoclassical tradition of the purely formal, empirically empty, "revealed preference" view are that the maximization of equations, a central, if not the central, part of the neoclassical tradition, is retained, and only ordinal, instead of cardinal, measurement of preferences is required. However, the disadvantage of "saving the equations" through the purely formal, revealed preference interpretation is that it leads to incoherence. That is, it is inconsistent for a research tradition to defend utility maximization as an empty abstraction and then proceed to use the substantive, self-interest interpretation of utility in such areas as agency theory, game theory, transaction cost economics, and public choice economics. Research and policy recommendations in all these areas, among others in the neoclassical tradition, treat utility maximization as a substantive thesis that implies self-interest maximization. Incoherence in a research tradition is not a technical nicety; it violates the norms of science.

The second response to the empirical falsity of the substantive interpretation of utility maximization is to expand the concept of "self" in self-interest. As Etzioni (1988, 25) put it, "when a person acts altruistically, this is explained by the suggestion that the pleasure of the person who benefits from this act has become a source of the doer's pleasure, part of his or her utility." For example, "those who give gifts are said to seek reciprocal gifts, reputation, status, approval, or some other goods the doer desires."

Numerous defenders of utility maximization expand the "self" in self-interest. For example, Boulding (1981, 6) stated, "All we have to suppose is that the perception of one party, A, of the welfare of the other, B, is a variable in A's utility function such that when A perceives that B is better off, A's utility rises." Similarly, Margolis (1982, 1) pointed out that it is now "fairly common" to incorporate altruism into utility maximization because "We have no more need to distinguish between the bread Smith buys to give to the poor and that which he buys for his own consumption, than to distinguish his neighbor's demand for sugar to make cookies from his demand for sugar to make gin in the cellar." As a third example, Azzi and Ehrenberg (1975, p. 28) attempted to incorporate religious activities into utility maximization through the concept of "afterlife consumption" and maintained that "this variable . . . [is] at least partially a function of the household's investment of members' time in religious activities during their lifetimes." As a fourth example, Lipsey and Steiner (1975, 142–143) defended the utility maximization assumption thusly:

> The assumption is sometimes taken to mean that individuals are assumed to be narrowly selfish and devoid of any altruistic motives. This is not so. If, for example, the individual derives utility from giving his money away to others, this can be incorporated into the analysis, and the marginal utility that he gets from a dollar given away can be compared with the marginal utility that he gets from a dollar spent on himself.

Stigler (1966, 57) pointed out that expanding the "self" in self-interest to include altruism is to "turn utility into a tautology." That is, expanding "self" to incorporate, post hoc, all conceivable behaviors removes the empirical content from both utility and its maximization. Tautologies are true by linguistic convention, not by empirical test. Therefore, as with the empty abstraction defense, it is incoherent to defend utility as a tautology and then to proceed, as do the various research programs in the neoclassical tradition, to use the substantive, self-interest interpretation in research and public policy.

As a third response to the empirical falsity of the substantive interpretation of utility maximization, some writers return to Friedman's (1953) "close enough" argument. For example, Williamson's (1975, 255) transaction cost economics assumes that "economic man . . . is thus a more subtle and devious creature than the usual self-interest seeking assumption reveals." For transaction cost economics, *homo economicus* not only maximizes self-interest but does so with opportunistic "guile." Williamson argued for assuming universal opportunism because it is "ubiquitous" (1981, 1550), since "even among the less opportunistic types, most have their price" (1979, 234), and opportunistic "types cannot be distinguished ex ante from sincere types" (1975, 27) or, at the very least, "it is very costly to distinguish opportunistic from non-opportunistic types ex ante" (1981, 1545). The assumption of opportunism is so important to transaction cost economics that, in its absence, "the study of economic organization is pointless" (1981, 1545). Indeed, "the interesting problems of comparative economic organization vanish if either hyper rationality or faithful stewardship is ascribed to economic actors" (1996, 365).

Clearly, transaction cost economics treats utility maximization as neither an empty abstraction nor a tautology but a substantive concept that stresses self-interest. Equally clear is its acknowledgment of the falsity of the view that all economic agents engage in malfeasance (see Williamson 1994, 7) as well as the acknowledgment that "faithful stewardship" is separate and distinct from self-interest (see Williamson 1996, 365). That is, ethical behavior and faithful stewardship are neither assumed away nor tautologized as "warm glow," self-interest maximizing.

Why, then, for transaction cost economics, would assuming opportunism to be nonuniversal make the study of economic organization pointless? Why, then, would the "interesting" problems of economic organization vanish? Indeed, how does one justify universal opportunism in the face of its (acknowledged) empirical falsity? Answering these questions, we suggest, shows the power of a research tradition. Because universal self-interest maximization is central to the neoclassical tradition and because the tradition itself, not the characteristics of real-world economies, defines what constitutes "interesting" problems and when such problems "vanish," then the absence of the assumption of universal opportunism would make the study of the interesting problems of economic organization pointless within the neoclassical tradition. Therefore, universal opportunism is defended because the assumption of nonuniversal opportunism would place transaction cost economics outside the neoclassical research tradition.

However, since the time of Galileo, science has not accorded legitimacy to the "not in my research tradition" argument. Therefore, although neoclassical economists may be satisfied with "not in the neoclassical tradition," nonneoclassical scholars require a second justification. For such scholars, transaction cost economics attempts to defend universal opportunism on the grounds that it is common—that is, in Williamson's words, it is "ubiquitous," opportunistic "types cannot be distinguished" or "it is very costly to distinguish opportunistic" types, and "most [people] have their price." In short, for outsiders, transaction cost economics defends universal opportunism because it is "close enough" (Friedman 1953).

Let us now return to the issue of personal moral codes and the use of the H-V model to understand the personal moral code implied as the basis for human motivation in the neoclassical economics research tradition. When "utility" is used as a substantive concept in neoclassical economics, business, and marketing, it implies that all people have a personal moral code that includes only a teleological evaluation (TE). That is, the deontological evaluation (DE) is zero. Within the teleological evaluation (TE) portion of the H-V model, the self-interest maximization interpretation of utility implies that the importance weights (e.g., in the previously described, teleological evaluation formula) given to all stakeholders other than "self" are zero.[1]

In normative, moral philosophy terms, when "utility" is used substantively, the thesis of utility maximization equates with the doctrine of ethical egoism. This philosophy is often associated with philosophers such as Thomas Hobbes (1588–1679) and Frederick W. Nietzsche (1844–1900), who held that self-interest maximization is, and ought to be, the guiding principle underlying ethical codes. Furthermore, the utilitarianism associated with Jeremy Bentham and John Stuart Mill (1806–1873) would, like utility maximization, also ascribe zero influence in ethical decision making to the deontological evaluation (DE). However, unlike utility maximization, "utilitarianism" would assign equal importance weights to all stakeholders in teleological evaluation (TE). Thus, utilitarianism should never be used as synonymous with "utility maximization." Indeed, utilitarianism, because of its focus on the importance of all stakeholders, may be argued to share more with deontologically oriented ethical codes (e.g., Kantianism) than it does with utility maximization.

Conclusion

The objectives of this chapter have been to use the Hunt-Vitell (H-V) theory of ethics to explicate the concept of "personal moral code," show how "why" questions involving ethical judgments can be understood by means of the H-V theory, and show how the H-V theory can help in understanding the "utility maximization" concept in neoclassical economics. In the process of doing so, it has been reemphasized that the H-V theory is a positive rather than a normative model. Thus, it is not designed to give prescriptions as to how people should resolve ethical conflicts. Rather, it is designed to explain and predict how people actually do attempt to resolve ethical issues. The chapter has shown, however, how the theory helps us understand the basis for the ethical conflicts embedded in the examples involving admissions policy, intellectual property, and gifts to purchasing agents. We maintain that understanding how ethical decisions are made can serve as a starting point for discussions that might eventually resolve some of these ethical conflicts.

Contrary to neoclassical economic theory, this chapter argues that utility maximization is not the personal moral code of all, or even most, individuals. Indeed, we show that utility maximization is most aptly described, in ethical terms, as ethical egoism, which is only one of several teleological theories of ethics. Because empirical tests of the H-V theory have shown that deontological considerations are equally important to, if not more important than, teleological considerations in determining ethical judgments, ethical egoism appears not to be the moral code of most individuals. Furthermore, as pointed out, ethical egoism differs significantly from other teleological perspectives, most particularly utilitarianism. The former is concerned only with the consequences for self, whereas the latter is concerned with the consequences for all stakeholders.

In conclusion, the Hunt-Vitell theory's constructs and relationships were originally designed to guide empirical research in ethics, help in our understanding of ethical decision making, and provide a model that would be useful to instructors of marketing and business ethics. The theory's empirical, theoretical, and pedagogical successes over its first two decades lead us to believe that future tests, explications, and classroom uses will likewise be fruitful.

Note

1. The resource-advantage (R-A) theory of competition assumes that human motivation is best described as "constrained self-interest seeking" (Hunt 2000, 106). The constraint on self-interest seeking is the personal moral code of the individual. Therefore, R-A theory explicates the process by which such macrolevel, trust-promoting institutions as moral codes can contribute to, or detract from, firm-level, superior financial performance (see Hunt 2000, 235–237).

3

Why Do Good People Do Bad Things?

Challenges to Business Ethics and Corporate Leadership

Patricia H. Werhane

Since the time of Aristotle, people have been debating why good people engage in questionable behavior and even repeat their mistakes. For example, Arthur Andersen was commonly cited as the best, as well as the largest, audit company in America (e.g., Collins and Porras 1994). Andersen was always profitable; it was a company that was constantly evolving to meet changing global demands; and books have been written about the ethical demeanor of its founder as setting the gold standard for behavior in the audit community. Even so, just before the Enron scandal that brought the company down, Andersen was involved in questionable auditing practices at Waste Management, at Sunbeam, and even at the Baptist Foundation of Arizona. Why did such incidents recur in a company allegedly as fine and well-managed as Arthur Andersen?

For their 1994 book, *Built to Last: Successful Habits of Visionary Companies,* Collins and Porras studied the characteristics of "visionary companies" (as identified by a poll of CEOs of 700 major corporations) and examined how these companies differed from other "comparison companies." Collins and Porras defined a visionary company as the premier organization in its respective industry, as being widely admired by its peers, and as having a long track record of making a significant impact on the world around it. Each of the visionary companies chosen in the CEO poll had faced setbacks, and each had made mistakes. Still, the long-term financial performance of each has been remarkable. A dollar invested in a visionary company stock fund on January 1, 1926, with dividends reinvested, and making appropriate adjustments for when the companies became available on the stock market, would have grown by December 31, 1990, to $6,356. That dollar invested in a general market fund would have grown to $415.

What was the difference between visionary companies and the comparison companies? Each operated in the same market and each had the same relative opportunities. What was critical for the visionary or successful companies, according to Collins and Porras's findings, was that a visionary company was driven by an ideology that "it lives, breathes, and expresses in all it does. . . . A visionary company almost religiously preserves its core ideology—changing it seldom, if ever" (Collins and Porras 1994, 8). Moreover,

> [c]ontrary to business school doctrine, "maximizing shareholder wealth" or "profit maximization" has not been the dominant driving force or primary objective through the history of the visionary companies. Visionary companies pursue a cluster of objectives, of which making money is only one—and not necessarily the primary one. Yes, they seek profits, but they are equally guided by a core ideology—core values and a sense of purpose beyond just making money. Yet, paradoxically, the visionary companies make more money than the more purely profit-driven comparison companies.

Despite the Collins and Porras study and its claims that the most profitable companies are run from a strong values ideology, the last two years have witnessed a plethora of bad corporate behavior. Beginning with Enron and including, most recently, questionable market timing, stale pricing, and late trading by allegedly reputable mutual funds, the tales of corporate misdeeds seem endless. In this chapter, some of the commonly cited reasons for these misdeeds will be examined. It will be argued that the primary reasons for these misdeeds were not self-interest or greed but rather an inability to take ethics seriously in economic transactions, the separation of ethics from compliance, and a weak definition of corporate social responsibility. Using concepts from systems thinking and the idea of moral imagination, the chapter will conclude with a case study that illustrates how a company might address ethical issues in practice.

A number of reasons are commonly cited as to why misdeeds occur in allegedly legitimate businesses run by well-educated and seemingly ethical people. Consider the following illustrative reasons:

- First, no one is perfect; everyone makes mistakes. So in large companies with thousands of managers (such as WorldCom), there are bound to be errors of judgment.

- Second, it is alleged that people are primarily motivated by self-interest, so managerial or corporate preoccupation with their own interests, sometimes even greed, accounts for questionable and even egregious behavior in business.
- Third, at least in certain instances, some of these people act primarily without much regard to social or legal networks of relationships and in disregard of untoward consequences, either to themselves or to their company.
- Fourth, each of these recent instances of misdeeds occurred within a complex network of professional, managerial, and legal relationships. It is sometimes argued that corporate culture, the particular roles and role responsibilities of managers and professionals where responsibilities are diluted, or built-in conflicts of interest constrain what outsiders might consider as morally appropriate behavior for managers and professionals, and preclude the consequential avoidance of harms.
- Fifth, the media relish bad news, so any mention of the thousands of good companies and fine mutual funds engaged in respected corporate practices escapes to the back pages or the late night news.
- Finally, it is sometimes argued that many companies and their managers either are unaware of the moral dimensions of their activities or lack skills in moral reasoning. Proper moral education could raise the level of individual and institutional moral awareness, enhance moral development, and give managers theoretical tools from moral theory with which to deal with ethical issues. If managers are trained in moral reasoning and moral theory, the argument is that they would apply such training to their decision processes with more positive results.

Each of these reasons is examined in more detail.

Some Good and Bad Reasons

Oversimplifying a bit, there are both "good" and "bad" reasons why misdeeds occur in legitimate businesses. Many of these reasons can be classified under headings of human nature and self-interest, disregard of others, role definitions of job responsibilities, and training in moral reasoning.

Human Nature and Self-Interest

All companies are made up of people. It follows that companies, like individuals, will make moral mistakes. This seems obvious, and it is also obvious that some people repeat their mistakes at least some of the time. What seems less clear is why and how collections of managers or professionals repeat their mistakes when faced with issues that are similar to those they have faced in the past, and when those former issues were public incidents that received media, regulatory, and/or public attention. Arthur Andersen apparently repeated its mistakes at Waste Management, then at Sunbeam, then with the Baptist Foundation, and finally at Enron. Former Federal Reserve chair Paul Volcker has contended that the common thread in all these scenarios is "good, old-fashioned greed" (Bacon and Salwen 1991). In other words, the audit partners at Andersen, Andrew Fastow, the CFO of Enron (and other managers there), WorldCom executives, and others simply acted in their own self-interest by manipulating the system in order to accumulate wealth for themselves. This is an interesting accusation and surely partly true.

However, acting in one's own self-interest is not necessarily evil. Many self-interest actions, even greedy ones, do not necessarily harm others. If, for example, it was true that some of Enron's executives wished to amass a fortune, they would not be alone in that motivation nor would they necessarily be bad people. It is only when that interest overwhelmed any sense of propriety, fiduciary responsibilities to shareholders and other stakeholders, or law that such actions became unconscionable. While one might wince at Ivan Boesky's alleged famous statement that "greed is good," it is important to avoid misidentifying all self-interest with greed and proclaiming that self-interest always entails questionable behavior.

Even if personal greed was the only motivation in the cases that were cited, most of these executives and managers would not get "A" grades in the successful practice of greed. Arthur Andersen partners lost everything when the company went out of business. Others, such as Bernie Evers of WorldCom, have virtually worthless stock, and Andrew Fastow, the CFO of Enron, has been indicted on 200 counts of fraud. So analyzing corporate or managerial wrongdoing or unintentional harms from the perspective of self-interest or greed does not always get at the cause of such behavior.

Disregard of Others

Still, it is tempting to imagine that the top managers at Enron gauged their moral judgments mostly by focusing on their own personal gain as the object of their self-interest, basing their actions on whether they would get caught. People deal with moral issues differently—some more naively than others; some primarily out of self-interest; some depending on law and convention; and others seeking ideal or universal principles on which to ground and evaluate moral decisions. Moreover, human relationships play central roles in morality, moral decision making, and moral evaluation. People are affected by human relationships, even in acts of solitude and rejection, and these relationships are part of what is defined as being moral or immoral.

What theories of moral development have more difficulty explaining is why an intelligent, well-educated person such as Andrew Fastow would get so involved in his job, his company, or himself that he did not perceive that he was very likely to get caught. Fastow may have been responding to company and role expectations for executives at Enron. But such an explanation places Fastow in disregard of social convention and the law, belying the expectations of that level of moral development. Fastow cleverly created perfectly legal off-book partnerships at Enron. But these partnerships became vehicles for unprofitable Enron ventures, and they did not meet the legal requirement of "arm's length" distance from the parent company. Fastow himself convinced the board of directors of Enron to suspend its conflict of interest rules so that he and some of his friends could direct these partnerships for their own financial benefit. Fastow admitted that he made over $45 million on the partnerships between 1999 and 2001 (*The Economist* 2002).

Fastow, a religious, practicing Jew who created a charitable foundation and coached his son's Little League team, had everything to lose by instigating and participating in the off-book partnerships he created. Similarly, at Arthur Andersen, the auditors could only lose when the cited situations went awry, and many executives found themselves in jail. There was no self-interest "payoff," either in the short run or the long run, and little in the way of conventional explanation to account for these misdeeds.

Role Definitions of Job Responsibilities

An important factor affecting managerial moral judgment is how managers and professionals prioritize client, corporate, and professional responsibility. The dilemma of which constituency should take precedence is well illustrated in the WorldCom case. At WorldCom, whose outside auditor was Arthur Andersen, the vice president of internal audit, Cynthia Cooper, began to question Andersen's method of financial audits. Following the mandate of WorldCom's CFO, Scott Sullivan, billions of dollars in operating expenses were being booked as capital expenses, thus allowing WorldCom to show a profit instead of a loss for 2001. At least two sets of accounting professionals played key roles in this case: the accountants at Arthur Andersen, and WorldCom's internal auditors, led by Cynthia Cooper. Both sets of professionals were CPAs and members of the American Institute of Certified Public Accountants (AICPA). The AICPA code proscribes certain actions of its members, and at least some of these code proscriptions are meant to override personal inclinations and institutional or corporate demands, even for inside employee auditors. Specifically, the AICPA code (Section 102.01) states:

> A member who knowingly makes, or permits or directs another to make, false and misleading entries in an entity's financial statements or records shall be considered to have knowingly misrepresented facts in violation of rule 102. (American Institute of Certified Public Accountants 1992)

Both Sullivan and the Arthur Andersen auditors violated their professional code when they countenanced booking ordinary expenses as capital expenses. Arthur Andersen seems to have treated the demands of WorldCom as more important than its independent professional obligations. Indeed, in a recent article, Bazerman, Loewenstein, and Moore (2002) argued that this prioritization, which is an obvious conflict of interest with AICPA rules, is a major cause of the code violations. Because the client was the paying customer, auditors and audit companies placed the client's interests first, despite the alleged independence asserted by the profession.

What is most troubling in many of these cases is that there is little evidence to suggest that either set of professionals, lawyers or auditors, considered a possible conflict of interest between their professional codes and what they were engaged in at any of these companies. They allowed client demands to override professional codes to which they were committed. Only Cynthia Cooper, who redid the Arthur Andersen audit and eventually went to the board of WorldCom with her finding of fraud, prioritized the code of the auditor before her loyalty to WorldCom.

As Toffler and Reingold (2003) have argued, Arthur Andersen's corporate culture decision dynamics may have obscured the clarity of individuals' independent judgments such that they did not take place or were ineffective. The fact that the Waste Management, Sunbeam, and Baptist Foundation incidents, for which Andersen was reprimanded and fined by the Securities and Exchange Commission, did not seem to play a role in its Enron activities supports this contention. It would be a gross exaggeration, at best, and indeed false, to say that a number of auditors at Arthur Andersen did not think of themselves as independent, morally responsible individuals and merely did as they were told. Yet in every institutional setting there are some practices that do not encourage independent decision making nor provide avenues for questioning what might be, by standards outside the institution, unacceptable activities. Sometimes, too, professionals as well as managers become so involved in their roles and what is expected of them by their clients or company that their judgments become identified with their perceptions of their role responsibilities.

By definition, people are enmeshed in a collection of overlapping social, professional, cultural, and religious roles, each of which makes moral demands. This overlap becomes problematic when the demands of a particular role become confused, when these demands come into conflict with another role, or when role demands clash with societal norms or common-sense morality. For example, the lawyer who protects a known repeat murderer, the psychologist or priest who honors the confidentiality of a criminal's confession, and the reporter who witnesses a spouse committing a crime respectively face role conflicts because of the contradictory demands of their profession, personal ties, and commonly held societal moral norms. In business, as illustrated by the behavior of some mutual fund managers, the pressure to be competitive, efficient, and profitable can often conflict with demands of common morality not to lie, steal, or cheat.

Role morality can constrain ordinary moral reactions. Sherron Watkins, a former manager at Enron, observed what she believed to be unethical and illegal activities when Enron booked losses to off-book partnerships. She wrote an anonymous letter to Kenneth Lay, then CEO of Enron, stating her doubts about these activities. Although Watkins saw herself as a manager with the important role of flagging improprieties, she did not blow the whistle outside Enron, despite her accumulation of good data to support her suspicions. She placed company loyalty rather than public and shareholder interests first (Swartz and Watkins 2003).

There is an attendant problem, a problem that many call "limited rationality." It is possible, within a particular institutional or theoretical context, to develop limited objectivity so as to create a closed loop of decision making. At WorldCom, Scott Sullivan defended his accounting practices as in the best interest of preserving shareholder value, and he claimed that he was going to correct the expense booking errors during the next fiscal year. He was able to justify these improprieties to himself because of his preoccupation with preserving WorldCom's standing as a reputable company with profitable returns. His goals, then, were those that every manager aspires to, but the means to attain them were fraudulent. Sullivan's behavior suggests that what seems to be a rational perspective, while crucial to moral decision making, may create a disconnect between what appears, in theory, to be correct and what, in particular fact, is correct. Therefore, what seems to be a rational perspective may be mere rationalization and thus not enough, by itself, to avoid moral disasters.

It could be the case, however, that these reasons are merely excuses. People are not exhaustively defined by their roles. Individuals should be able to distance themselves from, and evaluate, their roles and role responsibilities. Tools for evaluation include the precepts of common morality, which most individuals would regard as rules for how to behave, such as respecting others, avoiding harm, showing regard for rights and fairness, honoring contracts, and honoring property, however particularly defined.

Individuals can and should use these same tools of common morality for judging institutions, particularly those institutions in which they are involved. In such evaluations, as the Enron and Andersen scenarios suggest, individuals need to distance themselves from the institution and its decision-making habits. A less biased perspective is crucial, because unless managers and institutions can disengage themselves from the context of a specific problem, decisions are parochially imbedded so as to result in an iteration of the very kinds of activities that invite repeated moral failure. Scenarios such as accounting fraud tend to repeat themselves when managers lack moral perspective on their roles and the demands of the institution.

Obviously, it is difficult to evaluate every action taken in every role without becoming consumed with evaluation as a full-time activity, and there are limits to human impartiality and disengagement. But the act of stepping back and creating a distance from institutions in which people are deeply involved can put into perspective the relative importance of the institution and its role demands. Such evaluation activities are crucial to avoiding problems such as those in which Andersen found itself embroiled, and even the demise of a company.

Thus, the priority of institutional or managerial demands over professional codes (or just good sense, role morality, and rationalization posing as good reasoning) explain, at least in part, why good managers engage in questionable behavior. These explanations serve as pathological descriptions. But role morality does not explain all moral or immoral behavior, nor does it offer avenues for resolving conflicts of interest or professional or legal dilemmas.

Training in Moral Reasoning

There is another temptation in trying to answer the questions "Why do good people or fine institutions engage in questionable behavior?" and "Why do we repeat our mistakes?" Given limits of role morality and complications in arguing that managers are primarily motivated by personal gain or even greed, people are faced with the contention that what is missing in these companies is traditional moral education. Managers at Enron, WorldCom, Adelphia Cable, and elsewhere are morally responsible for what happened on their watch. So, this argument continues, it is necessary to talk to the managers of these companies about professional and moral responsibilities through the introduction of moral theory, locate the moral culprits, and begin moral education. This would be followed by testing their stage of moral development (whether they are egoists, conformists, rule-followers, law-abiders, precedent-setters, or philosophers) and offering them workshops on moral reasoning. In the workshops, professional and institutional codes of ethics would be discussed, the limits of role responsibilities and role morality demonstrated, some ethical theories presented (e.g., utilitarianism, deontology, virtue theory, and some theories of justice), and managers would be engaged in a series of practice sessions that apply moral theories to cases studies.

Therein lies the problem. Like the professional codes of ethics to which auditors are bound, most of the *Fortune* 1000 companies in the United States have codes of ethics and credos. At least one-third of them have ethics officers and ethics programs in place. Even so, as with the auditing profession, improprieties continue to occur. Enron, for example, had a clear credo of "Respect, Integrity, Community, and Excellence." Yet, according to Enron employees, the practice was "Rank or Yank," that is, "make your numbers or be fired."

Some Other Reasons

There are some other reasons why apparently good people and reputable companies engage in questionable behavior. There are other interesting role phenomena that affect behavior. Sometimes people simultaneously adapt contradictory roles without perceiving possible conflicts of interest. The most obvious examples are members of the U.S. crime syndicate who are known to be exemplary church members and good family people, but use a decision model in business dealings that contradicts the values of church and family. "Mafia mentality," as this phenomenon is often crudely labeled, is the ability to function in such contradictory roles simultaneously. That this phenomenon is limited to criminal activities is belied by cases such as Adelphia Cable. Adelphia Cable was founded by John Rigas and grew from a small family company to the sixth largest publicly traded cable television provider. The Rigas family was always extremely generous to the local community, and even today the family is revered in the town of Coudersport, Pennsylvania, where the company was located. According to Leonard (Leonard et al. 2002), John Rigas is considered "our Greek god" in Coudersport. Despite these good works, in recent years the family borrowed but did not repay hundreds of millions of dollars from the company. The company itself engaged in a series of accounting improprieties and grossly inflated the number of its cable subscribers. What accounts for the disparity between the Rigas family's "good works" in the community and fraud at the corporate level? Somehow John Rigas and his sons were able to compartmentalize their ethics, separating community social responsibilities from their commitment to shareholder interests.

This sort of "division of morality" also occurs, although less dramatically, in corporate compliance programs. In many companies, particularly those that deal regularly with government contractors, compliance and compliance rules and regulations are the guiding principles for behavior. Still, as Weaver and Trevino (1999) have demonstrated in a series of studies of corporate compliance programs, companies with ethics programs have better success at employee compliance than those that have only compliance programs. This is because the division of compliance from ethics allows managers to avoid the question "Is this the right thing to do?" and merely work on the edge of regulatory constraints.

A second reason for misdeeds is the confusion of means and ends. Although companies are in business to create value for their shareholders, shareholders do not expect that the companies will "do anything" to create that value. At WorldCom, the CFO seemed to have gotten means and ends mixed up. In order to keep up the share price, Sullivan instructed his internal auditors to book ordinary expenses as capital expenses. He is quoted as saying that he did this to preserve shareholder value while he worked on rectifying this audit error. However, his means for creating or preserving value were illegal and bad accounting practice, and ultimately caused the shareholders to lose their investments. The separation of ethics from economics was the downfall of WorldCom.

A third reason for misdeeds is the separation of corporate social responsibility from moral responsibility. Corporate social responsibility is often thought of as an add-on—something nice to do for the community. Enron, like Adelphia Cable, was one of the largest donors to its home city, Houston. Similarly, HealthSouth and its CEO were large benefactors of Birmingham. Charity and philanthropy are nice and part of being a good citizen. But such giving does not replace a company's primary responsibilities to produce quality products or services, engage in fair trading practices with its customers, suppliers and competition, and create value for shareholders. Indeed, companies that focus on what they do well will create good products, jobs, and increased share prices, and that is their primary social responsibility. Their moral responsibility is to do all of this without lying, cheating, or stealing—that is, with high moral standards throughout the company and its operations.

Mobil (now ExxonMobil) has funded *Masterpiece Theatre* on PBS for more than forty years. But such largesse cannot replace its moral responsibilities to operate aboveboard. The PBS program cannot cover up or excuse what *Forbes* magazine has reported as a bribery or extortion scheme with government officials in Kazakhstan (Fisher 2003). Again, this separation of corporate social responsibility from corporate moral responsibility allows companies and their managers to imagine that they can be philanthropic and cheat at the same time, just as Mafia members tried to be religious and family-oriented while simultaneously engaging in criminal behavior and even eliminating a family member.

The separation of ethics from commerce only exacerbates the possibility of misbehavior and perhaps even encourages it. No code of ethics, credo, ethics officer, or ethics program will work unless a company is committed to consistently behaving morally. And that behavior has to be exemplified in business practice, not merely in the annual statement.

This conclusion, while morally satisfying to some, leaves open the question, "Can a company engage in morally and socially responsible behavior and still be profitable?" Companies have been doing so for at least a century, although they are only infrequently publicized. In the next section, a contemporary example of one such company attempting to engage in morally and socially responsible behavior will be considered. It will be argued that what is needed for such an achievement is not merely good will, but also a great deal in the way of moral imagination and a systems approach to corporate thinking.

Moral Imagination, Systems Thinking, and Moral Change: ExxonMobil in Chad and Cameroon

Consider a case that takes a different model for thinking about corporate behavior (Mead, Wicks, and Werhane 2003). Subsequent to the behavior in the Kazakhstan case, ExxonMobil now appears to be following a different model. ExxonMobil, in partnership with ChevronTexaco and Petronas (a Malaysian company), is investing $3.5 billion in oil drilling in Chad and building a 600–mile pipeline through Cameroon. The project would generate over a billion barrels of oil, $5.7 billion in revenues for ExxonMobil, $2 billion in revenues for Chad, and $500 million in revenues for Cameroon over an estimated twenty-five years. The pipeline would go through Cameroon's rain forest, an ecologically fragile but important environmental outpost in Africa. Several tribes of Pygmies and Bantus, whose lifestyles depend on forest products, inhabit that area. The project is a challenging one and has attracted a great deal of world attention.

Chad and Cameroon are two of the poorest countries in the world. Per capita income in each country is less than $1 per day. As a comparison, ExxonMobil's 2001 revenues were $190 billion, whereas Chad's GDP was $1.4 billion. According to the nonprofit organization Transparency International, Chad and Cameroon are also known for their corruption, and they repeatedly come out near the bottom of Transparency International's annual corruption list (www.transparency.org).

Originally, the Chad-Cameroon project was to be a joint venture involving Shell, TotalFinaElf, and ExxonMobil. However, Shell and TotalFinaElf withdrew from the venture. According to sources close to these companies, Shell feared another Ogoniland, its often-sabotaged oil fields in southeast Nigeria. Ogoniland proved to be Shell's nemesis for environmental, social, cultural, and political reasons, generating years of alleged environmental and social degradation and very bad press for Shell.

Shell has drilled for oil in Nigeria since 1937 and until recently was the largest oil operator in that country. Its joint venture with Elf and Agip produced over 900,000 barrels of oil a day in the early 1990s, primarily from a region inhabited by an ethnic group called the Ogoni. At the same time, between 1982 and 1992, approximately 1.6 million gallons of oil were spilled in the Nigerian oil fields (some due to dissident Ogoni unhappy with the oil venture), the environment was degraded, and there was a negative impact on family values in the local villages and communities. Although Shell claimed to have invested over $100 million on environmental projects in Nigeria, there was little to show for this investment. Indeed, the *Wall Street Journal* (Brooks 1994) described Ogoniland as "a ravaged environment." Finally, when Shell did not try to intervene or protest the government's assassination of a number of prominent dissidents, including Ken Sari-Wiwa, worldwide media attacked Shell for what was perceived to be complicity in these deaths (Newberry and Gladwin 2002).

Despite $300 billion earned from oil since 1975, Nigeria's per capita income has decreased 23 percent in that time period. In 1993, Shell shut down its operations in Ogoniland, but it still drills for oil and gas in other parts of Nigeria. Shell has dramatically revised its code of ethics, invested at least $100 million in cleaning up Ogoniland, and has pledged over $500 million to explore alternate energy sources (www.shell.com).

Shell, like many oil companies drilling in remote areas or in less developed countries, had approached the Ogoniland project using its standard operating procedures for oil drilling. Such an approach, as Shell now admits, was too simple. A company would locate prospects for oil; get government permission to drill; bring in drilling equipment and foreign drilling experts; hire a few local people for menial temporary jobs; drill, lay pipeline, pump out oil; and pay royalties to the government in question. More enlightened companies took into account the local communities that were affected by the drilling by, for example, building a school or hospital. Recently the pipes themselves have been improved to minimize spills that, even under the best conditions, account for 2 to 3 percent loss of oil every year at every site. Still, at least according to protesters living in Ogoniland, local living conditions, cultural values, governmental structures or the lack thereof (except when sensitive payments were required), environmental issues, and the long-term effects of these projects on the people, the area, and the country were not always taken into account by the company.

ExxonMobil is a new company formed by the merger of Exxon and Mobil. Each had been economically successful in drilling in less developed countries in the past, and each had developed well-proven formulas for drilling and extracting oil. Why should the company change its modus operandi? The history of Shell in Ogoniland, Mobil's alleged payoffs to government officials in Kazakhstan, and Exxon's *Valdez* disaster were probably reason enough for the company to rethink its approach to new drilling in less developed countries with reputations and environmental challenges of the ilk of Chad and Cameroon.

The Chad-Cameroon project presented a challenge, not to ExxonMobil's drilling expertise, but to its thinking about how to expedite this venture while avoiding the problems of previous explorations. To do this required that ExxonMobil revise its traditional mental models for oil exploration that have worked well in developed countries. ExxonMobil needed a new approach for drilling in places such as Chad and Cameroon, and that approach would create a template for future corporate activities. Consequently, it needed to employ a great deal of moral imagination and conceive of this and future projects using a systems approach.

What is meant by moral imagination? Elsewhere, I (Werhane 1999, 93) have defined moral imagination as "the ability in particular circumstances to discover and evaluate possibilities not merely determined by that circumstance, or limited by its operative mental models, or merely framed by a set of rules or rule-governed concerns."

The notion of moral imagination is, by and large, a facilitative reasoning process that helps people think outside of a particular framing box, leading them to refocus their attention, critique, revise, and reconstruct other operative mental models, and develop more creative normative perspectives. Moral imagination requires the ability to disengage—to step back from the situation and take another perspective, or at least be able to begin a critical evaluation of the situation and its operative mental models. Thus, part of being morally imaginative is to perceive the ethical dimensions of a managerial or corporate situation and its operative mind-sets. Of course, no one can ever disengage completely or take a "view from nowhere." Revisions, critiques, and evaluations are still context-driven by history, circumstances, culture, education, and personal framing choices. However, just as children playact, so too can managers devise ways to disengage and step back to examine themselves and their projects from a somewhat disinterested or distanced perspective.

Unlike other forms of imagination, moral imagination deals not with fantasies, but with possibilities that, if not practical, are at least theoretically viable and actualizable. Further, because the conceptual focus is on *moral* imagination, these possibilities have a normative or prescriptive character; they are concerned with what one ought to do, right and wrong, virtue, positive and negative outcomes, or what common morality calls "good" and "evil." That is, moral imagination involves principle-based reasoning.

ExxonMobil's oil project in Chad and Cameroon requires another dimension in its thinking. The project is involved in a complex network of relationships imbedded in a complex set of systems and subsystems, including the cultures of two countries and their diverse indigenous populations, environmental issues, financing, pressures from nongovernmental organizations (NGOs), and, it will turn out, the World Bank. To develop rich decision-making skills may require what the organizational and scientific literatures call "systems thinking" or a systems approach.

For present purposes, systems thinking presupposes that most thinking, experiencing, practices, and institutions are interrelated and interconnected. Almost everything people can experience or think about exists in a network of interrelationships such that each element in a particular set of interrelationships affects the other elements in that set and the system itself. Almost no phenomenon can be studied in isolation from all relationship with at least some other phenomenon.

A systems approach should include the following (Mitroff and Linstone 1993; Werhane 2002):

- Concentration on the network of relationships and patterns of inter-action, rather than on individual components of particular relationships, and spelling out the networks of relationships from different perspectives
- A multiperspective analysis attempting to understand the various perspectives of the manager, the citizen, the firm, the community, the state, law, tradition, background institutions, history, and other networks of relationships
- An evaluative perspective that asks "What values are at stake for which stakeholders?" and "Which take priority, or should take priority?"
- A proactive approach both within the system and in initiating structural change
- Thought about whether and what organizations or individuals within the system might be capable and willing to risk challenging bits of the system in order to carry out change

Figure 3.1   **ExxonMobil's Alliance Model**

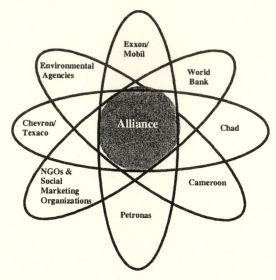

Source: Model Courtesy of Mary Ann Leeper, COO, Female Health Company.

Coupled with moral imagination, systems thinking encourages networked systems analyses that are engaged and critical, creative and evaluative; and values grounded in and encouraging constructive change within a network of relationships.

The Chad and Cameroon Project

Given the character of Chad and Cameroon, overridden with poverty, corruption, environmental challenges, fragile indigenous cultures, and the checkered history of oil exploration in less developed regions, ExxonMobil made the decision to experiment with a new, more systemic approach to oil exploration. The company has created a new model for oil exploration based on an alliance model. This model is shown in Figure 3.1.

Rather than simply drilling for oil on its own or with other corporate partners, ExxonMobil first created an alliance with the Chad and Cameroon governments, the World Bank, and a number of NGOs. Before signing on as a partner, the World Bank conducted an extensive series of environmental studies to determine if this project could be carried out without drastic environmental degradation. It concluded, in a thorough and enlightening 2,000–page report, that with careful drilling and care to the surrounding landscape, and with safety measures that would prevent illicit tapping into the pipeline, the project was environmentally safe. The World Bank then put pressure on the Chad and Cameroon governments to pledge to use the profits they would receive from the project to improve the standard of living of their citizens.

The World Bank's interest was in improving the well-being of the people in Chad and Cameroon. The rationale for considering and then approving the project was that, according to the World Bank (2003b), "[t]his project could transform the economy of Chad. . . . By 2004, the pipeline would increase Government revenues by 45–50% per year and allow it to use those resources for important investments in health, education, environment, infrastructure, and rural development necessary to reduce poverty." The World Bank also ensured that there would be sound fiscal management of the revenues received by Chad and Cameroon, set up strict environmental and social policies, and consulted with a number of NGOs involved in the project.

According to a World Bank (2003b) report, by the middle of 2002 the project employed over 11,000 workers, of whom at least 85 percent were from Chad or Cameroon. Of the local workers, more than 3,700 received high-skills training in construction, electrical, and mechanical trades, and 5 percent of the local workers held supervisory positions. In addition, local businesses benefited from the project to a total of almost $100 million. Through the World Bank, microlending projects were developed that were accompanied by fiscal and technical training. The aim was to establish permanent microlending banks.

ExxonMobil and the World Bank also created alliances with various NGOs to assist with hands-on protection of indigenous populations. The goals of the NGOs are to improve the economies of Chad and Cameroon and to protect indigenous traditions and the environment.

ExxonMobil hired a former prime minister of Chad to coordinate the project and an anthropologist, Ellen Brown, who was in Chad in the Peace Corps some years ago. Under Brown's and other NGO supervision, ExxonMobil is building schools, funding clinics, digging water wells, fielding AIDS education units, and providing antimalarial mosquito nets. In some areas, where sacred trees are in the way of the pipeline, villagers must give permission to remove the trees, and Brown orchestrated chicken sacrifices to preserve the spirit of the trees (Useem 2002).

Evaluating the Project

The alliance model and the various partnerships that ExxonMobil developed are highly imaginative. The model exemplifies a systems approach to this sort of project, and its aim is both to do good and do well in Chad and Cameroon. Still, the project is not without its problems and critics. Despite good intentions, environmental hazards are inescapable. In any oil drilling project, even with the strictest safety measures, there will be oil spills. According to World Bank estimates, annual spill rates will be between 1 and 4 percent. There will be increased greenhouse gas emissions, although the level of the emissions has not been accurately calculated. There will also be forestry and bush product losses (e.g., nuts, herbs, and fruit), for which the indigenous populations are to be compensated. In addition, large projects such as these frequently spawn an increase in HIV infections and other health risks. Agricultural and livestock losses for displaced farms will also occur, although ExxonMobil has guaranteed compensation and/or relocation.

According to the Cameroon Environmental Defense (2002) report, this project has a number of almost insurmountable negative aspects. First, as ExxonMobil, the World Bank, and NGOs working in the region are well aware, there exists no sound rule of law in either country, so that any contracts or promises are not backed with a well-developed legal system to enforce them. Not only is this problematic in terms of agreements between ExxonMobil and the governments, but there is no legal guarantee that money given to the governments will actually be spent on citizen welfare. Indeed, despite World Bank protests, the president of Chad bought arms with his first payment of oil revenue. (He promised not to do this in the future, but there is no legal framework by which to hold him accountable.)

The Cameroon Environmental Defense report questions whether adequate compensation is being provided for land use and displacement of people. There have been some intertribal wars between Pygmies and Bantus concerning whose land is actually being compensated. This sort of quarrel upsets the delicate balance between these tribes, and again, there are no enforcement mechanisms to remedy any injustices or thefts. Consequently, questions arise concerning the protection of rights and cultural values of indigenous peoples in this region. *Fortune* (Useem 2002) reports that not every citizen will be satisfied with ExxonMobil's efforts. For example, locals are complaining that they are not getting jobs, and worries about Pygmy (i.e., the Baka and Bakola tribes) rights abound (Useem 2002).

Both the Cameroon Environmental Defense and the Rainforest Action Network challenged the environmental viability of the project. They argued that issues of water pollution and rain forest protections had not been adequately addressed, so part of the ecosystem may be negatively impacted. Many of the local tribes depend on the forest for food, and changing this ecostructure may not preserve these traditional food supplies.

Project Uncertainty

The moral risk involved in ExxonMobil's oil project cannot be eliminated, since it is hard to calculate, in advance, whether producing oil will create more harm than good in the two countries. Indeed, the moral risk may never even be determined with certainty. Because the project deals with multiple stakeholders in a situation in which there are no enforceable legal mechanisms, ExxonMobil and the World Bank cannot control or mitigate all risks, although the company (as well as Chad and Cameroon or, at least, their governments) will likely profit extensively from this very rich oil source and expand the oil supply for its customers. However, doing nothing will not bring prosperity to Chad or Cameroon. If ExxonMobil sticks to its alliance model and tries to do the right thing while engaged in profitable oil exploration, it will have attempted to apply a morally imaginative systems approach with some success while trying to avoid morally questionable behavior.

Conclusion

A number of factors contribute to moral mistakes. Self-interest or greed may be a contributing factor. Conflicts of interest between professional and institutional commitments, conflicts of role responsibilities, and/or the identification of moral responsibility with role responsibility may lead to the subsequent abdication of individual moral responsibility to institutional or client demands. Analyses such as those discussed earlier are helpful in pinpointing weaknesses in individual, managerial, and corporate decision making. But such analyses do not successfully attack the problem of repeated moral errors. The problems may be in other places, specifically in confusing compliance with ethics, in imagining that social responsibility is merely an add-on, or in separating economic concerns from moral concerns.

Moral imagination coupled with systems thinking is necessary to understand, evaluate, and institute structural, organizational, and individual change. Organizations, institutions, and political economies are dynamic and revisable phenomena, created and changed by individuals. Only when the complexity of the systemic interrelationships is understood can the issues in question be successfully evaluated and changes made that are critical for moral progress.

4

Corporate Governance and Ethical Leadership

Debbie Thorne McAlister and O.C. Ferrell

The events leading to the bankruptcy of Adelphia Communications Corporation highlight the misconduct that can occur when a firm's corporate governance system is weak and ethical leadership is barely existent. In the first years of the twenty-first century, Adelphia was the sixth-largest cable television company in the country. Brothers John and Gus Rigas founded it in 1952, and nearly fifty years later, John's sons, Michael, Tim, and James, were executives at Adelphia. Along with their father, they sat on the company's board of directors.

Adelphia filed for Chapter 11 of the U.S. Bankruptcy Code in June 2002 due to a failure in corporate governance and ethical leadership. Consider the following actions and the effects on stakeholders. A relative was paid nearly $13 million for furniture and design services in 2001. In addition to the use of corporate jets for personal business, off-balance-sheet loans were made to family members. For example, Adelphia helped fund the family purchase of a golf course and the Buffalo Sabres. John Rigas's daughter, Ellen, and her husband lived rent-free in a Manhattan apartment owned by Adelphia. Ellen's husband served on Adelphia's board of directors. A Rigas-owned farm made most of its revenue by performing snow removal, landscaping, and related services for Adelphia.

In late 2002, John Rigas, Michael Rigas, Tim Rigas, the former vice president of finance, James R. Brown, and the former assistant treasurer, Michael Mulcahey, were indicted on twenty-four counts of conspiracy, bank fraud, securities fraud, and wire fraud. All the executives originally pleaded innocent, but Brown later pleaded guilty to three charges in exchange for his testimony against the Rigases. Adelphia is pursuing its own lawsuit in federal court that charges Rigas family members and twenty companies controlled by the family with violation of the Racketeer Influenced and Corrupt Organizations Act (RICO), including a breach of fiduciary duty, abuse of control, waste of corporate assets, and substantial self-dealing. Ethical leadership did not exist, and there appeared to be little concern for stakeholders.

Adelphia sued its external auditor, Deloitte & Touche, for fraud and negligence in failing to uncover the personal gain afforded the Rigas family. The auditing firm countered that Adelphia's board of directors knew of and approved some of the transactions under complaint. Three insurers that provided liability coverage for Adelphia's directors and officers of the firm sued to rescind the contract on the basis that these leaders were aware of the fraud when they applied for coverage. Other stakeholders potentially harmed by Adelphia's bankruptcy are Scientific-Atlanta Inc., Fox News, In Demand, FX, and other channels. These companies are waiting for collections from Adelphia. Share prices of leading cable firms fell as a result of the Adelphia scandal. The cable industry became wary of the misconduct's effect on its reputation and worried that investors might lose confidence because of the situation at Adelphia and other companies like WorldCom.

The central problem is that several executives acted in their own self-interest at a company whose control, risk, and governance system was ineffectual at detecting and preventing such misconduct (Grover 2002; Hahn 2002; Leonard et al. 2002). There was neither a value system nor an ethical compliance program to buffer illegal actions by top management or board members. Today, corporate leaders must be ready for scrutiny and accountability in their communications and decisions (Pagano and Pagano 2003). Through corporate governance, executives and boards ensure that a firm has an effective system of checks and balances for fulfilling responsibilities to stakeholders and society.

Before the governance crises of Enron, WorldCom, and other firms, the editor of Corporate Governance.Net commented on corporate governance as follows: "Despite its still relatively low profile, it's where much of the real action is going on when it comes to positively changing corporate behavior" (McRitchie 1999). By 2002, however, corporate governance was a major issue for business and the public. The effects of the Arthur Andersen, Qwest, Tyco, Global Crossing, and other high-profile scandals were seen in the stock market, in the economy, in the growth of public cynicism and distrust, and even in the job prospects for new college graduates (Russ 2003). The egregious oversights that left thousands without jobs or retirement savings, saw executives being led away to court, prompted federal legislation, and sparked major reform in the accounting and auditing fields challenged the tenets of our economic system (*BusinessWeek* 2002).

In this chapter, we define corporate governance and briefly trace its evolution in the United States. We examine primary issues that should be considered in the development and improvement of corporate governance systems, including the roles of boards of directors, shareholders and investors, internal control and risk management, and executive compensation. Finally, we indicate how strong governance is tied to ethical leadership and consider the future of corporate governance.

The Nature of Corporate Governance

We define corporate governance as the formal system of accountability and control for ethical and socially responsible organizational decisions and use of resources. Accountability relates to how well the content of workplace decisions is aligned with a firm's stated strategic direction. Control involves the process of auditing and improving organizational decisions and actions. The philosophy of business ethics and social responsibility that a board or firm holds directly affects how well accountability, control, and corporate governance work in an organization. Until recently, business ethics was considered a separate field from corporate governance, and the word "ethics" was rarely used in discussing the nature and purpose of corporate governance (Russ 2003).

Discussions of corporate governance often center on executive compensation, auditing and control, organizational performance, disclosure and transparency, executive succession plans, mergers and acquisitions, composition and structure of a board of directors, risk management, and shareholder rights. These issues normally involve strategic-level decisions and actions taken by boards of directors, business owners, executives, and others with high levels of authority and accountability. Although these groups have been relatively free from scrutiny in the past, changes in the business environment have caused stakeholders to demand greater accountability on issues such as ethical compliance, executive pay, risk and control, resource accountability, shareholder rights, and other decisions made on behalf of the organization (McAlister 2003).

From a control perspective, firms need cohesive values and policies in order to achieve consistency across organizational decisions and practices, including financial reporting, human resources, and the establishment of an ethics program. Accountability for organizational decisions and resources begins with a strategic mission and vision that create a responsible organization responsive to stakeholders. From this strategic directive, it is possible to account for and assess decisions made on behalf of the organization. Thus, corporate governance is about the process and content of ethical decision making in business organizations.

Corporate Governance Models

There is variability in how individuals, industries, and even nations approach business accountability and control. In order to understand the role of corporate governance in business, it is important to consider how governance relates to fundamental beliefs about the purpose of business organizations. Some people believe that as long as a company is maximizing shareholder wealth and profitability, it is fulfilling its core responsibility. Although this must be accomplished in accordance with legal and ethical standards, the primary focus is on the economic dimension. Other people, however, take the view that a business is an important member, or citizen, of society and must assume broad responsibilities. This view assumes that business performance is reflexive, meaning it both affects and is influenced by internal and external factors. In this case, performance is often considered from a financial, social, and ethical perspective. From these assumptions, we can derive two major conceptualizations of corporate governance—the shareholder model and the stakeholder model (Maher and Anderson 1999).

The shareholder model of corporate governance is founded in classic economic precepts, including the maximization of wealth for investors and owners. For publicly traded firms, corporate governance focuses on developing and improving the formal system of performance accountability between top management and the firms' shareholders (Demb and Neubauer 1992). Thus, a shareholder orientation should drive management decisions toward what is in the best interests of investors. Underlying these decisions is a classic agency problem, where ownership (i.e., investors) and control (i.e., managers) are separate. Managers act as agents for investors, whose primary goal is shareholder value. However, investors and managers are distinct parties with unique insights, goals, and values with respect to the business. Managers, for example, may have motivations beyond shareholder value, such as market share, personal compensation, or attachment to particular products and projects. Ethical leadership from a shareholder perspective is providing transparency so that shareholders have an opportunity to form a fair judgment about the performance of the corporation (Leaf 2002; Pagano and Pagano 2003). Because of differences in the goals of managers and shareholders, corporate governance mechanisms are needed to ensure an alignment between investor and management interests. Although the shareholder orientation is primarily relevant to publicly held businesses, it also has implications for private firms. However, the shareholder model has been criticized for its restrictive view of the corporation, its constituencies, and its responsibilities (Maher and Anderson 1999).

In the stakeholder model of corporate governance, the purpose of business is conceived in a broader fashion. Although a company has a responsibility for economic success and viability, it must also answer to other parties, including employees, suppliers, government agencies, communities, and groups with which it interacts. This model presumes a collaborative and relational approach to business and its constituents (McAlister 2003). Because management time and resources are limited, a key decision within the stakeholder model is to determine which stakeholders are primary. Once primary groups have been identified, appropriate corporate governance mechanisms are implemented to promote the development of long-term relationships (Organization for Economic Cooperation and Development 1999). Primary stakeholders potentially include shareholders, suppliers, customers, employees, the government, and the community. Governance systems that consider stakeholder welfare in tandem with corporate needs and interests characterize this approach. There is no generic stakeholder group that can be identified for all firms. The characteristics of primary stakeholders and a firm's obligations to specific stakeholder groups will vary considerably (N. Craig Smith 2003).

Although these two approaches seem to represent both ends of a continuum, the reality is that the shareholder model is a more restrictive precursor to the stakeholder model. Many businesses have evolved into the stakeholder model as a result of government initiatives, consumer activism, industry activity, and other external forces. In the aftermath of corporate scandals, the polarity between the two views was narrowed, as it became clear how even the economic accountability of corporations could not be detached from other responsibilities and stakeholder concerns.

The shareholder model focuses on a primary stakeholder—the investor—whereas the stakeholder model incorporates a broader philosophy toward internal and external constituents. Ethical leadership includes understanding what differentiates an organization—its mission, values, ethics, and core business activities (N. Craig Smith 2003). According to the World Bank (World Bank Group 2003a), a development institution whose goal is to reduce poverty by promoting sustainable economic growth around the world, corporate governance is defined by both internal (i.e., long-term value and efficient operations) and external (i.e., public policy and economic development) factors. We are concerned with the broader conceptualization of corporate governance in this chapter.

Brief History of Corporate Governance

In the United States, a discussion of corporate governance draws on many parallels with the goals and values held by the nation's founders (Monks 1996). As mentioned earlier, governance involves a system of checks and balances, a concept associated with the distribution of power within the executive, judicial, and legislative branches of the U.S. government. The U.S. Constitution and other documents have a strong focus on accountability, individual rights, and the representation of broad interests in decision making and resource allocation.

In the late 1800s and early 1900s, corporations were headed by such familiar names as Carnegie, DuPont, and Rockefeller. Because these individuals owned their businesses, there was less reason to talk about corporate governance as the owner of the firm made strategic decisions. The owner primarily bore the consequences—positive or negative—of decisions made. During the twentieth century, however, an increasing number of public companies and investors brought about a gradual shift in the separation of ownership and control. By the 1930s, corporate ownership was dispersed across a large number of individuals. This dispension raised new questions about control and accountability for organizational resources and decisions.

One of the first known incidents that helped shape current understanding of accountability and control in business occurred in 1932, when Lewis Gilbert, a stockholder in New York's Consolidated Gas Company, found his questions repeatedly ignored at the firm's annual shareholder meeting. Consequently, Gilbert pushed for reform, which led the brand-new U.S. Securities and Exchange Commission (SEC) to require corporations to allow shareholder resolutions to be brought to a vote of all stockholders. Because of the Gilbert brothers' activism, the SEC formalized the process by which executives and boards of directors respond to the concerns and questions of investors (McRitchie 1999).

Since the mid-1900s, the approach to corporate governance has involved a legal discussion of principals and agents in the business relationship. Essentially, owners are "principals" who hire "agents," the executives, to run a company. A key goal of businesses is to align the interests of principals and agents so that organizational value and viability are maintained. Achieving this balance has been difficult, as evidenced by cases where the long-term value and competitive stance of organizations were traded for short-term financial gains or rewards. The results of this short-term view included workforce reduction, closed manufacturing plants, struggling communities, investor losses, and a generally negative perception of corporate leadership.

Many stakeholders called for change and looked to the federal government for resolution.

The Sarbanes-Oxley Act of 2002 provided the most significant piece of corporate governance reform in over sixty years. Under the act, both the chief executive officer (CEO) and chief financial officer (CFO) of a company are required to certify that their quarterly and annual reports accurately reflect performance and comply with requirements of the SEC. Among other changes, the act also requires more independence of boards of directors, protects whistle-blowers, and establishes the Public Company Accounting Oversight Board. An independent board audit committee and a code of ethics for top financial executives are supposed to provide ethical principles to prevent financial misconduct. The New York Stock Exchange (NYSE) and NASDAQ overhauled the governance standards required for listed firms and submitted the changes for review, comment, and approval by the SEC. Business codes of ethics, director qualifications, unique concerns of foreign firms, loans to officers and directors, internal auditing, and many other issues are part of the NYSE and NASDAQ reforms (Cifrino and Smith 2002).

Issues in Corporate Governance Systems

Organizations that strive to develop effective corporate governance systems consider a number of internal and external issues. In this section, we look at four areas that need to be addressed in the design and improvement of governance mechanisms. We begin with boards of directors, which have the ultimate responsibility for ensuring a governance focus. Then, we discuss the role of shareholders and investors, internal control and risk management, and executive compensation within the governance system. These issues affect most organizations, although individual businesses may face unique factors that create additional governance questions. For example, a company operating in several countries will need to resolve issues related to international governance policy.

Boards of Directors

Members of a company's board of directors assume legal and ethical responsibility for the firm's resources and decisions, and they appoint its top executive officers. Board members have fiduciary duty, meaning they have assumed a position of trust and confidence that entails certain requisite responsibilities, including acting in the best interests of those they serve. Thus, board membership is not designed as a vehicle for personal financial gain; rather, it provides the intangible benefit of ensuring the success of the organization and the stakeholders affected and involved in the fiduciary arrangement.

"There has been a massive failure in corporate governance," according to William W. George, retired chairman and CEO at Medtronic Inc. and currently a director at Target Corporation, Novartis AG, and Goldman Sachs Group Inc. (Hymowitz 2003, R1). George goes on to say that boards will have "to ratchet up their level of oversight, and make sure management is held to strict codes of conduct" (Hymowitz 2003, R1). The failure of boards to provide oversight is widespread. It is alleged that Kmart executives inflated profit forecasts in order to obtain board-approved executive loans for $24 million just one month before the company filed for bankruptcy. The company's creditors tried to force then-CEO Charles Conaway to repay millions in severance pay and a $5 million loan that was forgiven (Elliot Blair Smith 2003).

The traditional approach to directorship assumed that board members managed the corporation's business, but research and practical observation have shown that boards of directors rarely, if ever, perform the management function (Eisenberg 1997). Because boards meet only a few times a year, there is no way that time allocation would allow for effective management. Today, boards of directors are concerned primarily with monitoring the decisions made by managers on behalf of the company. This includes choosing top executives, assessing their performance, helping to set strategic direction, evaluating company performance, developing CEO succession plans, communicating with stakeholders, maintaining legal and ethical practices, ensuring that control and accountability mechanisms are in place, and evaluating the board's own performance. In sum, board members assume the ultimate authority for organizational effectiveness and ethical performance. A recent study by The Conference Board asked ethics officers about the role of their board of directors in the firm's ethics program. Fifty-five percent believed that their directors were not engaged enough in ethics issues. While over 80 percent of the respondents indicated that employees received ethics training, only 27 percent said that their board of directors had been through ethics training (Conference Board 2003).

Independence

The desire for independence is one reason that firms are studying whether to split the powerful roles of chair of the board and CEO. While the practice is common in the United Kingdom and activists have called for this move for years, the idea has only recently been considered by U.S. and Canadian firms. Chubb Corporation, Midas, Pathmark Stores, Toronto Dominion Bank, and Closure Medical have already made the transition. In addition to independence concerns, it is unlikely that one person can devote the time and energy it takes to be effective in both roles. The National Association of Corporate Directors is in favor of splitting the roles, whereas other experts suggest that a "presiding" chair take over most of the chair's and CEO's duties with respect to the board. Finally, opponents believe the new rules and practices emerging from governance reform may negate the role split debate by improving other aspects of the board's membership and impact (Byrne 2003; Lublin 2002b).

Traditionally, board members were often retired company executives or friends of current executives, but the trend throughout the 1990s was toward outside directors who had valuable expertise yet little vested interest in the firm before assuming a director role. Thus, directors today should be chosen for their competence, motivation, and ability to bring enlightened and diverse perspectives to strategic discussions. Outside directors are thought to bring more independence to the monitoring function because they are not bound by past allegiances, friendships, a current role in the company, or some other matter that may create a conflict of interest. However, independent directors who sit on a board for a long time may eventually lose some of the outsider perspective. A related concern is interlocked chairmanships, where corporate chairs sit on each other's boards. According to a *USA Today* study, there are over twenty pairs of interlocked corporate chairs. While this practice does not currently violate any laws or rules, it may spark the interest of shareholders and other constituents (Jones and Hansen 2003).

Although insiders traditionally represented approximately 20 percent of members on most boards of directors, many dot-com high-technology companies filled their boards with insiders who were heavily invested in the firm. In addition to higher percentages of inside directors, these boards were often smaller than those found in large, traditional businesses. Yahoo!, for example, once had a board of six, including three company executives. Directors of new high-tech firms were usually brought in to add management and strategic expertise to the business, whereas traditional firms tended to choose board members who understood governance, succession planning, and other oversight roles. The dot-com crash brought complaints that many new technology companies had not adequately or carefully considered the importance of strong governance to their long-term success. As legal expert Charles M. Elson noted, "It's really not until something goes wrong that people focus on [governance]" (Reingold 1999).

Quality

Finding board members who have some expertise in the firm's industry or who have served as chief executives at similar-sized organizations is a good strategy for improving the board's overall quality. On the other hand, few directors are trained or certified in their knowledge, and according to one CEO, "Directors can do a lot of damage to shareholder interest and yet don't have to demonstrate any ability to be able to do the job" (Shmukler 2003, R6). Directors with competence and experiences that reflect some of the firm's core issues should bring valuable insights to bear on discussions and decisions. Directors without direct industry or comparable executive experience may bring expertise on salient issues, like ethics programs, executive compensation, and succession planning. Directors also need time to read reports, attend board and committee meetings, and participate in continuing education that promotes strong understanding and quality guidance. For example, directors on the board's audit committee may need to be educated on new accounting and auditing standards. Experts recommend that fully employed board members sit on no more than four boards, whereas retired members should limit their memberships to seven boards. Directors should be able to attend at least 75 percent of the meetings (Lavelle 2002).

Performance

An effective board of directors can serve as a type of insurance against the business cycle and the natural highs and lows of the economy. A study by *Business Week* showed that during robust economic times, the stocks of firms with strong governance and boards outperformed companies with weaker governance by a two-to-one margin. During the economic slowdown in 2000 and 2001, however, the stocks of companies with strong governance bested weakly governed firms by four to one. A similar study by Governance Metrics International demonstrated that firms with strong governance greatly outperform Standard & Poor's (S&P) 500–stock index, while those with weak governance significantly underperform the index (Lavelle 2002). Strong boards ask the tough, yet strategic, questions of management to ensure long-term performance. For example, many Internet businesses found that customer acquisition costs were as much as four times higher online than offline. Other firms soon learned that brand recognition is a long way from brand loyalty and the financial benefits of repeat customers. In hindsight, the high cash burn rate and other problems in dot-com businesses that failed might have been noticed and remedied under more robust governance structures.

Board independence, along with board quality, stock ownership, and corporate performance, is often used to assess the quality of corporate boards of directors. Several factors stand out about the best boards of directors. These boards are generally more independent and have greater accountability to shareholders than the boards of other corporations. Their directors own company stock, making them more sympathetic to shareholder concerns. Moreover, these directors encourage innovative practices and take a more active role than directors of other firms. Apria Healthcare's board includes three shareholder activists and a separate chair and CEO. At 3M, all investors receive user-friendly communications regarding the rights and responsibilities of shareholders, along with an explanation of basic board processes and rules. The head of 3M's audit committee is the former chief financial officer of a leading retailer. Home Depot's ten outside directors visit twenty stores in the chain every year; these visits give them a stronger sense of what is going on within the company, as well as the opportunity to address issues before they become problems. Medtronic's board has been praised for its strong evaluation system, which rates board members on their ability to hold management accountable and on their meaningful participation in meetings (Lavelle 2002).

Rules promulgated by the Sarbanes-Oxley Act and various stock exchanges now encourage a majority of independent directors on the board; regular meetings between nonmanagement board members; audit, compensation, governance, and nominating committees either fully made up of or with a majority of independent directors; and a financial expert on the audit committee. The governance area will continue to evolve as the corporate scandals are resolved and the government and companies begin to implement and test new policies and practices. Regardless of the size and type of business for which boards are responsible, a system of governance is needed to ensure effective control and accountability. As a corporation grows, matures, enters international markets, and takes other strategic directions, it is likely that the board of directors will evolve and change to meet its new demands.

Shareholders and Investors

Because they have allocated scarce resources to the organization, shareholders and investors expect to reap rewards from their investments. This type of financial exchange represents a formal contractual arrangement that provides the capital necessary to fund all types of organizational initiatives, such as developing new products and constructing new facilities. Shareholders are concerned with their ownership investment in publicly traded firms, whereas "investor" is a more general term for any individual or organization that provides capital to a firm. Investments include financial, human, and intellectual capital.

Shareholder Activism

Shareholders, including large institutional ones, have become more active in articulating their positions with respect to company strategy and executive decision making. Activism is a broad term that encompasses engaging in dialogue with management, attending annual meetings, submitting shareholder resolutions, bringing lawsuits, and other mechanisms designed to communicate shareholder interests to the corporation.

Shareholder resolutions are nonbinding, yet important, statements about shareholder concerns. A shareholder that meets certain guidelines may bring one resolution per year to a proxy vote of all shareholders at a corporation's annual meeting. Recent resolutions brought forward relate to auditor independence, executive compensation, independent directors, environmental impact, human rights, and other social responsibility issues. In some cases, the company will modify its policies or practices before the resolution is ever brought to a vote. In other situations, a resolution will receive less than a majority vote, but the media attention, educational value, and other stakeholder effects will cause a firm to reconsider, if not change, its original position to meet the resolution's proposal. The accounting scandals prompted many resolutions about executive compensation among shareholders who believe that improper compensation structures are often a precursor to accounting mismanagement (Burr 2002). The resolution process is regulated by the SEC in the United States and by complementary offices in other countries; some critics of the process claim the process is more favorable to the corporation than to shareholders.

Other shareholder concerns reach the legal realm. For example, the California Public Employees' Retirement System (CalPERS) led a suit against W.R. Grace & Co. after officers and directors paid a $20 million severance package to a CEO who resigned amid sexual harassment allegations in 1995. Known as an aggressive institutional investor, CalPERS bolstered the lawsuit effort because it demanded stronger corporate governance mechanisms, including a sexual harassment policy. The lawsuit, finally settled in 1999, included a recovery of nearly $4 million, to be divided among all company stockholders. The insurer that covered the company's board of directors paid the $4 million. In addition, the company agreed to develop a progressive policy against sexual harassment and to appoint more independent, outside directors on the board of directors' auditing, nominating, and compensation committees (Anderson 1999).

Social Investing

Many investors believe in the stakeholder model of corporate governance and follow a strategy of social investing in which social and ethical criteria are formally integrated into their investment decisions (Kinder, Lyndenberg, and Domini 1992). Roughly three-quarters of U.S. investors take social responsibility issues into account when choosing investment opportunities. Twelve percent indicate that they are willing to take a lower rate of return if the company is a strong performer in the social responsibility area (SocialFunds.com 2003). However, most social investors do not have to worry about a poor return on their investments. Over the past decade, the Domini 400 Social Index, the benchmark for social investing, had an average annualized 14.02 percent return versus a 13.27 percent return for the S&P 500–stock index. While social investing has traditionally been conducted through managed mutual funds, like those with Domini Social Investments, TIAA-CREF, Vanguard, and Calvert Group, some individual investors are using Web-based research to venture out on their own. Web sites such as FOLIOfn, SocialFunds.com, and Morningstar Inc. provide information and services to help the socially conscious investor in decision making (Scherreik 2002).

Thus, individuals have a number of opportunities to demonstrate an active strategy with respect to investing and social responsibility. Whereas a passive investor is mainly concerned with buying and selling stock and receiving dividends, social investors are taking a variety of stakeholder issues into account when making investment decisions. Social investors take the social responsibility of "ownership" seriously since a firm in which they invest implements plans and tactics on behalf of its owners. It could be argued that the dishonest actions of a firm are carried out on behalf of shareholders; thus, an investor in the firm would also be responsible. Conversely, it could be argued that a firm implementing a strong social responsibility strategy and agenda is doing so on behalf of its owners (Langtry 2002). Shareholder activism is the strategy for ensuring that owners' perspectives on social responsibility are included on the corporate agenda.

Investor Confidence

Shareholders and other investors must have assurance that their money is being placed in the care of capable and trustworthy organizations. These primary stakeholders are expecting a solid return from their investment but, as illustrated earlier, have additional concerns about social responsibility. When these fundamental expectations are not met, the trust that investors and shareholders have in corporations, market analysts, investment houses, stockbrokers, mutual fund managers, financial planners, and other economic players and institutions can be severely tested. Part of this trust relates to the perceived efficacy of corporate governance. In 2003, over 300 nonbinding shareholder proposals sought to modify excessive executive pay and uncover the mystifying link between CEO pay and performance. According to a survey by Mercer Human Resource Consulting, although the total return of the

S&P 500 decreased by nearly 25 percent in 2002, CEO total annual compensation (base salary and bonus) increased by a median of 10 percent in that same year (Calabro 2003).

Bankruptcies and financial misconduct in the early 2000s shook investor confidence. In the days after each major scandal broke, volatile, intraday market swings of 200 to 300 points were common. Mutual fund managers with sizable investments in firms accused of misconduct were questioned about their aptitude in choosing and selling stocks. Consumers, financially uneasy and cautious about spending, saw their portfolios and retirement accounts dwindle. At Charles Schwab, the largest discount brokerage in the United States, annual trades per account dropped to an average 3.6, compared to more than 8 per account the previous year. A group of finance ministers from twenty-four countries, known as G24, asked the United States to take quick action to restore investor confidence and ensure the continuation of global growth. The malfeasance at Global Crossing, Tyco, and other firms had effects throughout the global economic system. Essentially, stakeholders were calling for boards of directors and others with access to financial records and the power to demand accountability to tighten the control and risk environment in companies (Schepp 2002).

Internal Control and Risk Management

Controls and a strong risk management system are fundamental to effective operations because they allow for comparisons between the actual performance and the planned performance and goals of the organization. Controls are used to safeguard corporate assets and resources, protect the reliability of organizational information, and ensure compliance with regulations, laws, and contracts. Risk management is the process used to anticipate and shield the organization from unnecessary or overwhelming circumstances, while ensuring that executive leadership is taking the appropriate steps to move the organization and its strategy forward. A recent study revealed that this area of governance, which deals with organizational processes, is a top priority for executives. The survey reported that 76 percent of the surveyed executives were improving internal controls, 64 percent were reviewing relationships with auditors and accountants, and 55 percent were revising their codes of conduct (Corporate Reputation Watch 2003).

Internal and External Audits

Auditing, both internal and external, is the linchpin tying risk, controls, and corporate governance together. Boards of directors must ensure that the internal auditing function of the company is provided with adequate funding, up-to-date technology, unrestricted access, independence, and authority to carry out its audit plan. To ensure these characteristics, the internal audit executive should report to the board's audit committee and, in most cases, the chief executive officer (*Internal Auditor* 2002).

The external auditor should be chosen by the board and must clearly identify its client as the board, not the company's chief financial officer. Under Sarbanes-Oxley, the board audit committee is directly responsible for the selection, payment, and supervision of the company's external auditor. The act also prohibits an external auditing firm from performing some nonaudit work for the same public company, including bookkeeping, human resources, actuarial services, valuation services, legal services, and investment banking. The friendly relationship that can develop between an external auditor and the firm's financial team may affect the auditor's ability to maintain independence in the auditing process and report. For example, in more than half of the largest bankruptcies since 1996, the external audit report provided no hint of the pending financial downfall. The external audits conducted on Kmart, Global Crossing, and Enron issued clean audit perspectives just months before the companies' respective bankruptcies. Part of the problem relates to the sheer size and complexity of organizations, but these factors do not negate the tremendous responsibility that external auditors assume.

Control Systems

The area of internal control covers a wide range of company decisions and actions, not just the accuracy of financial statements and accounting records. Controls also foster understanding when discrepancies exist between corporate expectations and stakeholder interests and issues. Internal controls effectively limit employee or management opportunism, or the use of corporate assets for individual or nonstrategic purposes. Controls also ensure that the board of directors has access to timely, quality information that can be used to determine strategic options and effectiveness. For these reasons, the board of directors should have ultimate oversight for the integrity of the internal control system (Eisenberg 1997). Although board members do not develop or administer the control system, they are responsible for ensuring that an effective system exists. The need for internal controls is rarely disputed, but implementation can vary. Thus, internal control represents a set of tasks and resource commitments that require high-level attention.

Although most large corporations have designed internal controls, smaller companies and nonprofit organizations are less likely to have invested in a complete system. For example, a small computer shop in Columbus, Ohio, lost thousands of dollars due to embezzlement by the accounts receivable clerk. Because of the clerk's position and role in the company, she was able to post credit card payments due her employer to her own account and then later withdraw the income. Although she faced felony theft charges, the owner of the computer shop admitted feeling ashamed and did not want his business associated with a story on employee theft (Hoke 1999). Such crime is common in small businesses because they often lack effective internal controls. These techniques are not always costly and they conform to best practices in the prevention of ethical and legal problems that threaten the efficacy of governance mechanisms.

Risk Management

A strong internal control system should alert decision makers to possible problems, or risks, that may threaten business operations, including worker safety, company solvency, vendor relationships, proprietary information, and environmental impact. Risk is always present within organizations, so executives must develop processes for remedying or managing its effects. A board of directors should expect the top management team to have risk management skills and plans in place. In reality, crisis-prepared companies are in the minority. At least 75 percent of *Fortune* 500 companies are not equipped to manage an unfamiliar crisis (Mitroff and Alpaslan 2003).

There are at least three ways to view risk as either a potentially negative or positive concern for organizations (Billington 1997). First, risk can be categorized as a hazard. In this view, risk management focuses on minimizing negative situations, such as fraud, injury, or financial loss. Second, risk may be considered an uncertainty that needs to be hedged through quantitative plans and models. This type of risk is best associated with the term "risk management," which is used in the financial and business literature. Third, risk also creates the opportunity for innovation and entrepreneurship. All three types of risk are implicitly covered by our definition of corporate governance because there are risks for both control (i.e., preventing fraud and ensuring accuracy of financial statements) and accountability (i.e., innovation to develop new products and markets). For example, the Internet and electronic commerce capabilities have introduced new risks of all types to organizations.

Regular audits permit shareholders and investors to judge whether a firm is achieving the goals it has established and whether it abides by the values it has specified as important. A significant benefit of ethics auditing is that it may prevent public relations crises resulting from ethical or legal misconduct, crises that potentially can be more devastating than traditional natural disasters or technological disruptions. Just as companies develop crisis management plans to respond to and recover from natural disasters, they should also prepare for ethical disasters, which can result not only in substantial legal and financial costs, but also disrupt routine operations, paralyze employees and reduce productivity, destroy organizational reputation, and erode stakeholder confidence.

CEO Compensation

How executives are compensated for their leadership, organizational service, and performance has become an extremely troublesome topic. Leading business publications, including the *Harvard Business Review*, weighed in on excessive compensation, perhaps the most controversial aspect of corporate governance in recent memory (e.g., Elson 2003; Martin 2002). Indeed, 73 percent of respondents in a *Business Week*-Harris poll indicated they believe that top officers of large U.S. companies receive too much compensation (Bernstein 2000). Many people believe that no executive is worth millions of dollars in annual salary and stock options, even one who has brought great financial returns to investors. The reality, however, is that some executives continue to receive extremely high pay packages while their companies fall into ruin. A study by United for a Fair Economy and the Institute for Policy Studies found that CEOs in twenty-three firms under federal investigation received compensation averaging $62 million over three years. These firms laid off 162,000 employees, and their combined stock values plunged $530 billion in the same period (Bauder 2002; Grant 2002).

Unease over executive compensation often centers on the relationship between the highest-paid executives and median employee wages in the company. If this ratio is perceived as too large, then critics believe that either rank-and-file employees are not being compensated fairly or high executive salaries represent an improper use of company resources. The average executive now earns nearly 600 times the average worker's salary, up from forty times the average salary in the 1960s. Critics have asked whether business executives are generating such strong performance that they deserve this striking movement in pay over the last thirty or forty years. The usual answer is a resounding no (*Across the Board* 2002).

Because of the enormous difference between CEO and employee pay, the business press is careful to support high levels of executive compensation only when it is directly linked to strong company performance. Most of the business press has criticized compensation packages over the last few years. Although the issue of executive compensation has received much attention in the media of late, some business owners have long recognized its potentially ill effects. In the early twentieth century, for example, the capitalist J.P. Morgan implemented a policy that limited the pay of top managers in businesses he owned to no more than twenty times the pay of any other employee (Anderson et al. 1999).

It has been argued that because executives assume so much risk on behalf of a company, they deserve the rewards that follow from strong company performance. In addition, many executives' personal and professional lives meld to the point that they are on call twenty-four hours a day. Because not everyone has the skill, experience, and desire to become an executive and assume so much pressure and responsibility, market forces dictate a high level of compensation. When the pool of qualified individuals is limited, many corporate board members feel that offering a large compensation package is the only way to attract and retain a top executive to ensure their firm has strong leadership. In an era where top executives are increasingly willing to move to other firms that offer higher pay, potentially lucrative stock options, bonuses, and other benefits, such thinking is not without merit (Lavelle 2002).

The E*Trade Group CEO, Christos M. Cotsakos, returned $21 million in pay after shareholder complaints about his $80 million pay package. Cal Turner Jr., the CEO of Dollar General, gave back $6.8 million after the firm's financial results were restated (Strauss 2002a). These examples show that executive compensation is an important, yet potentially explosive, issue for boards of directors and other stakeholders to consider. Under new NYSE rules, the compensation committee must be entirely made up of independent directors and must establish goals and responsibilities, member qualifications, and a process of self-evaluation. The NASDAQ revisions require independent directors' approval of CEO compensation, either through an independent compensation committee or through a majority of independent directors meeting in a closed session.

Regardless of the structure, an integral matter for boards and compensation committees to consider is the extent to which executive compensation is linked to long-term company performance. Plans that base compensation on the achievement of several performance goals are intended to align the interests of owners with management. However, many executives are rewarded through stock options and other programs that provide an incentive for managing stock price and short-run gains. When executive wealth is heavily tied to the short-term performance of the company's stock, it can drive aggressive and misrepresentative accounting and related practices, as revealed in recent corporate scandals. Other points for review include the evaluation criteria for executive performance, use of compensation consultants to help determine appropriate pay, disclosure of executive compensation, industry standards for remuneration, the ability to attract top talent, and incentives for superior performance (Conference Board Commission on Public Trust and Private Enterprise 2002).

Linking Corporate Governance and Ethical Leadership

As the issues discussed in the previous section demonstrate, corporate governance is primarily focused on strategic-level concerns for accountability and control. Although many discussions of corporate governance still revolve around responsibility in investor-owned companies, good governance is fundamental to effective performance in all types of organizations. A system of checks and balances is important for ensuring a focus on multiple perspectives and constituencies; on proper distribution of resources, power, and decision authority; and on the responsibility for making changes and setting direction.

Given the increasing complexity of governance and corporate responsibility, the relationship between corporate governance and ethical leadership is an important one to consider. As recent scandals have illuminated, ethical leadership, whether embodied by top executives or a board of directors, has significant effects on stakeholder relationships and subsequent performance. Much like the classic chicken-and-egg dilemma, this section will explore the role of ethical leadership in promoting strong governance and the influence of corporate governance on ethical leadership.

Role of Ethical Leadership

Most experts agree that the CEO establishes the ethical tone for the entire firm. Lower-level managers and employees obtain their cues from top managers and then, in turn, impose some of their personal values on the company. This interaction between corporate culture and executive leadership helps determine the ethical value system of the firm. However, obedience to authority can also explain why many people resolve workplace issues by following the directives of a superior. An employee may feel obligated to carry out the orders of a superior, even if those orders conflict with the employee's values of right and wrong. If that decision is later judged to have been wrong, the employee may justify it by saying, "I was only carrying out orders" or "My boss told me to do it this way."

A recent study of ethics officers and corporate executives revealed that ethical leadership is described as people-oriented, modeled through visible ethical actions and traits, focused on setting ethical standards and accountability, based on broad ethical awareness, and indicative of a strong decision-making approach (Trevino, Brown, and Hartman 2003). Table 4.1 elaborates

Table 4.1

Characteristics of Ethical Leadership

Characteristics	Practices
People oriented	Cares about people
	Treats people with respect
Modeled through visible ethical actions and traits	Serves as role model of ethical conduct
	Is consistent and predictable
Focused on setting ethical standards and accountability	Does not tolerate ethical lapses
	Practices values-based management
Based on broad ethical awareness	Serves the greater good
	Acknowledges interests of multiple stakeholders
Indicative of a strong decision-making approach	Uses fairness criteria
	Employs other heuristics, such as the golden rule and "newspaper test"

Source: Trevino, Brown, and Hartman (2003).

on these characteristics and associated best practices in the workplace. However, articles have also examined the lack of ethical leadership and its effects on corporate culture (e.g., Sims and Brinkmann 2002; Trevino, Weaver, Gibson, and Toffler 1999). Leadership influences many aspects of organizational behavior, including employees' acceptance of and adherence to organizational norms and values. Leadership that focuses on building strong organizational values among employees creates agreement on norms of conduct. Leaders in highly visible positions in the organization play a key role in transmitting values and diffusing norms and codes of ethics (Brass, Butterfield, and Skaggs 1998).

The two dominant leadership styles are transactional and transformational leadership. Transactional leadership attempts to create employee satisfaction through negotiating for levels of performance, or "bartering" for desired behaviors. Transformational leaders, in contrast, try to raise the level of commitment of employees and create greater trust and motivation (Burns 1985). Transformational leaders attempt to promote activities and behavior through a shared vision and common learning experience. Table 4.2 describes the fundamental values and assumptions of these two leadership approaches.

Transactional Leadership

Transactional leadership focuses on making certain that the required conduct and procedures are implemented. The use of negotiation as barter to achieve the desired outcomes results in a dynamic relationship between leaders and

Table 4.2

Leadership Approaches

	Transactional leadership	Transformational leadership
Relations to others	Independent	Interdependent
Rights and obligations	Actions to protect individual rights are valued	Actions that meet social obligations are valued
Nature of goals	Pragmatic goals	Idealistic goals
Evaluation of means and ends	Ends justify means (outcome or teleological orientation)	Means justify ends (process or deontological orientation)
Behavioral strategy to influence others	Social contract and exchange of resources as basis for influence	Cultivating personal virtues and empowerment of others as basis of influence
Nature of ethics	Emphasis on purpose and on particulars	Emphasis on duty and on universals

Source: Kanungo (2001).

employees in which reactions, conflict, and crisis are more influential than ethical concerns. Transactional leaders produce employees who achieve a negotiated level of required ethical performance or compliance. As long as employees and leaders find the exchange mutually rewarding, the compliance relationship is likely to be successful. However, transactional leadership is best suited to changing ethical climates quickly or reacting to ethical problems or issues. Michael Capellas used transactional leadership to change his firm's culture and ethical conduct when he took over as CEO and chair after an accounting scandal forced the company into bankruptcy proceedings. Capellas sought to restore WorldCom's—now called MCI—credibility in the marketplace by bringing in a new board of directors, creating a corporate ethics office, enhancing the code of ethics, and launching new financial reporting and ethics training initiatives for employees (*Wall Street Journal* 2003).

Transformational Leadership

Transformational leaders communicate a sense of mission, stimulate new ways of thinking, and enhance as well as generate new learning experiences. Transformational leadership considers the employees' needs and aspirations in conjunction with organizational needs. Therefore, transformational leaders have a stronger influence on coworker support and building of an ethical culture than transactional leaders. Transformational leaders also build a commitment to and respect for values that provide agreement on how to deal with ethical issues. Transformational leadership is best suited for higher levels of ethical commitment among employees and strong stakeholder support for an ethical climate. A number of industry trade associations, including the American Institute of Certified Public Accountants, Defense Initiative on Business Ethics and Conduct, Ethics Officer Association, and Mortgage Bankers Association of America, are helping companies provide transformational leadership (Greenwood, Suddaby, and Hinings 2002).

Our position is that both transformational and transactional leaders can effectively influence the organizational climate, although some scholars have suggested that transformational leadership is more successful in positively managing the ethical climate (e.g., Bass 1998; Burns 1985). As Kanungo (2001, 263) noted, "the two types of leadership behaviors have to be judged for their moral standing by using two fundamentally different ethical perspectives." Further, the efficacy of each style may be dependent on current organizational needs, industry type, employee characteristics, and other factors. The relationship between ethical leadership and corporate governance is inherently reflexive. A CEO's leadership approach will affect the ways in which priorities develop and decisions are made. Concurrently, the governance environment may allow or restrict a particular leadership approach. Most executives believe it is their own personal responsibility to manage the company's reputation, which is largely affected by the ethical standards demonstrated to both internal and external stakeholders. These executives also believe that the board has responsibility, as well, in managing the firm's reputation (Corporate Reputation Watch 2003).

Although boards of directors exercise ultimate authority in organizations, they are removed from daily decision making and the administration of strategy, stakeholder relationships, and other management tasks. Thus, executives are the fundamental nexus between the board and its broader constituents, including customers, employees, business partners, and the community. In this role, executives ensure that all forms of strategic decisions—from setting ethical standards to selecting new business ventures—are considered and implemented with board-approved methods and philosophy. CEOs focused on ethical leadership recognize and reap the benefits of governance, including control, accountability, strategy, and collaboration (Taylor 2003).

Role of Boards of Directors

Regardless of a CEO's particular leadership approach, boards of directors must expect the CEO and other executives to emphasize ethics, along with many other aspects of strategy. The governance philosophy that a board of directors assumes affects the degree to which a CEO demonstrates a verbal and tangible commitment to ethics. The "yes man" boards of the past will not suffice in developing a connection between ethics and governance. Although ethics is an element of the Sarbanes-Oxley legislation, boards will need to be proactive in asking questions about the firm's ethics program and ensuring that communication and strategic decisions are clearly focused on building an ethical climate. In a report titled *The Role of the Board of Directors in Enron's Collapse*, the United States Senate Subcommittee on Investigations pointedly blamed the board of directors for a host of governance infractions, including fiduciary failure, high-risk accounting, excessive compensation, and conflicts of interest. The subcommittee "identified more than a dozen red flags that should have caused the Enron Board to ask hard questions, examine Enron policies, and consider changing course. Those red flags were not heeded" (United States Senate Committee on Governmental Affairs 2002, 61).

Ethics as a Business Goal

Inducing ethical behavior and/or reducing unethical behavior are business goals no different from increasing profits or satisfying customers. Boards should expect these ethics-related goals to be on the corporate agenda. If progress is not being made toward creating and maintaining an ethical culture, boards must require that executives determine why and take corrective action, either by enforcing current standards more strictly or by setting higher standards. If the code of ethics is aggressively enforced and becomes part of the corporate culture, it can be effective in improving ethical behavior within the organization. If a code is merely window dressing and not genuinely part of the corporate culture, it will accomplish very little. Corporations involved in recent high-level scandals, such as Enron and WorldCom, often had codes of ethics that were not integrated into the corporate culture.

Ethics Programs

Boards must expect top management to provide a plan for developing and maintaining an ethical corporate culture that affects decision making at all levels. If boards and executives do not explicitly address these issues, a culture may emerge in which unethical behavior is sanctioned and rewarded—whether in the boardroom or on the manufacturing line. To be most successful, ethical standards and expected behaviors should be integrated throughout every organizational process, from hiring, training, strategic planning, implementing, and rewarding to firing. Boards must adhere to the same code and set even higher standards for themselves. In addition to ensuring that organizational ethics are codified, the board will need to consider its own values and ethics in managing itself and overseeing corporate behavior and outcomes. A strong ethical culture within the board should enable responsible decision making on the key governance issues discussed earlier.

An organization needs a comprehensive ethical compliance program that includes a code of ethics, ethics training, an ethics officer, ongoing communication, an employee assistance "hot line," and other systems to monitor and assess the program's effectiveness (Ferrell, Thorne, and Ferrell 1998). A prescribed, customized ethics program may guide organizations in helping employees from diverse backgrounds understand acceptable behavior within the organization. Many complex issues in business require organizational agreement regarding appropriate action. Top executives and boards of directors must provide the leadership and a system to resolve these issues. The Ad Hoc Advisory Group on the Organizational Sentencing Guidelines (United States Sentencing Commission 2003) made the following recommendations related to ethical compliance and corporate governance:

- Emphasize the importance of an organizational culture that encourages a commitment to compliance with the law.
- Specify the responsibilities of an organization's governing authority and organizational leadership for compliance.
- Include training and dissemination of training materials and information within the definition of an "effective program."
- Add "periodic evaluation of the effectiveness of a program" to the requirement for monitoring and auditing systems.
- Provide for the conduct of ongoing risk assessments as part of the implementation of an "effective program."

Future of Corporate Governance and Ethical Leadership

Because governance is concerned with the decisions made by boards of directors and executives, it has the potential for far-reaching positive—and negative—effects. Until recently, governance was one area in the business literature that had not received the same level of attention as other issues, such as environmental impact, diversity, and sexual harassment (Carver 2002). Over the next few years, however, ethical leadership and corporate governance will emerge as operational centerpieces of corporate responsibility. The future will require that business leaders have a different set of skills and attitudes, including the ability to balance multiple interests, handle ambiguity, manage complex systems and networks, create trust among stakeholders, and improve processes so ethical leadership is pervasive throughout the organization (*Harvard Management Update* 1999). A majority of executives from Europe, Asia, and North America believe that diminished corporate reputations and corporate wrongdoing have permanently changed the business landscape (Corporate Reputation Watch 2003). There are several key forces and directions to consider.

First, business leaders and managers will need to embrace governance and ethical leadership as essential to effective organizational performance. Some of the elements of corporate governance, particularly executive pay, board composition, and shareholder rights, are likely to stir debate for many years. However, business leaders must recognize the forces that have brought governance and ethical leadership to the forefront as preconditions of management responsibility. Thus, they need to accept the "creative tension" that exists between managers, owners, and other primary stakeholders as the preferable route to mutual success (Monks 1996).

Second, government agencies and legislators have a key role to play in corporate governance. National competitiveness depends on the strength of various institutions, with primacy on the effective performance of business and capital markets. Strong corporate governance is essential to this performance, and governments will need to be actively engaged in affording both protection and accountability for corporate power and decisions. Just like the corporate crises in the United States, the Asian economic crisis years earlier prompted companies and governments around the world to consider tighter governance procedures. The positive return on governance goes beyond organizational performance to benefit the industrial competitiveness of entire nations. Further, as nations with large economies embrace responsible governance principles, it becomes even more difficult for nations and organizations that do not abide by such principles to compete in these lucrative and rich markets. There is a contagion effect toward corporate governance among members of the global economy, much as peer pressure influences the actions and decisions of individuals.

Third, stakeholders are becoming more willing to use governance mechanisms to influence corporate strategy, standards, and decision making (e.g., Equality Project 2003). Investors, whether they are shareholders, employees, or business partners, have a stake in decisions and should be willing to take steps to align various interests for long-term benefits. Many investors and stakeholders are willing to exert great influence on underperforming companies.

Finally, the past emphasis of governance systems and theory was on the conflicts of interest between management and investors (Daily, Dalton, and Cannella 2003). Governance today holds people at the highest organizational levels accountable and responsible to a broad, diverse set of stakeholders. Perhaps the greatest challenge is the power shift taking place between executives and board members. A key issue in the future will be the board's ability to align corporate decisions with various stakeholder interests (*Economist* 2003; Hymowitz 2003). According to Robert Monks (1996, 1), an activist money manager and leader on corporate governance issues, effective corporate governance requires understanding that the "indispensable link between the corporate constituents is the creation of a credible structure (with incentives and disincentives) that enables people with overlapping but not entirely congruent interests to have a sufficient level of confidence in each other and the viability of the enterprise as a whole."

5

Ethical Leadership and Creating Value for Stakeholders

R. Edward Freeman

We need a new way to think about business. Business executives in the last twenty or so years have witnessed unprecedented changes, and the dominant models and frameworks that are used to understand business cannot easily account for these changes. From the globalization of capital markets to the emergence of powerful information technologies, the very nature of the modern corporation has changed virtually beyond recognition.

The basic idea is quite simple. Business can be understood as a set of relationships among groups that have a stake in the activities that make up the business. Business is about how customers, suppliers, employees, financiers (stockholders, bondholders, banks, etc.), communities, and managers interact and create value. To understand a business is to know how these relationships work. The executive's job is to manage and shape these relationships.

Customers, suppliers, employees, financiers, communities, and managers are all key parts of today's business organization. Indeed, a thorough understanding of the very basics of capitalism will show that this has always been true. The relatively recent fascination with only one of these groups—stockholders—as necessary to business success is an aberration. The very nature of capitalism is putting together a deal, or a contract, or a set of relationships among all kinds of stakeholders so that all can win continuously over a long period of time.

Four Trends

Presently there are at least four major trends, each of which has had profound effects on business. First, few people are arguing that we need more government planning and control of private business. Indeed, around the world, governments have been exiting markets, leaving business to private parties, and selling their stakes in industry after industry through privatization. Markets have become much more open and liberal, and while there is still steady pressure for regulation, most policy makers around the globe realize that the basic processes of markets, companies, and investments are the keys to prosperity.

Second, along with the liberalization of markets has come a liberalization of political institutions around the world. The fall of communism, the pressure for more market-oriented reform in countries as different as Japan and Indonesia, the market reforms in China, and the openings of once closed societies have all had a tremendous impact on the opportunities available for businesses. Business today is global in unprecedented ways.

Third, over the last few decades we have "discovered" that we need to take better care of our environment. This environmental awareness, led by nongovernmental interest groups, has spread around the world. And it has led to a wealth of innovation in business. 3M sells products from its waste stream. Companies like Patagonia make useful products out of what once would have been garbage. Even U.S. automobile manufacturers are inventing new technologies that make the internal combustion engine cleaner. Many critics have argued that environmental values are only the beginning of a larger trend, namely, that business can and should pay attention to societal issues.

Finally, these three trends are fueled by a fourth one—the impressive advances in information technology. The information revolution has made it possible for businesses around the globe to see vast improvements in productivity and innovation. Today's world is connected, wired, plugged in, and turned on. Information technology has changed the very nature of the way that we work with each other, emphasizing knowledge shared among workplace locations.

Each of these trends has added a layer of complexity and intensity to stakeholder relationships. Whether, as IBM says, it is an "on-demand" world, or whether the interconnections among stakeholders make communication much easier, there are few secrets in today's world. Executives live in the fishbowl, on full display. They need a way of thinking that easily integrates the many changes that they face. Focusing only on stockholders and shareholder value is not helpful.

The Basic Framework of Managing for Stakeholders

Stakeholders are groups that can affect or be affected by the achievement of a business's core purpose. The idea is simple. A business is successful insofar as it satisfies key stakeholders continually over time. And it must be aware of potential influences from groups that may be at odds with its purpose. At the very heart of the process of value creation that is business, we find a profound concern with stakeholder interests and relationships. For most businesses, managers or entrepreneurs must minimally put together a deal (or agreement, or contract) so that customers, employees, suppliers, financiers, and communities jointly share in the value that is created. Over time, the function of an executive is to balance the interests of these groups and increase the value that is created for all of them (Freeman 1984, 1994; Donaldson and Preston 1994; Jones 1995).

Stockholders are one very important stakeholder, but there are others. I want to suggest that there are at least two important kinds. There are stakeholders that might be called "primary" or "definitional" stakeholders to signify that they are vital to the continued growth and survival of any business. These are customers, employees, suppliers, communities, and financiers. Take away the support of any one of these groups and the resulting business is not sustainable. This is perhaps less clear in the case of community, but remember that in a relatively free society, if community interests are not satisfied, activists often go to government for relief, and the result may be more and more regulation that may well threaten the business. Second, we need to look at the broader business environment on a routine basis, and in particular we have to be concerned with those groups that can affect primary relationships. Activists, competitors, governments, media environmentalists, corporate critics, and special interest groups are all "instrumental" stakeholders insofar as they can affect primary business relationships.

More important than the illustrative web of relationships is the mind-set that must accompany it. This stakeholder mind-set means understanding that business is merely creating value for stakeholders. From start-ups to large bureaucratic firms, business works when customers, suppliers, employees, communities, and financiers get their needs and desires satisfied over time. A key insight of the "managing for stakeholders" framework is that the interests of these groups must be considered together. A business that constantly trades off the interests of one group for another is doomed to fail.

Seeing stakeholder interests as joint rather than opposed is difficult. It is not always easy to find a way to accommodate all stakeholder desires. Indeed, it is easier to trade off one against another. Why not delay spending on new products for customers in order to keep earnings a bit higher? Why not cut employee medical benefits in order to invest in a new inventory control system? The stakeholder mind-set asks executives to reframe the questions. How can the business invest in new products and create higher earnings? How can it be sure employees are healthy, happy, and able to work creatively so that the benefits of new information technology such as inventory control systems can be captured?

The current way of thinking about business and management simply asks the wrong question. It asks the value allocation question: How should businesses distribute the burdens and benefits among stakeholders? The "managing for stakeholders" mind-set asks the value creation question: How can businesses create as much value as possible for all stakeholders?

In a recent book reflecting on his experience as CEO of Medtronic, Bill George (2003, 104) summarized the "managing for stakeholders" mind-set:

> Let me be very clear about this: There is no conflict between serving all your stakeholders and providing excellent returns for shareholders. In the long term it is impossible to have one without the other. However, serving all these stakeholder groups requires discipline, vision and committed leadership.

It is to these topics that we now turn.

Ethics, Values, and the Creation of Value for Stakeholders

The "managing for stakeholders" mind-set raises a host of new strategic questions. When executives focus on the process of creating value for stakeholders, they can no longer separate the ethics and values questions from the business questions. They must ask questions that deal with issues of purpose, vision, and values. What do we stand for? What are our aspirations? For whom do we want to create value and how? What do we want to leave behind for others?

Each of these questions deals simultaneously with issues of values, ethics, and the business. Indeed, one cannot meaningfully separate the business from values and ethics if these questions are addressed properly. We want to call this level of strategic thinking "enterprise strategy" or "enterprise strategic thinking" to distinguish it from the more traditional levels of strategic thinking about what businesses we should be in and how to compete in a particular market. There are at least three distinct parts to enterprise strategy: the basic value proposition, the principles of stakeholder cooperation, and societal standards of conduct.

The Basic Value Proposition

Managing for stakeholders starts with a basic value proposition: Why should stakeholders do business with this firm in the first place? How does it create value for stakeholders? For which stakeholders? What does it stand for? What are its aspirations? These are all questions that the basic value proposition must answer. It must provide a purpose that drives the firm to deliver value in the marketplace. It must be the inspiration for why stakeholders should choose to do business with the firm, and it must give a clear and concise statement of the value added.

To be successful, firms need to be clear about what they are contributing and how they go about it. Having a lucid vision of the fundamental value proposition of the firm—one that is constant and extends beyond any given strategy or product—is critical to the firm's capability to continue to make money and serve stakeholders.

The Principles of Stakeholder Cooperation

The basic value proposition does a great deal for the firm, both in terms of setting direction and getting like-minded people together in pursuit of a common goal. In particular, it does a great deal to foster stakeholder cooperation, precisely because people who are attracted to the firm's value proposition will be more inclined to work together to realize it. However, it leaves open the question of how the firm will go about achieving its aspirations. Firms need to work out the ground rules of how they are going to treat stakeholders as they pursue their value-creation ideals. These are the core principles that the firm develops that define the firm, how it treats others, and how it will develop relationships in order to create the value it envisions.

Notions of respect, fairness, integrity, trust, and other core values are commonly used in expressions of how we expect people to behave as they work with others to create value (Bowie 1996; Paine 1994). The principles should reflect the shared authentically embraced core values of organizational members and leaders. The principles of stakeholder cooperation should clarify stakeholder responsibilities and expectations, focusing on what should be done rather than on negative injunctions and a long list of detailed rules, and be morally defensible. They must be connected to the basic value proposition and should foster cooperation, even as circumstances change and problems arise, so that parties can look out for their interests and be confident that their partners will cooperate with them in a timely, responsive, and efficient way.

Societal Standards of Conduct

The last level of enterprise strategy requires that firms think beyond their value proposition and their basic principles to look at their external environments and ensure that their values and activities fit, or at least do not conflict with, the larger legal and ethical standards of the societies in which they operate. This is a true challenge for many companies, especially in a global economy.

Executives need to be able to analyze and understand the relevant standards of business conduct, regardless of where the company is operating. Legal and moral expectations can be complex and difficult to meet. Company practices need to be examined to ensure that they show the proper respect for standards of conduct. Executives need to be aware of company practices that go against prevailing standards and have a strategy in place to be effective (Donaldson 1989; De George 1993).

Paying attention to these three levels of enterprise strategy is part of the process of creating value for stakeholders in today's turbulent business world. However, there is a large missing ingredient—the idea of leadership. If executives must deal with turbulence, think about stakeholders, not just stockholders, and deal with the basic questions of enterprise strategy, then they must become leaders, not position holders and authority figures.

Ethics, Values, and the Concept of Leadership

No single topic takes up more space on business bookshelves than leadership.[1] The truth is, we do not know very much about leadership, despite all of the studies and examples from history. Some skeptics have even questioned the usefulness of "leadership" as a concept. We begin our analysis with a canonical interpretation of leadership as consisting of four variables and a set of outcomes.

Scholars have built an interpretation of leadership over the past one hundred years. As the study of leadership progressed, most theories built on prior theories, leading to this canonical interpretation. The four variables that have emerged are "the leader," "the follower," "leadership processes and skills," and "the situation or context." Most current leadership theories take some position on each of these variables, even if it is to say that, for example, "the situation" is not very important in understanding leadership. Relationships among the four variables are depicted in Figure 5.1.

While the leadership literature does not often separate the leader from leadership processes and skills, it is necessary to do so if leadership is to be understood in the context of values and ethics. Relating leadership to values and ethics permits an investigation of whether there is a moral question about the choice of processes and skills used by the leader, rather than simply limiting the moral question to one of individual character. Given this canonical interpretation of the leadership literature, there are three ways to connect values, ethics, and leadership. We shall take each in turn: amoral leadership, values-based leadership, and ethical leadership.

Figure 5.1   **A Canonical Model of Leadership**

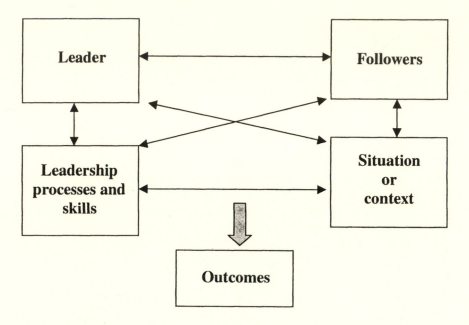

Amoral Leadership and Amoral Leadership Theories

During the first fifty years of the twentieth century, as scholarly attention to leadership intensified, ethics and values played no role in understanding effective leaders. Indeed, effective leaders were those viewed as capable of achieving effective outcomes. In turn, effective outcomes were defined as attainment of organizational objectives, such as efficiency, low turnover, high profitability, innovation, and client service. As long as the leader was judged by these measurable standards, the theories saw no need to understand how ethics and values might impact those outcomes.

For instance, "great man" and "trait" theories sought simply to understand those (universal) characteristics that great leaders embody. If the most common traits were intelligence, self-confidence, determination, authenticity, sociability, and the like, this genre of theories would make it difficult to distinguish between, say, Adolf Hitler and Mahatma Gandhi. While authenticity could possibly be viewed as having an ethical or value-based component, it is easy to speculate that Hitler was intelligent, determined, self-confident, authentic, and—to a lesser degree—sociable. Both Hitler and Gandhi were effective leaders according to this group of theories because the evaluation criterion was simply the accomplishment of stated objectives. But few people would argue that Hitler was a good leader. Hence, these theories do not enable us to evaluate the goodness, or rightness, of leadership.

Situational theories of leadership move from the descriptive to the prescriptive, but they remain morally neutral. Their basic premise is that different situations demand different styles of leadership. They stress that leadership is composed of both a directive and supportive dimension, and each has to be applied appropriately in a given situation (Hersey and Blanchard 1988). Situational theories demand that leaders match their style to the competence and commitment of subordinates. Effective leaders are those who can recognize what employees need and then adapt their own style to meet those needs. The theories are silent, however, on the ethics of those needs, the tools used to meet the needs, and the ends being sought.

Situational leadership theories have three main characteristics in common:

- They focus narrowly on leaders and followers. No mention is made of the situation or the skills that the leader employs.
- Each theory seeks to help leaders better motivate their constituents. An implicit assumption is made that workers need to be prodded into being productive. These discussions occur outside any consideration of values or ethics.
- Effective leadership is defined as the attainment of stated objectives, without concern as to the goodness of the end or the means.

Hence, in this group of theories, ethics and values are not a legitimate part of the study of leadership. The canonical interpretation suffices without moral or value assumptions. One can understand the outcomes produced by studying how the four variables—leaders, followers, leadership processes and skills, and situations—(or some combination thereof) interact, without addressing the ethical content of those variables. Hence, using these theories, we can talk about effective leadership, but we can make no statement regarding ethics or values.

The absence of values and ethics in amoral theories of leadership does not foster the exploration of certain interesting questions. Is the desired outcome desirable? Are the tools used ethically sound? Should followers be apprised as to how the leader is motivating them? On what basis can we distinguish a good leader from a bad leader? These leadership theories, therefore, are not satisfying. Although they have advanced the study of leadership and perhaps represent the inevitable starting point for understanding this complex process, their limitations are significant, especially if we look to organizations' leaders to help solve some societal problems.

Values-Based Leadership Theories

The values-based view of leadership attempts to explicitly bridge the gaps between ethics, values, and leadership. Here, values are taken as a central part of leadership. The argument is that if one wishes to understand how the outcome emerged, one must understand also the values of the leaders and followers. This view emphasizes the description of values (such as honesty and trustworthiness) and the causal role they play in determining desired outcomes. Ethics come into play only in that the question for the leader or follower concerns authenticity and integrity. Since values are treated primarily from a social scientific point of view, one hesitates to pass moral judgments.

Much of the recent, popular leadership literature can be categorized as highlighting the leader's and followers' values in determining the effectiveness of leadership. These theories claim that in order to understand the outcome, such as a highly successful business enterprise, one needs to determine whether the values of the leader are aligned with those of the followers. These popular treatises include those of Bennis (1989), Bennis and Nanus (1985, 1997), Covey (1990), and Kouzes and Posner (1993, 1995).

All of these treatises lament the absence of "true leadership." The authors ascribe all types of social and business ills to this leadership vacuum, and in so doing, they actively raise our anxiety level. They next observe that leadership is a human relationship. In order to understand leadership, it is necessary to understand this relationship. And in order to understand this relationship, it is necessary to understand first the leader's own values, motives, ethics, strengths, and weaknesses, and then understand the values of the followers. By understanding and respecting the followers' wants and needs, and fulfilling them, the leader gains the trust, loyalty, and commitment of the followers, who will then be empowered to achieve undreamed accomplishments.

These treatises do not debate the appropriateness of the goals; they do not query the rightness of the followers' values. They simply say that values are central to the leadership process. The leader must at all times be seen as honest, trustworthy, inspiring, confident, and attuned to the followers' dignity and values. Each of these treatises provides prescriptions for how to attain these qualities. Kouzes and Posner (1995) provided the "Ten Commitments of Leadership." Bennis (1989) claimed that there are five "ingredients" to leadership: integrity, dedication, magnanimity, openness, and creativity. Covey (1990) gave us one P and eight Ss: people, self, style, skills, shared vision, structure and systems, strategy, and streams. Bennis and Nanus (1985, 1997) claimed the need for five key skills: acceptance, forgiveness, courtesy, trust, and self-confidence.

The values-based view of leadership focuses attention on the values of the leader and on the skills and processes used to effect the desired outcome. It places at its center the observation that followers seek an honest leader above all else (Kouzes and Posner 1993). Gone are potentially manipulative strategies to elicit desired behaviors, as these authors make the assumption that followers are fully autonomous, ethical beings.

There are limitations to this perspective, however. The role that the situation plays in determining the outcome may not be adequately dealt with in moral terms. Are constituents truly free to exit the situation if their ethics require doing so? Further, it is difficult to ask the following question: Is it sometimes morally correct for the leader to withdraw from the leadership role? Sometimes the ethical choice may be for the leader to step aside, enabling followers to struggle, grow, and be fully autonomous moral beings.

The Ethical Leader and Theories of Ethical Leadership

While there is little work that concerns itself directly with the connection between ethics and leadership, other than in the manner described above, it is worth paying attention to the work of two political scientists, John William Gardner and James MacGregor Burns, for a description of what integrated, ethical leadership might look like in the business environment. Gardner approached the issue of ethical leadership through the lens of government, world problems, and community disintegration, with a lesser focus on corporations. Nonetheless, much of what he had to say is applicable to the business executive. Gardner argued that when we ask a question over and over again, and receive no satisfactory answer, perhaps we are asking the wrong question. He claimed, "attention to leadership alone is sterile—and inappropriate. The larger topic of which leadership is a subtopic is the accomplishment of group purposes" (Gardner 1990, xvi). Constraints on achieving group purposes include the availability of resources, the degree of agreement as to basic values and objectives, the situation faced by leaders and followers, their willingness to adapt and renew, and issues of moral and social cohesion.

Gardner discussed the types of leaders that "clearly transgress our moral standards" (1990, 67). First, there are leaders who treat followers cruelly, using them for personal ends. Then there are leaders who may treat their followers ethically but encourage them to do evil things. Some leaders exploit their followers' unconscious need for the all-powerful parent from early infancy, rendering them dependent and childlike. Finally, there are leaders who enflame bigotry and capacity for hatred. While we could think of examples of leaders who bear these characteristics in the extreme, it is important to remember that variations on these themes are relatively common.

The evaluation of immoral leaders is not confined to the leader, however.

Gardner stated, "It is easy to tell ourselves that in all of the [situations] . . . the sole source of evil was the leader. But the leader is never a sole causative factor. There is always, *in some measure,* the collaboration of those led. If a leader holds sway by exploiting our greed or our hatreds, the evil is in us too" (71).

Still, Gardner recognized that leaders have a significant role to play in the leader-follower interaction. How they should play that role, though, elicits more questions than answers. Noting that a simple answer has not emerged from the leadership research, Gardner suggested that perhaps no simple answers exist. There are, however, complex answers that are hedged by conditions and expectations.

One tool used by leaders is power. Noting that power is ethically neutral and that leadership is centrally concerned with the use of power, Gardner stated that the significant questions about power were these: "What means do [leaders] use to gain it? How do they exercise it? To what ends do they exercise it?" (57). Hence, Gardner incorporated ethics and values into all aspects of leadership.

For Gardner, the morally acceptable leader must have, at a minimum, the following objectives:

- Releasing the human potential of constituents
- Balancing the needs of the individual and the community or organization
- Defending the fundamental values of the community or organization
- Instilling in individuals a sense of initiative and responsibility

Leadership is not confined to questions of the leader-follower relationship. The leader must work to eliminate or reduce some of the more dehumanizing aspects of large organizations. A key task of leadership, according to Gardner, is to devise ways to offset the inevitable tensions between an organization's largeness and its vitality and creativity. Job redesign, autonomous working groups, schemes for performance feedback, and other techniques should be used to ensure that employees can find meaning in their work. Gardner characterized these leadership tasks not as a means of enhancing organizational effectiveness, but rather as a way to ensure the soundness of the organization's moral climate.

Like all leadership theorists, Gardner emphasized the leader's role in setting a vision for the organization. Even in this fundamental task, however, he believed that it was not possible to separate leadership and values:

> Leaders today are familiar with the demand that they come forward with a new vision. But it is not a matter of fabricating a new vision out of whole cloth. A vision relevant for us today will build on values deeply embedded in human history and in our own tradition. . . . The materials out of which

we build the vision will be the moral strivings of the species, today and in the distant past. (xi)

James MacGregor Burns's seminal work on transformational leadership is also considered an ethically integrated view. In *Leadership* (1978), Burns wrote:

I hope to demonstrate that the processes of leadership must be seen as part of the dynamics of conflict and of power; that leadership is nothing if not linked to collective purpose; that the effectiveness of leaders must be judged not by their press clippings but by the actual social change measured by intent and by the satisfaction of human needs and expectations; that political leadership depends on a long chain of biological and social processes, of interaction with structures of political opportunity and closures, of interplay between the calls of moral principles and the recognized necessities of power; that in placing these concepts of political leadership centrally into a theory of historical causation, we will reaffirm the possibilities of human volition and of common standards of justice in the conduct of people's affairs. (3)

Burns's writing was concerned with political leadership. But if we acknowledge that a business is simply a minicommunity, embodying all the aspirations and emotions of people and having an inevitable impact on them, we can certainly translate his teachings to the business community. Take, for instance, Burns's definition of leadership:

Leadership over human beings is exercised when persons with certain motives and purposes mobilize, in competition or conflict with others, institutional, political, psychological, and other resources so as to arouse, engage and satisfy the motives of followers. (18)

The key difference between both Gardner's and Burns's definitions relative to those of management scholars is that of mobilizing followers when they have a choice of whom to follow. Gardner argued that "leaders by choice" is the only interesting concept. Burns grounded the moral legitimacy of his transformational leadership theory in "*conscious choice among real alternatives.* Hence leadership assumes competition and conflict, and brute power denies it" (Burns 1978, 36; emphasis added).

We can build on the ideas of Gardner, Burns, and others to offer a view of the ethical leader and an ethical theory of leadership. In this view, leadership is seen as a full player in the moral discourse. Little can be said about leadership without at least implicitly making moral or value judgments. Ethics and values pervade each box in Figure 5.1. Skills and processes cannot be divorced from the outcomes they produce and hence cannot be seen as morally neutral. Followers make judgments and choices, project their wishes and dreams onto the leaders, and sometimes even hold them accountable. Situations are ripe with moral meaning, depending in part on how such contextual factors are framed.

Ethical leadership also notes the social legitimacy (and hence the implicit value judgment) that is conferred simply by calling someone a leader, so the very idea of leadership cannot be stated without ethical judgment. Presumptively, leaders are legitimate in business as well as the political sphere, and social legitimacy begins with the idea that one is acting from an ethical point of view. Of course, this may not turn out to be the case, so we may be left with a summary judgment of illegitimate leaders or immoral leaders, but the theories of ethical leadership imply that these issues have yet to be addressed.

The Tasks of the Ethical Leader in Creating Value for Stakeholders

The previous analyses can be used to create concrete tasks for business executives who lead the process of value creation. The argument has been that in such a process ethics and values are present at a number of levels. In fact, it would be disingenuous to try to separate out which tasks are ethical tasks and which are business tasks, for the idea behind managing for stakeholders is that one cannot and should not separate business from ethics.

The following set of tasks is based on the observations of and conversations with a host of executives and students over the past twenty-five years, and on a reading of the business literature, both popular and scholarly. However, it should be seen as tentative and open to revision.

- The ethical leader frames actions in ethical terms. In short, the ethical leader views leadership as a fully ethical task. This entails taking seriously the rights claims of others, the effects of one's actions on others (stakeholders), and how acting (leading) in a certain way affects one's character and the character of others. There is nothing amoral about the ethical leader, who recognizes that his or her values may well turn out to be a poor guidepost. The ethical leader takes responsibility for using sound moral judgment.
- The ethical leader articulates and embodies the purpose and values of the organization. It is one thing to tell a good story, one that is compelling and morally rich. But it is another thing to embody it and live it. Ethical leaders must do both, and it is difficult to do so in today's business environment where everyone lives in a fishbowl. Many political leaders fail to embody the high-minded stories they tell at election time,

and recently business leaders have produced cynicism through the revelations of numerous scandals and bad behaviors.

- The ethical leader connects the basic value proposition to stakeholder support and societal legitimacy. The ethical leader must think in terms of enterprise strategy, not separating business from ethics. Linking the basic raison d'être of the enterprise with the way that value gets created and society's expectations is a gargantuan task. But the ethical leader never hides behind the excuse of "It's just business."
- The ethical leader creates a vibrant conversation about ethics, values, and the creation of value for stakeholders. Too often business executives think that having a statement of values card or a compliance approach to ethics has solved the ethics problem. Suffice it to say that Enron and other troubled companies had all of this apparatus. What they did not have was a conversation across all levels of the business in which the basics of value creation, stakeholder principles, and societal expectations were routinely discussed and debated. There is a fallacy that values and ethics are the soft, squishy part of management. In organizations that have a lively conversation about ethics and values, people expect everyone to really live the values. And they expect the leaders of the organization to do the same. Having a lively conversation means that people must have knowledge of alternatives, must choose every day to stay with the organization and its purpose because it is important and inspires them. How to bring to life such a conversation is beyond the scope of this chapter, but it is essential if one is to lead ethically.
- The ethical leader creates mechanisms for dissent. Most people know the story of how Johnson and Johnson responded to the Tylenol incident in the 1980s. Fewer know that J&J had held a series of challenge meetings all around the world, at which managers debated the corporate credo, a statement of the company's purpose and principles. There was an explicit way to push back if someone thought that a particular market, region, or internal process was out of line with the principles. Other companies have used anonymous e-mail and telephone processes to allow employees to bypass the levels of management that inevitably spring up as barriers in large organizations. Most of the current scandals could have been prevented if there had been more creative ways for people to express their dissatisfaction with the actions of their bosses and others in the companies. Creating these mechanisms of dissent will vary by company, by leadership style, and by culture, but it is a crucial task in leading the creation of value for stakeholders.
- The ethical leader finds the best people and develops them. This task is pretty standard for all models of leadership. The ethical leader pays

special attention to it precisely because there is a moral imperative to developing people, helping them lead better lives that create more value for themselves and for others.

- The ethical leader makes tough calls while being imaginative. The ethical leader inevitably has to make a lot of difficult decisions, from reorienting the company's basic value proposition to helping employees exit the organization. There is no way for the ethical leader to duck these decisions since "I'm doing this for the business" is not an excuse. The ethical leader must put together "doing the right thing" and "doing the right thing for the business." And, as Patricia Werhane (in Chapter 3 in this volume) has so eloquently argued, sometimes exercising moral imagination is the most important task. The idea that ethical leadership is just being nice is very far from the truth.

Ethical leadership is about raising the bar, helping people realize their hopes and dreams, creating value for stakeholders, and doing these tasks with the intensity and importance that ethics connotes. That said, there must be room for mistakes, for humor, and for a humanity that is sometimes missing in our current leaders. Ethical leaders are ordinary people who are living their lives as examples of the ability to make the world a better place while reaping benefits for themselves. Ethical leaders speak to us about our identity, what we are, and what we can become.

Implications for Business Schools

If the ideas in this chapter are taken seriously, there are at least four implications for business schools and their curricula. First, and most important, business schools must center themselves on the practice of value creation and trade. That is, we need to put "business" back into "business schools." Since the attempts in the 1960s to adopt a more "scientific" approach to the study of business, business schools have gradually moved away from teaching the art of judgment, which is crucial in a world of turbulence where it is not always clear what the right thing to do really is. Substituting analytical frameworks for judgment is akin to teaching physicians physiology without teaching them how to deal with patients or that individual patients differ even though they share the same basic physiology. It is akin to teaching lawyers that every client has the same motive. It is akin to teaching architects that setting and aesthetics do not matter.

Second, we have to see the creation of value in its most complete sense, the creation of value for stakeholders. We need to put an end to the hegemony of finance professors and economists who pronounce (without argument or evidence) that the only purpose of the firm is to maximize shareholder value. Such ideology is bad business and leads to bad judgments, a reactive and harmful public policy, and a theory of business that is severely impoverished.

Third, we need to reemphasize courses that have a basis in the humanities, and we have to rescue the teaching of leadership from those overly committed to a social sciences approach. Business and business leadership are fundamentally human activities. The great thinkers who have dealt with the human condition have much to add. William Shakespeare is as important as Peter Drucker. Sartre's ideas about relationships are as important as the path-goal or least preferred coworker theories. Rawls (1971), for example, has as much to say about fairness as he does equity theory. Social science frameworks can be helpful, but so too can studying literature, ethics, drama, and the arts.

Finally, we need to return to John Dewey's idea of experimentalism. After all, this is really the key insight of any scientific method. We try things that might work to make our lives better. We keep what works and abandon what does not, rather than pretending that we are engaged in some purist search for Truth. The goal of inquiry, especially in professional schools, must become making our lives better, helping us cope with the world as we find it, or some other slightly more noble calling than maximizing shareholder value. Indeed, if the arguments above are roughly correct, the only way to maximize shareholder value is to pay attention to creating value for stakeholders and the process of leadership, both of which have values and ethics through and through. There is much work to be done. We cannot sit idly by and wait for things to work out. Preserving human freedom, especially in our most important institution, value creation and trade, is our most noble calling.

Notes

This chapter is the result of a number of collaborations over the years. Robert Phillips (University of San Diego), Jeff Harrison (Cornell University), and I are exploring these ideas about managing for stakeholders in more depth in a forthcoming book, *Managing for Stakeholders*. My colleague Patricia Werhane and I are tackling the issue of the connection between ethics and leadership in *The Ethical Leader*. Margaret Cording (Rice University), Patricia Werhane, and I are developing the theoretical connections between ethics and leadership in a working paper titled "Connecting Ethics and Leadership." Andrew Wicks, Bidhan Parmar, and I are developing the connection between managing for stakeholders and business ethics in a working paper titled "Business Ethics in an Era of Corporate Crisis." This chapter draws on all of these accounts, and I wish to thank my coauthors for their ideas and support.

1. The ideas in this section are explained in more detail in the working paper "Business Ethics in an Era of Corporate Crisis." I am grateful to my coauthors for permission to discuss the ideas here.

6

Mindfulness and Integrity

The Ongoing Challenge of Leadership Development

Sandra Waddock

In a recent *Harvard Business Review* article, Charles Handy (2002, 50) opined:

> The American disease is not just a matter of dubious personal ethics or of some rogue companies fudging the odd billion. The country's whole business culture may have become distorted. This was the culture that enraptured America for a generation, a culture underpinned by a doctrine that proclaimed the market king, always gave priority to the shareholder, and believed that business was the key engine of progress and thus should take precedence in policy decisions.

Why did this so-called American disease arise? To what extent was business education responsible? And what are the implications of changing this perspective to something broader that works for all stakeholders, societies, and future generations? Arguably, the problems of management and business education are not about bad apples or even bad companies. They are about a system that puts inordinate and narrowly defined performance pressures on managers and their companies (cf. Cavanagh et al. 2002). Company leaders focused narrowly on shareholder considerations are not likely to make decisions in the best interest of other stakeholders and the societies within which they operate, and may even shortchange shareholders (Collins and Porras 1996).

Business education has tended to foster, or at least support, a narrow focus on financial performance. Consequently, MBAs have a narrow focus on solving reasonably tractable problems while ignoring more complex, bigger-picture considerations, even overlooking important strategic considerations, not to mention considerations relating to human beings, society, and the environment.

Ethics in Business Education

Business education is typically designed with finance and economics at the center and with shareholder considerations given first priority. Disciplinary strengths exist in marketing, operations, accounting, and management information systems, and in quantitative subjects like decision analysis, management science, and statistics. Recently, strategic management has lost some of its integrative character and taken on disciplinary strength.

Managerially focused courses like organizational behavior and business-in-society (and certainly business ethics) are marginalized in students' minds, although "management" is what they are ostensibly studying. A striking example is students' negative comments in response to an initiative that asked the Association to Advance Collegiate Schools of Business (AACSB), the business education accrediting organization, to make ethics a core component of business education. The exchange between professors and anonymous MBA students occurred on a Social Issues in Management Division of the Academy of Management listserver in early 2003. The students stated, among other things, that "[s]tudents want jobs not lectures on morals. Discussions of ethics . . . are a waste of the 50 minute class we paid good money for." They further argued that "[t]here is no value added to us from your ethics lectures." Unfortunately, that view is widespread among business students, albeit somewhat diminished in the wake of the corporate scandals of the early 2000s.

The good news is that a 2002 study by the Aspen Institute's Business & Society Initiative concluded that "[w]hile attracting and keeping good employees and providing excellent customer service are still considered hallmarks of a well-run company, operating according to corporate values and a strong code of ethics has gained importance for students in 2002" (Aspen Initiative for Social Innovation through Business 2002, 3). The bad news of the Aspen survey is that less than 50 percent of the surveyed students viewed investing in employees as a primary responsibility of businesses and even fewer (less than 30 percent, albeit a slightly higher percentage than in the previous survey) believed that compliance with the law was part of a company's primary responsibilities. Further, environmental concerns were barely on the radar screens of the primarily American students, with only about 6 percent perceiving environmental sustainability as an important responsibility of businesses.

In the same survey, however, more than 70 percent believed that (lack of) individual ethics was an important contributor to the recent spate of corporate scandals in the United States, whereas nearly 70 percent thought external performance pressures might have contributed to the scandals, suggesting that about 30 percent of the surveyed students were apparently clueless about these factors. Corporate responsibility, from the perspective of the students surveyed, is largely a public relations or reputational issue, and although more than 50 percent recognized that customer loyalty might be enhanced by heightened responsibility, fewer than 40 percent thought that corporate responsibility was relevant to employee retention and productivity (Aspen Initiative for Social Innovation through Business 2002). While there was an attempt to put a positive spin on these results by the Aspen Institute, it is clear that ethical and general business-in-society considerations hardly seem mainstream to the business students surveyed.

Good News and Bad News

Business education seems to work (Gioia 2002). If nothing else, business education teaches critical problem-solving skills. At the same time, it provides a perspective on what is important to do in order to be successful in business—an attitude regarding "how business is done." For what it is worth, some students do recognize the importance of ethics in management. Yet business students seem to come away from their education having absorbed shareholder capitalism, skills in problem solving for reasonably tractable problems (Hayes and Abernathy 1980), and a considerably narrowed sense of what managing businesses is all about (Aspen Initiative for Social Innovation through Business 2002).

While the Aspen study indicates that many students believe that most functional courses should address ethical and corporate responsibilities, there is an absence of data suggesting that those courses actually do address those concerns in any systematic or rigorous way (see chapter 12 in this volume). In fact, most discipline-based business educators would probably attest that the breadth of coverage needed simply to convey their discipline's content "prevents" them from incorporating ethical content into their courses. Further, most business educators would likely acknowledge little capability to teach ethics even within their content domain (hence, the somewhat ironic efforts of now-defunct Arthur Andersen to teach ethics to business educators during the 1980s). Even if issues of corporate responsibility and ethics are included in functional courses, they are likely to be viewed as add-ons finding their way into an "ethics day" dismissed by the students as relevant.

One need hardly explore the critiques of business education to know that ethics, integrity, and a broader conception of the role of business in society have been given little attention in business education (Adler 2002).[1] Yes, there is the odd business ethics or business-in-society course in the curriculum, always at risk of being eliminated in favor of more rigorous, "relevant," or quantitatively demanding courses that most business educators and students regard as more important to the management mission. Further, despite years of arguments about the need for values-based business education, the dominant economics-based model of investor capitalism combined with free market globalization still claims to be value neutral, all the while holding wealth maximization for shareholders, profitability, and growth as obvious central values.

The absence of a values perspective in business education, promoted and reinforced by the narrow functionalism that still pervades it, subjected it to criticisism in the early 1980s (e.g., Hayes and Abernathy 1980). Early critiques gave way to demands for change leading to greater integration, teamwork, and broader perspectives in the late 1980s (Porter and McKibbin 1988). Particularly in light of recent corporate scandals, some change toward greater integration has indeed taken place, but numerous problems remaining suggest a lack of attention to the well-being or integrity of the system as a whole (Bartunek 2002; Clegg 2002; Hinings and Greenwood 2002; Kochan 2002; Trank and Rynes 2003).

Although there have been (sometimes Herculean) efforts to institutionalize more integrated curricula, such initiatives are too frequently thwarted by faculty problems identified in a major and largely negative assessment of business educators by the AACSB in the mid-1990s (Association to Advance Collegiate Schools of Business 1996). In its report, the AACSB claimed that faculty limitations impeded real change because, among other things, business educators had insufficient real-world contact, lacked an understanding of the global and technological contexts of business, and possessed narrow disciplinary orientations and an "if it ain't broke, don't fix it" attitude. Little of significance with respect to ethical grounding or understanding of the broader historical and social contexts in which businesses operate has changed in business education or in the recognition of faculty members regarding their own responsibilities since that report. If anything, pressures for faculty "performance," narrowly defined as publishing in prestigious, discipline-focused journals, has only intensified, further enhancing disciplinary specialization. When combined with the apparently ever-increasing demand for MBA programs to be highly ranked by prestigious surveys (e.g., *U.S. News & World Report, BusinessWeek*) that emphasize graduates' salaries and recruitment, faculty prestige, and physical facilities rather than actual education, the likelihood of integrated curricula being institutionalized seems rather remote.

Management Practice

What happened to management practice in this context? The scandals of the first years of the twenty-first century, the public uproar over exceedingly high levels of executive compensation (now estimated to be 450 times that of the average worker), and anticorporate and globalization activism are only a few factors that lend credence to the notion that something is rotten in business and, by extension, business education. Students, for one group, seem to fail to see any problems whatsoever with the multiples in executive salaries, arguing rather vociferously that CEOs must, after all, be worth their salaries since that is what they are being paid (a notably circular argument).

However, it seems likely that there may be not just a few isolated rotten apples (unethical individuals) but an entire barrel of rotten apples. The rotten barrel perspective (cf. Handy 2002) proposes that there are systemic problems creating pressures that push even good people into bad actions to satisfy the demands of a marketplace hungry for ever-increasing bottom lines, ever greater market share, and ever larger companies to demonstrate continued growth.

The inevitable answer to the question regarding what went wrong with many of the companies involved in scandals is that short-term pressures from the financial community for continuous performance improvement and growth were dominant in fostering an atmosphere where just about anything goes to produce results. There seem to be few incentives to slow growth, to "root" companies locally within their communities, to provide "adequate" returns to shareholders, to honor the service of employees and suppliers, or to reward the loyalty of customers with better quality products that add more value. Instead, there are the Enrons, the WorldComs, the Tycos, the Halliburtons, and the Putnams, more corrupt practices that destroy trust among stakeholders, more arguments for free trade and globalization at the expense of community values (Cavanagh et al. 2002) and whatever employee interests and ecological good might be in play.

These problems do not arise purely as a result of individual ethics. They are a product of systemic pressures and dynamics that thwart mindful approaches to managerial decision making, that fail to value the integrity of individuals, organizations, and societies, and that fail to take into consideration the good of the system as a whole. These pressures put well-meaning individuals into an ethically questionable pressure cooker, where short-term performance in the interests of improving share price is a major, sometimes the only, goal. In a radical form of prisoner's dilemma, these problems focus on the apparent good of individuals or their organizations to the detriment of the system. As such, they represent system failures—failures of wisdom, failures to understand the long-term consequences of today's management decisions (Ackoff 1999), failures to focus on multiple rather than one group of stakeholders, and, indeed, failures of integrity in its broadest sense. However difficult system change is, it may well be time for a more integrated approach to business education and, ultimately, to the purpose of the firm in serving the interests of society.

An Integral Approach to Business Education

The question posed by the title of Handy's (2002) article, "What's a Business For?" provides a useful starting point for what might be needed to foster greater integrity and mindfulness through business education. Handy asks whether, if we were beginning again, we would invent the corporation and capitalism as they are today. In the context of business education, the rhetorical question is, What is business education for?

If we were starting over with business education, would we design it as a set of separate, functionally oriented, specialized, and quantitatively oriented disciplines with little overlap and little attention to the actual processes and implications of managing the important relationships that constitute the organization? Would we design it with virtually no attention to issues of ecological sustainability, community values and culture, aesthetic appreciation, nor to real valuing of families? Would we ensure that profit and growth orientation superseded other values related to individual, community, and societal well-being or respect for the intrinsic worth of stakeholders, nature, and even future generations? Or might we develop more ethical managers by developing an integral perspective (Wilber 1996) that could foster individual, organizational, and system integrity? The challenges of integrity framed by an integral vision of business education exist in the three perspectives outlined in Wilber's (1995, 1996, 1998) integral model, where the gamut of possible perspectives of any nested system can be found: I, we, and it/its. Wilber also framed these perspectives as self, culture, and world; the Beautiful, the Good, and the True; and Art, Morals, and Science (see Wilber forthcoming). Wilber (1995, 1996, 1998) used a two-by-two matrix to explain the four different perspectives available for understanding living systems. The right-hand, objective side of the matrix represents "it" and "its" dimensions or the individual and collective perspectives, which Wilber more recently collapsed into it/its dimensions of Science or the True, or what is knowable through observation and empirical study. But that is only half of life; the rest is subjectively experienced and, Wilber argued, all perspectives are needed to fully understand any given system. The left-hand, subjective side of the matrix, the "I" dimension, focuses on an individual's subjective experiences, emotions or feelings, aesthetic appreciation, values, visions, thoughts, or dimensions of the Beautiful, Art, and self. In the collective intersubjective dimensions can be found group experiences like culture, values, and norms within societies, or the Good, morals, and culture.

The key to applying Wilber's framework to business education is to recognize that typically any given discipline or subject is approached from only one perspective. However, a complete comprehension of any subject or system —an integral perspective—requires understanding all four perspectives (Wilber 1996, 1998): the individual and collective observed/objective perspectives (or right-hand side), and the individual and collective subjectively experienced (or left-hand side) perspectives. Business and business education, with some exceptions, generally emphasize the objective individual and collective perspectives ("it" and "its" perspectives), with subjectively experienced aspects (even the managing of people) given less attention. From the objective perspectives, individuals seek to understand things through objectively measurable or empirical data because the emphasis is on more or less observable or measurable factors like financial performance, market share, productivity and output measures, and share price. In the collective sense at the system level, indicators include macro measures along similar dimensions: GDP, national productivity, and economic growth. Most management courses are geared toward teaching about these objective and reasonably measurable aspects of doing business. Much less taken into account are the left-hand side perspectives (Wilber 1998), the "I" and "we" (subjective) perspectives as experienced by individuals and groups. These subjective experiences include how people feel about being managed, the quality of relationships as experienced by various stakeholders, and how corporate activities are experienced emotionally, aesthetically, or meaningfully.

Corporate success in the context of society, where stakeholders and the environment are given due weight, and where integrity matters, lies not only on the objective dimensions side of the equation (Collins and Porras 1996). Much of what makes managers or leaders successful has to do with how they incorporate the qualitative, so-called soft issues found on the left-hand side of Wilber's framework. These perspectives include the ways in which stakeholders experience their company relationships, the compassion with which employees and others are treated (Dutton and Heaphy 2003), and the experience of connection and relationships with stakeholders that actually constitute the business and with others whose actions and inputs affect the business (Freeman 1984). Certainly, issues of values, ethics, culture, aesthetics, meanings, and corporate responsibility, as well as stakeholder relationships, fall into this subjective domain of business activities. Further, although not widely acknowledged, good stakeholder relationships are at the heart of what companies do and are (Freeman 2003) and require different ways of understanding and managing than simply focusing on achieving the much-vaunted numbers without regard to how they are achieved.

Objective dimensions related to managerial leadership are dominant in typical measures of performance and in the largely siloed functional courses offered in business education—sales figures, market share, number of customers, products sold, throughput in a production process, profitability, and share price. These measures do not get at the subjectively experienced impacts of management decisions on stakeholders, yet stakeholders consistently raise concerns about these exact dimensions. Until quite recently, however, business education largely ignored the left-hand side issues related to individual experiences, such as meaning and inspiration, emotion, aesthetic appreciation, and subjective group-level or community concerns like health, human rights, working conditions, and labor rights. As business education evolves, these subjective dimensions deserve integration into the curriculum.

As we consider what shifts are needed in business education—and to the extent that we want to instill a broader understanding of the need for integrity and mindfulness in leaders—we need to incorporate subjectively experienced perspectives as well as those that are empirically observable. Since objective factors are already well covered, what follows will focus on ways to incorporate more subjectively experienced elements into business education.

The Integrity Challenge

Integrity means soundness, firm adherence to a code, principles and values, and openness and honesty (i.e., transparency, accountability, and responsibility). Without integrity at the individual, organizational, or system level, there is no trust and there can be no social, competitive, community, or ecological sustainability, nor effective business transactions. The market system itself cannot survive without a foundation of participant trust in the integrity of the transactions that are taking place and the reporting that is being done by companies and their auditors. Without trust, the system tends toward chaos. If integrity is about wholes, honesty, and adherence to standards, then integrity challenges to business education exist at three important levels of leadership: individual, organizational, and societal, each nested as "holons" (wholes and parts simultaneously) within the other (Wilber 1996).

Individual Leadership

At the individual level, business education arguably needs to provide more ways for students to understand the importance of individual integrity and honesty, to explore personal values and to study standards, and the role of the individual in fostering a climate of integrity within an organizational context. It is in the exploration of individual values and purpose in the broadest (and probably spiritually relevant) sense that individual ethics and personal meaning are to be found. This is where a business ethics course is most useful.

Individual ethics are arguably not to be found in someone else's preaching about what is right and wrong (as the students previously quoted suggest happens too often). Nor will this capacity necessarily develop through endless discussions about the ethical challenges faced by Peter Green in the Harvard Business School business ethnics case, "Peter Green's First Day," useful as such discussions might be in framing the business context of ethical decision making. Fundamentally, individuals cannot lead themselves or others unless they, like business enterprises, know where they are going, what they personally stand for (Freeman and Gilbert 1988), and what in life is meaningful to them. If correct, then vision and values are important at multiple levels, not just at the level of the organization.

The real work of individual ethics from this perspective lies in the exploration of how to live one's life with integrity, focus, and purpose within one's broader social context. It means knowing what really matters to oneself and those one cares about (including a company's stakeholders, presumably). Without such guideposts—personally developed guideposts shaped by ethnic, cultural, spiritual or religious, family, and educational contexts rather than those imposed by authoritative others—it is hard for people to stay true to their own convictions. It may well be that the real work of living a life of integrity lies in the personal exploration of purpose that goes beyond how one acts in one's career and in the recognition of the worth of the whole person, whether on the job or not. If this is correct, then the needed exploration goes well beyond simply how to act ethically in making a business decision; it demands that students orient toward the broader spectrum of what is personally meaningful to them in the nested group of personal stakeholder relationships within which they exist—families, communities, businesses and other organizations, and society. It requires helping students move through development stages so that they can see beyond what Kohlberg (1976) and many others (e.g., Wilber 1996) call conventional stages of moral reason to the postconventional stages that are needed for understanding systems, relationships, and the perspectives of others (Waddock 2001, 2002).

This type of exploration demands what Senge (1990) calls personal mastery and can include the development of a personal vision statement that explores the important values and balances in one's life. Of course, traditional ethical decision-making frameworks and guidelines can be helpful to students as they explore the rationale behind making good decisions. Students can extend these guidelines to encompass what type of organization and ultimately what type of society and world they really want to live and work in, thereby beginning an important conversation about the good life, about balances and relationships, and about systemic and individual integrity. The guidelines may also involve not just productivity and profitability, but also aesthetic and emotional considerations about work, life, and business activities as experienced individually and collectively. It may, in the end, require slowing down the pace of change in order to reflect on what really matters.

Organizational Leadership

Individuals, however strong their integrity, operate within organizations that are nested within industries and societies. Pressures from these broader systems influence what happens within each level in an interactive way. To be able to operate with integrity, businesses, like individuals, need to ask the "critical values" question: What do we stand for? (Freeman and Gilbert 1988). Asking employees this important question enabled Johnson & Johnson to act with integrity in the wake of the Tylenol scandals of the early 1980s and similarly later allowed Merck to give away Mectizan to combat river blindness when it became clear that there would be no profitable market for the drug.

A positive corporate vision can deal with how the organization will change the world for the better (Senge 1990; Waddock 2002), but vision needs to be underpinned by clearly articulated values that are communicated and implemented broadly throughout the enterprise. The values that potentially have the power to make organizations effective businesses and simultaneously honor important stakeholders are not a mystery. They can be found in most of the major management fads and fashions of the last twenty-five years (Liedtka 1998, 1999; Pfeffer and Veiga 1999), although they are infrequently fully implemented.

In productive business education, students might be asked to think seriously about what type of organization they would truly like to work for and what values that organization would honor. Further, they might be given tools to diagnose existing company values and, by examining failures caused by ethical lapses, explore the consequences for themselves—and their organizations—of not living up to stated, constructive values. Diagnosis might focus not just on examples of problematic decisions that companies have made with scandalous negative consequences, but also on inspirational and positive examples of companies that have struggled with decisions that ultimately benefit themselves, societies, and their stakeholders.

Searching for the linkages between such constructive decisions and business benefits can help students realize that being unethical is, in fact, not "how business is done," at least when businesses hope to be successful over the long term. They might then become aware that doing business with integrity and based on a sound set of constructive values not only benefits the business in the long term, but also enhances the societies within which it operates (cf. Liedtka 1998, 1999; Pfeffer and Veiga 1999). Future leaders need to be sufficiently self-aware and sufficiently cognitively and morally developed (cf. Torbert 2004; Waddock 2001) to understand not only how to develop a shared vision (Senge 1990) within their organizations, but also how to effectively communicate and implement it through organizational development and stakeholder engagement processes.

At the organizational level of leadership, business students need to have facility in creating shared organizational visions and values, disseminating them organizationally, and effecting system change as needed. Key to doing these things well might be enhancing future managers' capacities to engage productively with stakeholders who may hold quite different views from their own about the effectiveness and value of the firm's activities and impacts. Creating good stakeholder relationships (whether they are with employees, customers, shareholders, communities, suppliers, or critical nongovernmental organizations) demands that leaders possess the capacity to fully comprehend the position of the "other," whether the parties agree or disagree. Particularly in the emerging global context, the capacity to engage in productive dialogues with stakeholders (Calton and Payne 2003; Svendsen 1998) is a critical skill for making the organization an effective, productive participant in society.

Business Leadership in Society

Leaders who can act with integrity as stewards of their businesses in society need to understand what creates integrity in the system as a whole and what generates soundness in societies as well as in businesses and the environment. They need to know how adherence to standards that reflect core foundational values (Donaldson 1996; Donaldson and Dunfee 1994; Waddock 2003) fosters business success as well as economic and societal sustainability. Such leaders have the capacity to think through the systemic consequence of decisions, a capacity that Ackoff (1999) calls wisdom, and understand through perspective-taking how their decisions are being experienced by stakeholders outside the business. An integral approach to business education and business enterprises would include financial and otherwise measurable aspects, along with comprehensive understanding of the subjectively experienced impacts of business decisions on individuals, communities, and other stakeholders that reflect the multiple interests present in societies.

The anything-goes mentality of growth, size, and power dominance (Frederick 1995) that characterizes the modern corporation and the mentality of current business education may need to move toward a concept of a firm that is locally owned and operated (Cavanagh et al. 2002). Aesthetic, meaning-making, and emotional impacts may need to find their way into the decision calculus of businesses. Although how this might happen is unclear, movement toward triple (multiple) bottom-line accounting and reporting (Elkington 1997) is a step in that direction. Returns may need to be stated as achieving "reasonable" rather than maximal objectives, with consideration given to multiple stakeholder interests, not just those of shareholders.

Several topics in business education would be useful in providing insights into the broader contexts in which businesses operate. These would provide a truly integrative perspective to help students better understand issues of integrity as they relate to system and business soundness. One topic would focus on the historical context and development of business over time, providing an understanding of the benefits and limitations of industrialization, materialism, and consumerism as they have evolved. The historical and political contexts in which businesses operate are essential elements of a globalized world; relations among sectors and with stakeholders within those sectors are essential to providing what is now being called business's "license to operate" in society, a license granted when there is trust. A historical perspective would also highlight the reality that the corporation as we know it is a human construction that can be altered by humans through political and economic processes.

A second topic would focus on the views of a range of stakeholders about the implications of free trade and globalization for societies around the world, not just from the positive perspective of those already in business or the business press, but also from the more critical perspectives with which business students are currently unfamiliar. The trust that is missing in today's largely corrupt system, which emphasizes greed and accumulation of wealth above other values, can be restored or perhaps reinvented only if the relationships that actually constitute the firm are developed with integrity. Such critical views are too infrequently incorporated into business education, thereby limiting students' knowledge of the very real anticorporate forces in the world and preventing students from understanding and coping with these forces in a collaborative or symbiotic way. Understanding such different perspectives can also enhance the capacity and creativity of manager-leaders to foster truly workable business solutions that actually benefit society as well as the business.

The third topic would focus on developing a capacity for forward thinking and visioning. It would incorporate techniques like appreciative inquiry (Cooperrider et al. 2001), future search (Weisbord and Janoff 1995), open space (Owen 1997a, b), scenario planning (Schwartz 1991), and related "visioning" processes. Not only would attention to such processes and the issues they would raise provide a broader perspective on business's role in societies and its impacts on the environment, but it would also nurture creative thinking, perspective-taking, and integrative thinking capabilities.

The Mindfulness Challenge

"Wisdom," Russell Ackoff (1999, 16) wrote, "is the ability to perceive and evaluate the long-run consequences of behavior. It is normally associated with a willingness to make short-run sacrifices for the sake of long-run gains." This capacity relies on systems thinking, an integrative capacity to bring together the perspectives of all four of Wilber's quadrants and generate a holistic sense of the impacts, nature, and strategies of businesses. If Ackoff is right, then wisdom is exactly what business students need to gain if they are to manage mindfully. Emphasizing a similar point, management scholar Karl Weick spoke of the goals he saw for the future of business education:

> Our job is to prepare people so they see how vested interests work, see their universality in organizational life, speak up when the vested interest produces blind spots, and enact alternative vested interests. Students who are prepared to do this retain a place at the table despite their dissent because they are able to deal confidently with that which is fast, equivocal, situational, and exhausting. If situations weaken, then real worlds will be even more abundant, more pluralistic, and more idiosyncratic than they are now. But if we teach *wisdom* rather than a vocation, *character* rather than technicalities, and *mindfulness* rather than rationality, we will have done what we can to prepare people for the unknowable. (Weick 1999, emphasis added)

Mindfulness is a concept that relates to the issue of "presence" or self-awareness—awareness of what we are doing here now, today, and, implicitly, of how what we are doing impacts others through a connectedness that can be observed (e.g., Kabat-Zinn 1995, 2002; Torbert 1991, 2004). Although derived from the literature on meditation, mindfulness is increasingly relevant to the process of business education because it can provide for an expanded awareness that somehow seems sorely lacking in business students and leaders. Jon Kabat-Zinn, who has studied the effects of mindfulness for many years, recently explained what happens when it is achieved:

You come to see the possibility of being less reactive and less agitated through cultivating present-moment attention. . . . [Through what is called insight practice] you invite the field of your awareness to include a constantly changing field of objects. This is the cultivation of mindfulness—moment-to-moment, nonreactive, nonjudgmental awareness. Mindfulness can be thought of as penetrative awareness, a seeing underneath the surface or through the outer form of things to their truest nature. Behind surface appearances, we can perceive unsuspected dimensions of relationship and connectivity, a sense of the interconnectedness of things, including oneself. (2002, 69)

Mindful managers, aware of the connections that are important to sustain the diversity of life, community, and healthy societies, might focus on broader goals than short-term profit maximization and growth. They might be better able to engage with stakeholders even in potentially conflicting situations and be better able to hold and honor the personal, organizational, and societal values that are meaningful to them, even when under pressures to do otherwise. The capacity to do what is fundamentally important even in difficult circumstances is, in many ways, the essence of acting with integrity.

Business education, of course, needs to be concerned with designing and managing efficient, effective businesses. But efficiency and effectiveness alone fail to put business in its proper context—as a core element within healthy societies. When a business is disciplinarily fragmented into silos, efficiency considerations alone fail to provide for integrity. A more holistic conception of business in the broader system is needed. Fostering mindfulness among business students, however, might just give them the personal awareness, the courage of their own convictions, the capacity to see beyond the immediate results to the long-term consequences of their decisions, and the awareness of the impacts of their decisions on others that are needed to create system integrity. Strange as it might seem, the one thing business education might do to provide insights and access to the qualitative and subjectively experienced impacts of managerial decision making is to provide for, and even foster, some sort of mindfulness practice. The reasons for taking this perspective are briefly outlined in the concluding section in a context that suggests that vision, supported by values, results in value, not just for business enterprises but also for the system as a whole.

A Higher Purpose: Mindfulness and Integrity

This chapter ends as it began, with a quote from Charles Handy:

To survive, even to prosper, is not enough. We hanker to leave a footprint in the sands of time. . . . We need to associate with a cause in order to give purpose to our lives. The pursuit of a cause does not have to be the prerogative of charities. Nor does a mission to improve the world make business into a social agency. By creating new products, spreading technology, and raising productivity, enhancing quality and improving service, business has always been the active agent of progress. (Handy 2002, 54)

If Handy is correct, then business education might usefully put more attention on the fundamental purpose—and supporting vision and underlying values—of companies as contributors to successful societies, not just money-making machines focused on economizing and power aggrandizing (Frederick 1995). An integral approach to business education taps what truly inspires. The seminal work of Collins and Porras (1996) clearly delineated the relevance of vision and values for success (cf. Waddock 2002, 2003).

There is an enormous challenge to educating future leaders about integrity and mindfulness. It is not sufficient to believe that ethical individuals alone will solve problems of market and business integrity, nor even that individual businesses could do so by installing codes of conduct or sets of values while maintaining a narrow focus on maximizing shareholder wealth. However, mindfulness and integrity at the multiple levels described above have some potential for shifting the system, especially if the broader public policy system is engaged. Arguing for incorporation of the subjectively experienced aspects of business into business education is not to deny the importance of functional specialties, strategic thinking and decision making, and quantitative problem-solving. It is simply to argue that to focus solely on what is empirically measurable is to miss the human equation. Business education, as a human institution that supplies future business leaders, needs to inculcate a more holistic understanding to give meaning, inspiration, and values—integrity—to the roles and functions of business within societies.

Defining the purpose of the firm solely as maximizing shareholder value is myopic and requires a radical shift (Cavanagh et al. 2002), a broadening of purpose to encompass the interests of all involved stakeholders, and a refocusing on the health and well-being of all the human and other creatures that live in a world inextricably linked to the natural environment. The goals, purposes, and values of the firm and of business education need to reflect societal, ecological, organizational, and individual integrity as a set of wholes nested within each other (Wilber 1996) that are mutually dependent and constructively symbiotic.

Business education, like the concept of the firm itself, needs to rest on a new foundation that speaks to the health of society and the capacity of nature to sustain human civilization as a whole, not just on the competitiveness of businesses within an economic context. Business leaders are needed who truly understand the bases of their own integrity, their own core values, and what is truly meaningful to them. They need to have the courage to operationalize their values in their work and organizations, and in the ways that their organizations impact stakeholders and the environment. Both self- and other-awareness constitute the mindful—or wise—leader so much missing in the world today. The key for business education is to figure out new ways of educating such business leaders. In addition to the three topics articulated above, several other topics might be incorporated into business education.

First, business educators need to teach about wholes as well as holons, how holons are related to each other through systems thinking (Senge 1990), and how the interdependence within the system creates the need for integrity. They need to instill in their students, as the best companies do in their employees, a logic of "both/and" instead of "either/or" (Collins and Porras 1996).

Second, business educators need to be explicit about the moral foundations of business. Business and markets are all about trust. They cannot operate without trust. Trust implies integrity in all its meanings, especially in the relationships that constitute the business and the business system.

Third, business educators need to teach about ecology and sustainability from natural, social, and business perspectives. They need to integrate an understanding of the system dynamics and forces that exist in organizations, institutions, and societies, with the impact that individuals and groups can have.

Fourth, business educators need to figure out ways to teach ethical decision making in the context of discussions about personal integrity, vision, and values at multiple levels of leadership—individual, organizational, and societal. It is unrealistic to think that an honest individual alone can sustain integrity in a corrupt system simply through personal courage. Simultaneously, it is important to find new ways to identify and foster courage and a sense of self-efficacy, to build courage where it is lacking, and to encourage the capacity to bring issues out so that courage can effect system change.

Perhaps the words of Henry David Thoreau (1854/1990, 60), although offered in a context entirely different from business, best sum up what business and business education need. As one thinks about what truly inspires meaning in life, whether business life or some other aspect of an integrated, whole, and full life, one might usefully remember:

> Morning is when I am awake and there is a dawn in me. . . . We must learn to reawaken and keep ourselves aware, not by mechanical aids, but by an infinite expectation of the dawn, which does not forsake us in our soundest

sleep. I know of no more encouraging fact than the unquestionable ability of man to elevate his life by conscious endeavor. It is something to be able to paint a particular picture, or to carve a statue, and so to make a few objects beautiful; but it is far more glorious to carve and paint the very atmosphere and medium through which we look. . . . To affect the quality of the day, that is the highest of arts.

Note

1. See also the call to action posted on SIM and IABS listservers by Diane Swanson and William C. Frederick in 2002.

7

Benchmarking Student Attitudes Regarding Ethical Issues

Robert A. Peterson and Gerald Albaum

According to business ethicists such as Freeman (1984), Lozano (2000), and Mitroff (1983), a corporation has numerous stakeholders, groups whose support is essential to its well-being and even survival. These stakeholders have been variously categorized as internal and external, primary and secondary (e.g., Lozano 2000). Commonly acknowledged stakeholders that a corporation interacts with in one manner or another include employees, customers, shareholders, suppliers, government agencies, managers, creditors, and community groups.

One group that should be considered as a stakeholder consists of college students, especially business students, who collectively constitute the future leadership of corporations and will eventually become members of virtually all imaginable stakeholder groups. Even though college students are only rarely discussed or analyzed in what might be termed stakeholder theory, they are probably the stakeholder group most frequently studied by researchers undertaking empirical studies in business ethics. Indeed, perusal of articles in the *Journal of Business Ethics*, arguably the premier academic journal focusing exclusively on ethics issues in the business arena, reveals that more than 25 percent of the articles reporting empirical research in the past twenty years have utilized college students as study participants.

This chapter presents the results of a survey of undergraduate business students regarding certain ethics-related attitudes. As such, the chapter is intended to complement the remaining, more conceptually oriented chapters in the book and serve as a catalyst for future empirical research. The intent of the survey, in turn, was to provide insights into, and benchmarking information on, ethics-related attitudes of undergraduate college students majoring in business in the United States in the fall of 2003. As a consequence, the present survey represents the most exhaustive attempt to date to chronicle business students' ethics-related attitudes nationwide and overcome the lack of empirical ethics research observed by Hosmer (2000) in such a way that the criticisms of Randall and Gibson (1990) regarding empirical research on poor methodologies employed in business ethics are muted.

From a practical perspective, these students constitute the next generation of business and political leaders. Given the major and widespread ethical and legal lapses that have occurred in the past few years, as illustrated by such companies as Enron, WorldCom, Arthur Andersen, and Tyco, it is important to know where these future leaders stand on major ethical issues. Although basic values are likely formed by the time students enter undergraduate business programs, business ethics are specifically acquired by formal classroom education, observation of business practices, and informal education-related experiences. By studying the ethics attitudes of present undergraduate business students, it may be possible to predict the future ethical behavior of business (and political) leaders and perhaps even influence that behavior through appropriate business education.

Previous Related Research

The present research builds on a stream of empirical studies on business ethics that goes back nearly half a century. Of the previous empirical studies investigating business ethics issues, those of Beltramini, Peterson, and Kozmetsky (1984; Peterson, Beltramini, and Kozmetsky 1991) served as both inspiration and model for this study. Indeed, the present study can be viewed as an extension of their research; the same general research design was employed and many of the same business ethics issues addressed. Consequently, a brief review of their research is warranted.

In 1980, Beltramini, Peterson, and Kozmetsky (1984) conducted a survey to assess college students' concerns with respect to ten business ethics issues. Using a cluster-based sampling approach, they administered self-report questionnaires to 2,856 undergraduate college students enrolled in business, liberal arts or social science, and engineering or natural science majors. These students were drawn from twenty-eight different universities located in twenty-three states. Subsequent to their analyses, Beltramini, Peterson, and Kozmetsky concluded that the surveyed students appeared "somewhat more concerned about improving business ethics . . . than with 'finger pointing'" (199). They also concluded that "there was a consistent tendency for the females in the sample to express more concern than the males in the sample, regardless of the issue" (199).

Peterson, Beltramini, and Kozmetsky (1991) replicated their earlier survey in 1989–90. The replication consisted of surveying 1,681 college students enrolled in sixteen of the twenty-eight universities used previously as the sampling base. Concerns were elicited regarding five of the ten business ethics issues previously investigated. The results of the replication corroborated those of the 1980 survey but also suggested that there was a heightened level of concern among college students in 1989–90 with respect to the business ethics issues investigated.

Unfortunately, many of the other empirical studies undertaken to understand college students' attitudes toward, or perceptions of, common business ethics issues appear to possess limited generality. Consider the studies listed in Table 7.1. All of these studies were published in the *Journal of Business Ethics*, and all seem to employ stronger research designs, on average, than empirical studies of business ethics issues published elsewhere. Although these studies are not exhaustive, they collectively represent the empirical studies utilizing college students that have been published in the journal since its inception.

The median sample size of the studies contained in Table 7.1 is 213. Given the known and expected heterogeneity of college students with respect to the business ethics issues investigated (see, for instance, observed gender differences in attitudes and perceptions reported in Borkowski and Ugras 1998), many of the sample sizes seem a bit small. Furthermore, 62 percent of the studies only sampled students from a single university, typically by means of course-based convenience sampling. Because data collection frequently took place when many of the study participants were enrolled in a business ethics or business-and-society course, demand artifacts may well have been rampant. More than half of the studies, 57 percent, employed a scenario approach when collecting data; study participants were typically requested to respond to hypothetical ("decision") situations that were ethically ambiguous. To the extent that the scenarios employed were simultaneously unique and ambiguous, the interpretation of study participants' responses may be fraught with problems. In brief, the majority of prior empirical studies focusing on college students' attitudes toward, or perceptions of, business ethics issues leave much to be desired in terms of producing valid, reliable, and generalizable findings or meaningful inferences.

Research Methodology

The survey reported in this chapter is but one component of a global investigation of the attitudes of college students regarding capitalism and business ethics. Because one goal of the survey was to provide benchmark data, the

Table 7.1

Selected Characteristics of Illustrative Studies of Students' Ethics Published in *Journal of Business Ethics*

Study author(s)	Publication date	Sample size	Sample type	Number of universities sampled	Research design
Ameen, Guffey, and McMillan	1996	285	UB	4	scales
Arlow	1991	138	UG	1	scales
Betz, O'Connell, and Shepard	1989	213	UB, MBA	1	scales
Borkowski and Ugras	1992	130	UB, MBA	1	scenarios
Cole and Smith	1996	537	UB	9	scenarios
Galbraith and Stephenson	1993	107	UB	1	scenarios
Grant and Broom	1988	118	UB	3	scenarios
Jones	1990	134	UB	1	scenarios
Jones and Gautschi	1988	455	MBA	12	scales
Kennedy and Lawton	1998	490	UG	4	scales
Malinowski and Berger	1996	403	UG	1	scenarios
McCuddy and Peery	1996	171	UB	2	scenario
Rallapalli, Vitell, Wiebe, and Barnes	1994	295	UB	1	scales
Ruegger and King	1992	2,196	UB	1	scenarios
Shepard and Hartenian	1990	244	UG	1(?)	scenarios
Sikula and Costa	1994	211	UB	1	scales
Spain, Brewer, Brewer, and Garner	2002	410	UB	3	scenarios
Stanga and Turpen	1991	151	UB	1	scenarios
Stevens, Harris, and Williamson	1993	137	UB	1	scales
Stewart, Felicetti, and Kuehn	1996	892	UB	2	scales
Tsalikis and Ortiz-Buonafina	1990	175	UB	1	scenarios

Note: UG = both business and nonbusiness undergraduate students; UB = undergraduate business students; MBA = graduate students.

methodology employed in the survey is presented in some detail to facilitate any replications. In general, the present survey followed the research approach set forth in the Beltramini, Peterson, and Kozmetsky (1984) and Peterson, Beltramini, and Kozmetsky (1991) surveys and focused on several of the same ethical issues. However, unlike their surveys, the present one had as its universe only business students.

The present survey was designed to overcome many of the deficiencies characterizing previous studies of business ethics employing college students. For example, the present survey encompassed several thousand students drawn from dozens of colleges and universities throughout the United States. Moreover, generalizable rating scales tested for reliability were used to measure attitudes. Detailed information on the research methodology is presented in the following paragraphs.

Sample and Data Collection

A two-stage sampling design was employed in data collection. The first stage consisted of identifying a judgmentally representative sample of four-year colleges and universities in the United States. The second stage consisted of obtaining a cluster sample of business students in each of the stage-one colleges and universities.

Specifically, to obtain a nationally representative cross-section of business students, professors in sixty-four business schools across the United States were contacted in the summer of 2003. They were asked if their research or teaching assistant could administer about fifty questionnaires to undergraduate business students in an in-class setting at the beginning of the fall academic term. The professors were told that the questionnaires should not take more than five minutes to administer and that the assistant would receive an "honorarium" of $20 as a token of appreciation. Professors who agreed to participate in the survey were sent sixty blank questionnaires, a preaddressed, postage-paid return envelope, and the honorarium. An in-class setting was used to control for possible "noise" in data collection by having a common data collection environment. The timing of data collection was intended to control for the different subject matters in the courses in which data were collected.

Sixty of the sixty-four professors contacted agreed to assist in data collection. One professor only had access to graduate students, one was away from campus on sabbatical leave, and two did not respond to the request. Thus, the sample of students was derived from sixty different colleges or universities. These colleges or universities were located in thirty-two different states ranging from Maine to California, Washington to Florida, and Minnesota to Texas.

Table 7.2

Sample Profile

Characteristic	Percentage response
Gender	
Male	49.8
Female	50.2
Age	
Younger than 20	5.2
20–23	82.7
24 or older	12.1
Religious orientation	
Very religious	22.2
Somewhat religious	51.0
Not very religious	26.8
Employment status	
Work full-time	16.0
Work part-time	55.0
Do not work	29.0
Citizenship	
American	93.0
Other	7.0
Years at university	
One	11.5
Two	19.8
Three	36.7
Four or more	32.0

Eighty-eight percent of the business schools sampled were part of a public college or university.

The student sample consisted of 3,034 undergraduate business students, an average of 51 students per sampled business school. Due to the data collection approach, another 449 students completed questionnaires, but because these students were graduate students taking an undergraduate business course or undergraduate students who were not business majors, their questionnaires were excluded from further consideration. Approximately two dozen students did not respond to a sufficient number of the questionnaire items to be included in the final sample.

Table 7.2 presents a brief profile of the sampled students. Based on comparison data from the Association to Advance Collegiate Schools of Business and the United States Census Bureau, the gender, age, and citizenship characteristics of the student sample appear to be consistent with those of undergraduate (four-year) college students nationally as well as undergraduate business students generally. In addition to being used to assess the representativeness of the sample, the information in Table 7.2 was used to establish subsets of survey participants for analysis purposes.

Questionnaire

The questionnaire consisted of twenty-seven Likert-type items, the six items reflected by the Table 7.2 profile, and two items (academic classification and major field of study) used to ensure that the sample was limited to only undergraduate business students. Each of the twenty-seven items consisted of a declarative statement and a six-category "strongly agree" to "strongly disagree" rating scale; only the endpoints of the rating scale were labeled. Scale categories were labeled numerically from 1 to 6.

Survey participants were provided the following instructions:

> We are interested in your opinions about, and attitudes toward, several different issues. These issues are presented in the form of statements. Please read each statement as it appears and then indicate the extent of your agreement or disagreement by *circling* the appropriate number that represents your opinion or attitude. There are no right or wrong answers to any of the statements.

Of the twenty-seven items, only twelve are considered in this chapter; the other fifteen items were designed for use in the capitalism and non–United States components of the investigation.

The items used in the present survey were derived from several sources, including Beltramini, Peterson, and Kozmetsky (1984) and Hunt, Wood, and Chonko (1989). The items were pretested on a sample of twenty-five undergraduate business students at the University of Texas at Austin. The pretest included a qualitative evaluation of statement understandability and an assessment of two-week item test-retest reliability. The median (two-week) test-retest reliability of the twelve items was an acceptable .52.

The twelve items used in the present survey are presented in the appendix. Perusal of these items reveals that several different ethical issues are addressed as well as the existence of "pairs" of items. Some items were intended to document fundamental or underlying attitudes regarding business ethics. One was intended to obtain attitudinal insights moderated by business size, and one was utilized to provide guidance as to the delivery of ethics education in an academic setting. Certain pairs of items were designed to provide in-depth comparative insights into selected attitudes and to obtain inferences into the students' implied self-perceptions.

Results

Table 7.3 reports the response percentages for the total sample for each of the twelve items. These percentages can be aggregated in various ways to

Table 7.3

Response Percentages for Total Sample

Statement	Percentage response					
	Strongly agree					Strongly disagree
Business behavior that is legal is ethical.	4.9	11.0	19.4	24.2	27.0	13.5
Within a business firm, the ends justify the means.	3.2	9.0	24.9	27.9	22.0	13.0
Current ethical standards in business meet the needs of society.	4.3	15.8	31.3	25.8	18.4	4.4
Current ethical standards in business meet the needs of business.	5.1	21.0	38.3	22.4	11.1	2.1
If a manager in a company is discovered to have engaged in unethical behavior that results primarily in corporate gain (rather than personal gain), he or she should be terminated or fired.	29.2	29.3	17.8	13.1	6.9	3.7
If a manager in a company is discovered to have engaged in unethical behavior that results primarily in personal gain (rather than corporate gain), he or she should be terminated or fired.	46.1	29.4	12.5	6.6	3.0	2.4

The ethics of business people are worse than the ethics of people in government.	1.7	5.3	16.4	28.9	28.5	19.2
The ethics of business people are worse than the ethics of people in not-for-profit organizations.	11.5	25.0	26.8	19.2	10.9	6.6
The ethical standards of people working in large businesses are worse than the ethical standards of people working in small businesses.	4.6	19.0	28.6	25.9	15.2	6.7
Business ethics have deteriorated over the past ten years.	15.5	30.3	25.4	17.9	8.4	2.5
Business ethics will get better in the future.	7.2	17.8	31.4	27.2	12.2	4.2
I believe that all business students should take a formal course in business ethics.	35.7	29.5	18.1	9.7	4.6	2.4

facilitate their analysis and interpretation. To simplify the presentation of the response percentages, in the remainder of this chapter response percentages will be collapsed to reflect agreement (the first three or left-most scale categories anchored by "strongly agree") or disagreement (the last three or right-most scale categories anchored by "strongly disagree") with each statement. Despite this presentation simplification, however, all analyses were conducted at the individual scale-category level (i.e., when mean scale values were computed, they were computed using data from all six scale categories).

The response percentages in Table 7.3 can be interpreted in a fairly straightforward manner. It is interesting to note, for instance, that a substantial majority of the survey participants, about 5 out of 6, believed that "all business students should take a formal course in business ethics." Similarly, more than 70 percent of the survey participants believed that "business ethics have deteriorated over the past 10 years," even though nearly all of the survey participants were too young to have personally experienced the perceived decline. Of the twelve items, the one with the least variation in response percentages is "Current ethical standards in business meet the needs of business." The item with the greatest variability in response is "If a manager in a company is discovered to have engaged in unethical behavior that results primarily in personal gain (rather than corporate gain), he or she should be terminated or fired." In general, however, the dispersions of the item responses were relatively homogeneous across the twelve items.

Differences Across Subgroups

Although it is useful to analyze the responses of the total sample, it is more insightful to analyze the responses of certain sample subgroups. Tables 7.4 to 7.6 (see pp. 126–131) contain agreement percentages for each of the twelve items for various sample subgroups. In particular, response percentages are presented for six grouping variables:

- Gender (males and females)
- Age (younger than 20, 20 to 23, and 24 or older)
- Religiosity (very religious, somewhat religious, not very religious)
- Employment status (employed full-time, employed part-time, not employed)
- Citizenship (United States citizen, not United States citizen)
- Years at university (one, two, three, four or more)

A one-way analysis of variance was conducted for each item and grouping variable to determine whether a statistically significant relationship could be reasonably inferred between the attitude represented by the item response and the personal characteristic represented by the grouping variable. Because of the relatively large sample sizes of the subgroups analyzed, a conservative p-value of .001 was used as a statistical threshold when inferring whether a significant relationship exists between a particular attitude and personal characteristic.

In general, the business ethics–related attitudes investigated were held rather uniformly across the subgroups analyzed. Of the seventy-two analyses of variance conducted (12 items x 6 personal characteristics), less than a quarter suggested the existence of a statistically significant relationship (p <.001). There were virtually no significant relationships between business ethics–related attitudes and employment status or between business ethics–related attitudes and years at university. Significant response differences were observed most frequently between males and females; six of the twelve items exhibited statistically significant response differences. As indicated in Table 7.4, the responses of the females in the sample tended to reflect a greater degree of attitudinal ethicality than did the responses of the males in the sample.

Four of the items consistently produced response differences across multiple subgroups that were noticeable and/or statistically significant:

- "Business behavior that is legal is ethical."
- "Within a business firm, the ends justify the means."
- "If a manager in a company is discovered to have engaged in unethical behavior that results primarily in corporate gain (rather than personal gain), he or she should be terminated or fired."
- "I believe that all business students should take a formal course in business ethics."

Consider each of these items in turn. Female survey participants were significantly less likely than males to agree with the notion that "what is legal is ethical." Similarly, survey participants twenty to twenty-three years of age were less likely to agree with this notion than were survey participants who were younger than twenty years of age; survey participants who worked part-time were less likely to agree with this notion than were those who did not work; survey participants who were U.S. citizens were significantly less likely to agree with the notion than survey participants who were not U.S. citizens; and survey participants who had spent three years at their university were less likely to agree that "what is legal is ethical" than those survey participants who had spent only one year at their university.

Table 7.4

Percentage Agreement by Gender and Age

| | Percentage agreement | | | | |
| | Gender | | Age | | |
Statement	Males	Females	< 20	20–23	24 +
Business behavior that is legal is ethical.[a]	38.6	32.2	41.8	34.0	38.5
Within a business firm, the ends justify the means.[a]	43.0	31.9	39.9	37.1	36.6
Current ethical standards in business meet the needs of society.[b]	52.2	50.6	56.9	52.5	44.7
Current ethical standards in business meet the needs of business.	65.4	63.6	74.7	65.1	58.7
If a manager in a company is discovered to have engaged in unethical behavior that results primarily in corporate gain (rather than personal gain), he or she should be terminated or fired.[a,b]	73.6	78.5	62.3	76.0	81.2
If a manager in a company is discovered to have engaged in unethical behavior that results primarily in personal gain (rather than corporate gain), he or she should be terminated or fired.	87.3	88.6	83.8	87.7	90.6

127

The ethics of business people are worse than the ethics of people in government.	23.4	23.9	25.3	23.0	25.8
The ethics of business people are worse than the ethics of people in not-for-profit organizations.[b]	64.4	62.9	64.3	65.5	54.5
The ethical standards of people working in large businesses are worse than the ethical standards of people working in small businesses.	53.5	51.5	50.0	53.4	48.6
Business ethics have deteriorated over the past ten years.[a]	68.1	74.1	68.6	71.6	68.9
Business ethics will get better in the future.[a]	60.3	52.7	50.0	56.2	59.0
I believe that all business students should take a formal course in business ethics.[a]	80.7	85.9	79.6	83.2	85.0

[a]Significant relationship between attitude and gender ($p < .001$).
[b]Significant relationship between attitude and age ($p < .005$).

Table 7.5

Percentage Agreement by Religiosity and Employment

	Percentage agreement					
	Religiosity			Employment		
Statement	Very	Somewhat	Not very	Full-time	Part-time	Not
Business behavior that is legal is ethical.	35.2	36.4	33.5	35.6	33.2	39.1
Within a business firm, the ends justify the means.[a]	34.3	39.2	36.7	36.8	36.0	40.2
Current ethical standards in business meet the needs of society.	48.1	53.8	50.1	48.6	50.3	55.3
Current ethical standards in business meet the needs of business.	63.1	65.6	64.1	61.9	65.5	64.2
If a manager in a company is discovered to have engaged in unethical behavior that results primarily in corporate gain (rather than personal gain), he or she should be terminated or fired.[a]	81.4	74.4	75.0	78.2	76.8	73.6
If a manager in a company is discovered to have engaged in unethical behavior that results primarily in personal gain (rather than corporate gain), he or she should be terminated or fired.	87.5	88.3	87.8	88.7	88.6	86.4

The ethics of business people are worse than the ethics of people in government.[a]	25.8	24.8	19.5	26.5	23.2	22.9
The ethics of business people are worse than the ethics of people in not-for-profit organizations.	62.5	64.5	63.2	58.8	64.8	63.7
The ethical standards of people working in large businesses are worse than the ethical standards of people working in small businesses.	52.3	53.3	51.4	50.7	52.5	53.1
Business ethics have deteriorated over the past ten years.	73.4	70.9	69.6	74.0	71.1	69.5
Business ethics will get better in the future.	54.7	57.1	56.3	56.8	56.4	56.1
I believe that all business students should take a formal course in business ethics.[a]	86.9	84.0	79.1	82.8	84.1	82.2

[a]Significant relationship between attitude and religiosity ($p < .001$).

Table 7.6

Percentage Agreement by Citizenship and Years at University

	Percentage response					
	Citizenship		Years at university			
Statement	U.S.	Other	1	2	3	4+
Business behavior that is legal is ethical.[a]	34.4	42.7	39.6	36.8	33.8	34.3
Within a business firm, the ends justify the means.	36.6	42.2	43.3	40.9	35.8	34.7
Current ethical standards in business meet the needs of society.[a]	50.7	61.8	56.9	51.7	51.5	49.3
Current ethical standards in business meet the needs of business.[a]	63.6	76.6	67.8	66.8	63.2	63.6
If a manager in a company is discovered to have engaged in unethical behavior that results primarily in corporate gain (rather than personal gain), he or she should be terminated or fired.	76.6	70.9	70.2	74.7	76.4	78.9
If a manager in a company is discovered to have engaged in unethical behavior that results primarily in personal gain (rather than corporate gain), he or she should be terminated or fired.	88.3	84.1	83.1	87.6	87.9	90.2

The ethics of business people are worse than the ethics of people in government.	22.6	33.3	24.5	24.5	22.2	24.1
The ethics of business people are worse than the ethics of people in not-for-profit organizations.	63.5	66.0	58.3	66.9	64.1	62.8
The ethical standards of people working in large businesses are worse than the ethical standards of people working in small businesses.	52.6	53.3	50.7	52.4	51.5	54.2
Business ethics have deteriorated over the past ten years.	71.2	70.6	68.7	69.4	72.8	71.1
Business ethics will get better in the future.	53.2	61.4	56.8	53.9	55.6	58.6
I believe that all business students should take a formal course in business ethics.	83.6	81.0	82.4	81.9	84.4	83.3

[a] Significant relationship between attitude and citizenship ($p < .001$).

Female survey participants were significantly less likely to agree that "the ends justify the means" in a business than were male survey participants. Survey participants who reported themselves as being very religious were significantly less likely to agree that the "ends justify the means" than were survey participants reporting that they were somewhat religious. Survey participants who were U.S. citizens were less likely to agree that "the ends justify the means" than were survey participants who were not U.S. citizens, and survey participants who reported being at their university four or more years were less likely to agree with this proposition than were survey participants who reported being at their university for one year.

Survey participants who were females, and those who were twenty-four years of age or older, were significantly more likely to agree that a manager who engages in unethical behavior for corporate gains should be terminated than were, respectively, those survey participants who were males, and those who were younger than twenty years of age. Likewise, survey participants who reported that they were very religious reported more agreement with termination of the manager than did survey participants who stated they were somewhat religious or not very religious. Survey participants who were employed full-time were more likely to agree with termination than were survey participants who were not employed. Survey participants who were U.S. citizens were more likely to agree with termination than those who were not U.S. citizens, and the more time that survey participants had spent at their universities, the more they agreed with termination.

Female survey participants were significantly more favorably disposed toward all business students taking a formal course in business ethics than were male survey participants. Survey participants twenty-four years of age or older were more favorably disposed toward a formal course than were survey participants younger than twenty years of age. Survey participants who stated they were very religious were significantly more favorably disposed toward a formal business ethics course than were survey participants who stated they were not very religious.

Differences Across Items

As previously mentioned, and as can be observed in the appendix (see pp. 136–137), three "natural pairs" of items were included in the questionnaire. The purpose in doing so was to facilitate analyses that would elicit in-depth insights into the survey participants' attitudes regarding the ethics issues investigated. Responses to the three pairs of items are discussed here. For each pair of items, a repeated-measures t-test was computed so that each survey participant's respective responses to the two items were individually compared (that is, within an individual); this test, in combination with the correlation between the two responses, permitted an analysis that was sensitive to intra-individual response differences.

The first pair of items consisted of "Current ethical standards in business meet the needs of society" and "Current ethical standards in business meet the needs of business." Although the responses to these two items were moderately correlated ($r = .46$, shared variance = 21 percent), Table 7.3 reveals that, for the total sample, 51 percent of the survey participants agreed with the first item ("society"), whereas 64 percent agreed with the second item ("business"). The t-test reveals that this difference is statistically significant ($p < .001$). Thus, while a majority of the survey participants agreed that current ethical standards in business meet the needs of society and business, they also believed that current ethical standards in business were significantly *more likely* to meet the needs of business than meet the needs of society.

The second pair of items consisted of "The ethics of business people are worse than the ethics of people in government" and "The ethics of business people are worse than the ethics of people in not-for-profit organizations." Although the responses to these two items were correlated ($r = .21$), the shared variance was relatively minor (4 percent). As shown in Table 7.3, 22 percent of the survey participants agreed with the first item and 63 percent agreed with the second item. Thus, as might be expected, the difference in responses is very significant. The response percentages suggest that relative to the perceived ethics of business people, the survey participants possessed a much more positive belief about the ethics of people in not-for-profit organizations than they did about the ethics of people in government. Stated somewhat differently, survey participants tended to believe that the ethics of business people were not worse than the ethics of people in government, but that they were worse than those of people in not-for-profit organizations. Analysis of a related item revealed that 52 percent of the survey participants believed that the ethics of people working in large businesses are worse than those of people working in small businesses, a finding equivalent to "no difference" across business sizes.

The third pair of items consisted of "If a manager in a company is discovered to have engaged in unethical behavior that results primarily in corporate gain (rather than personal gain), he or she should be terminated or fired" and "If a manager in a company is discovered to have engaged in unethical behavior that results primarily in personal gain (rather than corporate gain), he or she should be terminated or fired." Responses to these items correlated more highly ($r = .62$) and reflected more shared variance (39 percent) than did the responses to the other two pairs of items. Whereas 76 percent of the survey participants believed that a manager should be terminated if he or she behaved unethically for the benefit of the corporation, 86 percent believed that the manager should be terminated if the unethical behavior was motivated by personal gain. As before, this response difference is very significant. Hence, survey participants appear to make a distinction regarding the intent of unethical behavior. Even though unethical behavior, per se, is not condoned, unethical behavior aimed at personal gain is perceived significantly more negatively than unethical behavior aimed at corporate gain. This finding is perhaps more vividly illustrated by the "strongly agree" percentages for the two items. Forty-six percent of the survey participants strongly agreed that a manager acting unethically for personal gain should be terminated, whereas 29 percent of the survey participants strongly agreed that such a manager should be terminated if he or she was acting unethically for corporate gain.

Observations

The observations gleaned from the survey corroborate certain previous conclusions regarding undergraduate business students' attitudes toward particular business ethics issues and complement other conclusions. Because of the research methodology employed, the results obtained from the survey should serve as a benchmark, both for comparing business students' attitudes regarding ethical issues obtained in specific settings as well as comparing business students' attitudes regarding ethical issues at future points in time. The survey results appear stable, valid, and generalizable within the parameters of the research methodology employed.

Although each reader will likely take away something different, and perhaps even something unique, from the survey results presented in this chapter, certain observations seem to possess generality. For example, in the context of the business ethics issues investigated, the results confirm prior research (e.g., Betz, O'Connell, and Shepard 1989; Ruegger and King 1992) indicating that, at least as measured by self-reports, female undergraduate business school students tend to possess attitudes that would be termed "more ethical" than corresponding male undergraduate business school students. (See the summary and meta-analysis of Borkowski and Ugras [1998] for similar conclusions. However, see also the empirical research of McCuddy and Peery [1996] and Sikula and Costa [1994] for opposite conclusions.) This "gender effect" was consistently the most pronounced set of differences observed. It is a bit disheartening to note that female survey participants were less optimistic about future improvements in business ethics than were male survey participants, especially given their increasing numbers in business schools and the demise of the "glass ceiling" in many corporations.

Beyond the gender response differences, the apparent homogeneity in the responses was a bit surprising. Given both intuition and anecdotal evidence, it was anticipated that there would be stronger relationships between attitudes and religiosity, employment status, and years at university. Perhaps some of the old shibboleths regarding the relationships between certain personal characteristics and ethics (e.g., that between religiosity and ethics) need rethinking. The results reported in this chapter might provide a starting point for in-depth explorations into relationships often taken for granted but seldom investigated empirically.

Some of the findings are subject to multiple and perhaps conflicting interpretations. Consider the finding that whereas 51 percent of the survey participants agreed that current ethical standards in business meet the needs of society, 64 percent agreed that current ethical standards in business meet the needs of business. Consequently, the finding provides support both for the "theory of moral unity" (there is only one set of moral standards) and the "theory of amorality" (different moral standards exist for business and society). This is because even though a majority of the survey participants agreed with both statements, there was a statistically significant difference between the two response percentages. (See Shepard and Hartenian [1990] for a discussion of the two theories.)

One survey finding that certainly merits reflection and discussion relates to the final item investigated: "I believe that all business students should take a formal course in business ethics." Approximately 83 percent of the survey participants agreed with this statement; more than one-third, 36 percent, strongly agreed with it. This finding is consistent with previous research on ethics education (e.g., Stewart, Felicetti, and Kuehn 1996). Thus, given that a large, nationwide sample of undergraduate business students has indicated that a formal business ethics course should be a course requirement, business school faculty members and administrators alike need to take this information into account when making curriculum decisions. Business ethics must be addressed in undergraduate business curricula, and the market for business ethics education, one critical business stakeholder group, has stated its preference. It now remains for business school faculties and administrators to respond.

136

Appendix

Items Used in Survey

Statement	Response categories					
	Strongly agree					Strongly disagree
Business behavior that is legal is ethical.	1	2	3	4	5	6
Within a business firm, the ends justify the means.	1	2	3	4	5	6
Current ethical standards in business meet the needs of society.	1	2	3	4	5	6
Current ethical standards in business meet the needs of business.	1	2	3	4	5	6
If a manager in a company is discovered to have engaged in unethical behavior that results primarily in corporate gain (rather than personal gain), he or she should be terminated or fired.	1	2	3	4	5	6
If a manager in a company is discovered to have engaged in unethical behavior that results primarily in personal gain (rather than corporate gain), he or she should be terminated or fired.	1	2	3	4	5	6

	1	2	3	4	5	6
The ethics of business people are worse than the ethics of people in government.	1	2	3	4	5	6
The ethics of business people are worse than the ethics of people in not-for-profit organizations.	1	2	3	4	5	6
The ethical standards of people working in large businesses are worse than the ethical standards of people working in small businesses.	1	2	3	4	5	6
Business ethics have deteriorated over the past ten years.	1	2	3	4	5	6
Business ethics will get better in the future.	1	2	3	4	5	6
I believe that all business students should take a formal course in business ethics.	1	2	3	4	5	6

8

Auditor Independence and the Scope of CPA Services

Roots and Recent Developments

Gary John Previts

The recent discoveries of capital market abuses and the unfolding of corporate scandals have led to the demise of Arthur Andersen as a member of the so-called Big Five auditing firms (Bartley 2002) and to significant changes in the scope of auditor services. The potential loss of credibility of the audit function, mandated for public companies as part of historic 1930s New Deal remedies for an ailing capital market, raises issues related to the governance of corporations and the proper conduct of parties using and seeking public investment funds.

This chapter explores the roots or origins of expectations about investor information in capital markets, the mandate for auditing publicly held companies, and the manner by which adjustments are made to auditor scope of services and independent behavior. From as early as the era identified with America's first large, interstate entities, the railroads, until the present, auditing as a function has evolved to ensure that where information was provided by those employing capital, it would be subject to a review process when communicated to capital providers. The need for financial technical expertise as part of this review, during the nineteenth century, led to the employment of specialist auditors. Eventually, as part of the 1933 Securities Act, an institutional role for external, independent auditors was mandated in federal law to safeguard the information rights of public investors (Previts and Merino 2003). Today, a few large CPA firms audit the majority of public companies.

In response to the original legislative mandate of the 1930s and 2002 legislation, CPA auditors are seeking to reorganize themselves to meet the requirements of registered firms overseen by the Public Company Accounting Oversight Board (PCAOB). The reorganization will provide the proper service amid continuing controversy regarding perceived spectacular audit failures and scores of financial restatements by public companies that had previously received clean audit opinions. Concerns caused by audit failures, such as those at Enron and WorldCom, led to consideration of the manner in which auditors maintain their independence from undue influence by their clients regarding economic and other conflicts of interest. The reorganization of auditor oversight follows the Public Company Accounting Reform and Investor Protection Act of 2002, commonly known as Sarbanes-Oxley, after two decades of CPA service expansion in response to market-driven demand for nonaudit services, most notably in the areas of taxation and advisory work (Freer 2002). As such, this market-driven scope of service approach, which emerged in the late 1970s and escalated in the 1990s, was a response to employment of global reach information technologies and the rise of the individual 401(k) investor.

Further, as business established the need to identify efficient outsourcing of noncore corporate support services, CPA audit firms responded because they were already operating as well-organized corporate suppliers of special knowledge services. Such a competitive market-based approach to allocating professional services markets reframed the issue of the extent to which such nonaudit services should be provided to an audit client without risking the protection provided to individual investors. Unlike the growing community of institutional investors, individual investors relied on the public accountant as the proverbial watchdog of operating company information reported about performance and the systems that provided it. CPA audit firms argued that an extended scope of service would be economically rational and efficient, permitting capture of scale economies. At the same time, though, critics expressed concerns about apparent and real conflicts of interest that could unfairly detract from the effective discharge of the responsibilities of an auditor.

Some pundits have asserted that any legislative and regulatory attempts to restore fairness fail to address the efficiency issues related to independence. At what point does one establish the precise limits of acceptable auditor service, especially since auditing every transaction is accepted as uneconomic? Is "independence," then, merely a code word for political negotiations leading to a legal mandate to allocate professional services market share to various highly skilled and compensated knowledge service providers? That is, do not consultants, accountants, and lawyers end up negotiating through legislation the extent to which they can provide certain services in the marketplace? And further, does not this create an environment contrary to competitive approaches that reward efficiency and discipline those who are inefficient?

Notwithstanding the paradox of employing regulation in a competitive market, recent legislation relating to publicly held companies, their audit committees, attorneys, financial executives, members of corporate boards, and auditors has raised expectations and penalties in the search to remedy the concerns of a new age of investment fund capitalism, wherein access to and information about public capital are almost instantly available. Individual investor participation has reached levels never before experienced. This is due in part to the financial intermediaries (mutual funds, insurance companies, and banks) moving capital into operating companies on behalf of tens of thousands of small investors who are now responsible for their own retirement funds in Individual Retirement Accounts (IRAs) and 401(k) plans. Learning more about the origins and development of capital formation, information, and investor expectations should provide a better understanding of the role of CPA auditors, their independence, and their scope of service as they affect corporate governance. Thus, this essay serves to inform those interested in the broader issue of corporate governance overall.

The topics in this chapter will be developed within the following framework:

- The U.S. Constitution as a social contract that influences auditing
- Roots of early auditing practice in U.S. corporations before the New Deal
- Post–World War II developments
- The politics of scope of services: the 1970s and after
- The new century: legislation to restore investor confidence
- Multidisciplinary firms: A bridge too far or the next horizon?

The U.S. Constitution as a Social Contract That Influences Auditing

The first ten amendments to the Constitution of the United States, the fundamental social contract between the American people and its government, are about personal freedoms, not personal property. So, while the Constitution protects an individual's right to own private productive property as wealth, these first amendments, collectively known as the Bill of Rights, preserve a free press, freedom of speech, and other individual democratic rights.

Property (Wealth) vis-à-vis People (Franchise)

A fundamental role of government is to balance the power of property and the power of people. The latter power, as individual rights, is voiced through franchise, or individuals casting their ballots or votes to shape government and the social contracts that government enacts and enforces. Regulation can be seen as a governmental response to balance the tendencies of those who have power based in property and can advance their interests by seeking the most efficient economic resolution, with the equitable claims of others who can employ only their voting power to obtain a fair social outcome. This trade-off between efficiency (self-interest) and fairness (public interest) is at the core of the incentives that mark social behavior in a free enterprise capital market system.

"Early capitalist theorists evidenced a strong bias against government encroachment in the economic sphere for political reasons. John Stuart Mill (1859/1956), for example, argued brilliantly in favor of restricting government regulation in order to avoid political evils. . . . But Mill, like [Adam] Smith, was driven by his own insight into the realities of the world to accept more governmental regulation than he would have tolerated in his more abstract philosophical concepts" (Steiner and Steiner 1988, 702–703). Therefore, it seems only appropriate to expect to find influences of what Mill would call "political economy" expressing themselves in the realities of the world regarding the extent to which self-interest behavior and public-interest behavior should be considered when those individuals given professional status are evaluated in society. Specifically, study of the trade-off of society's social power between property/wealth and people/franchise can be used to interpret private and public sector regulatory developments affecting accountancy through various industrial revolutions, including the steam revolution, the electrical revolution, the atomic revolution, and the personal computer revolution.

In the nineteenth and early twentieth centuries, many of the wealth and franchise contests were between those who had capital to lend and those who needed it for expansion. This was the case in the establishment of the eastern seaboard and the developing West. The eastern establishment favored sound and efficient money and limited credit expansion with control over monetary formation, as it had put its wealth to work in new sectors of the country where economic returns were anything but certain. The West championed expansion of credit and easy and fair money in multiple forms of currency, including currency backed by silver as well as gold.

Roots of Early Auditing Practice in U.S. Corporations
Before the New Deal

In the last decade, Flesher, Previts, and Samson (2000), Previts and Merino (1998a), Russ and Coffman (2002), and Samson, Previts, and Flesher (2003) have added to knowledge of colonial and antebellum auditing practices and the process by which the shareholder audit evolved to become a professional service. Capital providers in the nineteenth century, whether representing interests in the United States, Great Britain, or Europe, found that railroads were generally forthcoming with information. An early example is the Baltimore & Ohio (B&O) Railroad, established in 1827. The B&O Railroad provided substantial financial and operating information as a part of the established annual reporting requirements of its corporate charter. Indeed, Samson, Previts, and Flesher (2003) established that the B&O Railroad's bylaws required that an audit committee of directors undertake quarterly reviews of the corporate books so that merchants and other investor constituents, including the City of Baltimore and the State of Maryland (i.e., the public), would be informed. Russ and Coffman (2002) have also identified this type of audit committee function in a private investment entity, the Potomac Company, during the canal era preceding railroads. These informational activities and reports, while rudimentary by today's standards, provide evidence to support expectations about the right of investors to performance information as a contractual exercise in early corporate America.

Further evidence from Great Britain, a principal source of U.S. investment capital, supports the view that an expectation of auditing activity was well established before 1860, after which U.S. railroad investment and construction accelerated. The 1845 UK Railway Companies Clauses Consolidation Act, for example, provided for the appointment of an auditor (Worthington 1895). Also, in the 1850s, English bondholders of the Illinois Central Railroad formed an audit committee to oversee their investment in that company (Flesher, Previts, and Samson 2000).

Capital from Europe, especially Great Britain, which had been directed to the United States through New York financial houses, went into financing industrial securities throughout the nineteenth century, and many of today's *Fortune* 500 firms were formed through such securities. The consolidation of industries, beginning with the railroads and continuing with oil and tobacco and the creation of U.S. Steel in 1902, confirmed the need for an investment-grade industrial securities market and supported demand for financial statements as information useful to domestic and overseas capital sources to signal corporate performance. Early capital market leaders during the post–Civil War expansion of the economy, such as J.P. Morgan, were in the position to command the information they required when they contracted to invest. Morgan and his family had earned a reputation for trust and fiscal responsibility such that his association with a project or person was a near guarantee of financial stability. Morgan understood the value of proprietary information relative to the power of property, and he expressed concern about having to do business using "glass pockets," revealing too much information to the benefit of competitors (Jackson 1983, 237). However, as capital markets became more popular and began relying on individual investors, especially in the early twentieth century, more public forms of reliable corporate information and access to market information became necessary. Following Morgan's death and the start of the Federal Reserve System, the "Money Trust" identified with Morgan began to dissipate amid the growing influence of brokerage houses and investment trusts that competed for commission revenues from an expanding retail market for equities. Private sector information sources about credit, such as R.G. Dun, and railroad and industrial financial data, including those from Moody and from Standard & Poor's, had existed for some time and served commercial customers, but institutional arrangements to benefit small investors lagged.

Within sixteen years, criteria for chartered accountants and certified public accountants were established as evidence of professional status by royal charter in the UK (1880) and by state legislators in the United States (1896). This popularization acknowledged the informational expertise demanded by the capital marketplace so that property owners could assess how well their investments were performing. The concepts of chartered accountant and certified public accountant afforded stature to accountants and led to professional standing, which in turn marked the beginning of the public's awareness of auditors, both foreign and domestic, and the formation of expectations about auditor behavior, and hence, independence (Previts and Merino 1998a).

As early as 1898, independence for auditors was the subject of an editorial in *The Accountant*, published in England, at the crest of Lombard Street's sovereignty over world capital markets. The editorial discussed the refusal by UK auditors to sign the accounts of Sterling Gold Mines in Montana. Independence in this essay was about enabling auditors, who might be deemed "troublesome," to resist domination and dismissal by corporate directors. The editorial noted that "the hands of auditors require strengthening, and . . . [auditors] should be placed in a more independent position." Further, it stated that "auditors once appointed should remain in office for an extended period, unless for some palpable misconduct, and the removal should be by an extraordinary meeting of the shareholders." The editorial offered no resolution to the seemingly endless debate of how far management and director discretion properly extends before it becomes abusive. It did urge, however, that the Institute of Chartered Accountants look into the fact that another firm, perhaps too willingly, took up the Sterling Gold Mines engagement despite the first firm's refusal to issue a certificate (Previts 1985, 28).

Similar sentiments about the activities and responsibilities of accounting professionals surfaced in the United States during this period. Andrew Barr, chief accountant of the Securities and Exchange Commission (SEC), noted that in 1900, shortly after the passage of the Pennsylvania CPA law, *The Public Accountant* of Philadelphia, a trade journal, invited leading practitioners to define public accounting. There were twenty-nine responses to this invitation from eight different cities. Barr chose to emphasize the definition of one respondent, Charles C. Reckitt, a founder of the profession in Barr's home state of Illinois:

> A public accountant acknowledges no master but the public, and thus differs from the bookkeeper, whose acts and statements are dictated by his employers. A public accountant's certificate, though addressed to the president or directors, is virtually made to the public, who are actually or prospectively stockholders. He should have ability, varied experience, and undoubted integrity. (Barr 1959)

Disclosure and Public Markets

In the 1920s, individual investors, who were to become a dominant force and constitute the majority source of equity share ownership in the public capital market, were left to their own resources in the unregulated casino environment of the age. After the market failure of 1929 and disclosures about market manipulation, the ability to obtain information from corporations based on the tradition of laissez-faire practices would be altered by the securities acts. Into this gap between commercial information sources and the needs of a public market, audited general-purpose financial statements would evolve to satisfy the social contract for full and fair disclosure. The services and activities of an increasingly active group of analysts also would appear in the wake of Benjamin Graham's (1965) pathbreaking success in security analysis, which popularized as a public good individual investment based on publicly available information about corporate performance. The age of the individual as corporate property investor had dawned.

Along with this increased popular involvement in the stock market came terminology that reflected the accounting information environment of the times. Colloquialisms such as "in the red" and "in the black" came to represent being "in trouble" or being "okay." These meanings, of course, were derived from the bookkeeping practices of recording losses in red ink (i.e., "in the red") and profits in black ink (i.e. "in the black"). Later, just as the term "earnings per share" came to dominate personal and investment parlance, the term "bottom line" came to symbolize the measuring up of a situation, a sort of final analysis. The *Oxford English Dictionary* (2003) indicated that, in the United States, the term "bottom line" originated in accounting practices, not engineering, not medicine, not law. It means "the last line of the profit-and-loss account, showing the final profit (or loss)." Accounting and the role of auditors in providing information to individual investors have been woven into the fabric of business and culture and all of their representative idioms.

The New Deal: Mandated "Independent" Audits

The independent auditor gained new importance during the New Deal's reform of the capital markets. Not until 1933 did the federal government devise a legislative intervention to reform discredited capital market institutions. The devastating financial revelations about the Swedish industrialist known as the "Match King," Ivar Kreuger, after his apparent suicide in March 1932, forced legislative action by Congress (Flesher and Flesher 1986).

James M. Landis, who was asked by President Franklin Delano Roosevelt to work on drafting securities legislation, recalled, "Our draft remained true to the conception voiced by the President in his message of March 29, 1933 to Congress, namely that its requirements should be limited to full and fair disclosure of the nature of the security being offered and there should be no authority to pass upon the investment quality of the security" (Landis 1959). Described as the quintessential sunshine law, the 1933 Securities Act proposed by President Roosevelt moved to put the burden of telling the whole truth on the seller as a way to restore public confidence.

Berle (1963, 97) noted the context of the legislation: "On March 3, 1933, the closing of practically all the banks in the country paralyzed the supply of currency, and with it a large part of the production and distribution of the United States." The newly elected government was inaugurated on March 4, 1933.

Initially, the Federal Trade Commission (FTC) reviewed registration of new issues under the 1933 Securities Act. By 1934, concern that a "capital strike," a withholding of investment in opposition to federal intervention in the last bastion of laissez-faire, had subsided sufficiently and Congress established a separate Securities and Exchange Commission to administer the series of capital market laws forthcoming. President Roosevelt appointed Joseph P. Kennedy as the SEC's first chairman, to the dismay of some ardent reformers. In a radio address from the National Press Club on July 25, 1934, shortly after taking office, Kennedy set forth a "disclosure" message:

I conceive it to be an important part of the job we are trying to do here in the S.E.C. to reassure capital as to its safety in going ahead and to reassure the investor as to the protection of his interests by restricting certain practices which have proved to be detrimental to their interests, and by making available adequate information to the public upon which it can act intelligently. . . . Publicity will be an important element in the new conditions. Publicity not of an occasional nature, but regular and informative. (Kennedy 1934/1998, 322)

Post–World War II Developments

John L. Carey (1904–1987), perhaps more than any other single person, crafted the literature of CPA ethics and auditor independence from the 1940s until his retirement from the American Institute of Certified Public Accountants (AICPA) in 1968 (e.g., Carey 1940). SEC chief accountant Andrew Barr (1901–1995) established a basis for dialogue between the SEC and the organized profession during the significant years of expansion following World War II. The resolve of the SEC to advance its views, articulated in its own Regulation S-X, to define acceptable independence behavior, has been continuously demonstrated in key situations.

The establishment of a body of generally accepted auditing standards (GAAS) by the organized CPA profession after the end of World War II precipitated an expansion of audit services as the U.S. economy boomed, despite inflationary phenomena. Relative prosperity continued following the Korean War and into the period termed the Cold War. Increasingly, individual investors had sufficient wealth to invest in public equity capital markets, and this was supplemented by pension fund equity investment.

In an article in the *Journal of Accountancy*, Barr (1959) considered the developments leading up to the congressional hearings for the initial New Deal Securities Act. He began by observing Reckitt's definition of the duty of the accountant to the public. That Barr, the SEC's chief accountant at the time, should establish this historical premise while writing in the late 1950s is not surprising—this post–World War II expansion was a period of unprecedented growth for the capital market composed of individual investors. CPAs were paying increasing attention to the subject of auditor independence. Barr was therefore reorienting a new generation of accountants to their obligation to the public as a rationale for determining auditor independence. (Note that the organized CPA profession, as represented by the AICPA and its predecessors, had grown from less than 1,000 members in 1900 to approximately 9,500 at the end of World War II. Presently the AICPA has a membership approaching 340,000.)

Barr further asserted that other pre-1930 examples established that "the concept of independence was well developed, and the value of a review by independent accountants who are in no way connected with the business, was established *before* the passage of the Securities Act" (1959, emphasis supplied). Despite this assertion, not everyone agrees that the idea of an independent auditor was well established before the Securities Act was passed. According to McCraw (1984, 167–168), "the Federal Trade Commission and the Federal Reserve Board worked closely with the American Institute . . . to publish, in 1917, . . . *Uniform Accounting*, which proved to be a breakthrough. . . . Even so, the influence of accountants remained small before the New Deal, and their recommendations were often modified to fit the wishes of corporate management. The concept of the 'independent auditor' had not yet come of age in the United States."

Barr (1959) characterized the testimony of Colonel Arthur Carter, then president of the New York State Society of CPAs and senior partner of Haskins & Sells (currently Deloitte), as convincing Congress of the value of the involvement of the public accountant and thus securing passage of the proposal to require certification by independent public accountants in the 1933 Securities Act. The administrative regulations of the Act stated that accountants would not be considered independent under certain circumstances, such as if they were an officer or director of the audited company or had a substantial financial interest in it.

One oft-quoted passage from the April 1933 Senate Committee on Banking and Currency Hearings is the exchange between Arthur Carter, Senator Alben Barkley (D-KY), and Senator Robert Reynolds (D-NC) (United States Congress 1933, 58):

> Senator Barkley: You audit the controller?
> Mr. Carter: Yes, the public accountant audits the controller's account.
> Senator Barkley: Who audits you?
> Mr. Carter: Our conscience.

A pause at this point serves to emphasize the manner in which personal responsibility was thus established as the vehicle for the moral authority of the audit franchise, but the next statements are also informative:

> Senator Barkley: I am wondering whether after all a controller is not for all practical purposes the same as an auditor, and must he not know something about auditing?
> Mr. Carter: He is in the employ of the company. He is subject to the orders of his superiors.

Senator Barkley: I understand. But he has got to know something about auditing?

Mr. Carter: Yes.

Senator Barkley: He has got to know something about bookkeeping?

Mr. Carter: But he is not independent.

Senator Reynolds: Let me ask you a question, Colonel. These companies are going to arrive at these figures through your special auditors. All right. Now you want the members of your organization to check up on their figures?

Mr. Carter: As we do in many cases of industrial companies every year.

Senator Reynolds: All right. Then it goes to the Commission, does it not?

Mr. Carter: Yes.

Senator Reynolds: Have they got to check their accounts and your accounts?

Mr. Carter: I do not think so. I do not think they would have to go to that.

Senator Reynolds: Why should your members ask that they be permitted and empowered to check these accounts?

Mr. Carter: Because it is generally regarded that an independent audit of any business is a good thing.

John L. Carey, long-serving chief staff officer of the organized national CPA profession, recalled his understanding of the meaning of the term "independent" as contemplated in the 1933 Securities Act (Carey 1985, 6):

The word "independent" was first used in conjunction with "accountant" in the same sense as in the phrase "independent contractor"—as the dictionary says, "not subject to another's authority." But the noun form, "independence," also denotes the admirable quality of "not being influenced or controlled by others in matters of opinion or conduct." It was not difficult, by subtle thought transmission, for independent accountants, perhaps with some self-satisfaction, to invest themselves with this admirable quality of independence.

Many years earlier, in his capacity as editor of the *Journal of Accountancy*, Carey had responded to inquiries and criticisms regarding auditor independence and whether independence was possible given the ultimate question, Can a certified public accountant be wholly independent of the client who pays his fee and controls the tenure of his appointment? Later, Carey reopened the question in remarks to critics who held that "no profession ancillary to business no matter how high minded . . . can really be independent."

He responded as follows (Carey 1945, 93):

> The accountant in every auditing engagement has a co-employer, the pub-
> lic. If his work is not satisfactory to those who ultimately make use of it, he
> will no longer be useful to the client who pays his fee. It is therefore . . . not
> necessarily nobility or extraordinary strength of character which makes
> the accountant independent but primarily an instinct of professional self-
> preservation.

Some scholars in accounting argue that the admirable qualities of independence was always intended by Congress, but it is unlikely that there will
ever be a complete understanding of what it intended, semantic difficulties
aside (Committe 1989). After all, independent public accountants were to be
paid by the companies they audited, were they not? The admirable quality in
such cases would seem to be at risk from the very beginning. And in keeping
with a preference for private sector versus public sector direction in matters
of property and its informational components, an independently contracted
auditor, even at the risk of misunderstanding of meaning, was highly preferred in corporate and investment circles to a government auditor certifying
private company financial reports.

Then as now, one expects there could be the concern by corporations about
the quality and responsiveness of an IRS-type agency performing a credible
capital market assurance service. This is especially true today in an environment in which public companies are obligated to routinely produce comprehensive reports that may encompass dozens of country locations, languages,
currencies, and cultures and must be completed with an audit certificate in
hand within sixty days or less of the fiscal year-end closing date.

Auditor Independence: Meanings and Diverging Views

In 1947, the AICPA adopted a general statement on the concept of independence. The semantic distinction between the meaning of "independent" and
"independence" foretold differences about meanings that would begin to
develop in administration of the law and in practice. The arguments in most
cases were and are sufficient to continue the debate today.

Barr (1959) referred to the existence of a "double standard" in the profession. By this time, Carey (1965) pointed out, the concept of independence
had begun to create a great deal of confusion: "From the beginning, independent auditors . . . recognized that they would be useless to society unless they
were fair and objective in their attestations to financial data." Barr argued
that the AICPA's code of ethics and its rules of professional conduct required

public company auditors to observe one set of practices and private company auditors another.

This dichotomy reflected the SEC's revision of paragraph (b) of Rule 2.01 of Regulation S-X in 1950. Before this revision, with respect to the SEC's criteria for independence, "any substantial interest" in a client was considered evidence of lack of independence on the part of the accountant. As early as 1937, the SEC, through its *Accounting Series Release No. 2*, took the position that "an accountant cannot be deemed to be independent if he is or has been during the period under review, an officer or director of the registrant or if he holds an interest in the registrant that is significant with respect to its total capital or his own personal fortune" (Securities and Exchange Commission 1938). In the 1950 revision of this position, the word "substantial" was removed, meaning that an accountant could not have *any* financial interest in a registrant or any affiliate thereof.

Thus, according to the SEC, the existence of any financial interest, not the degree of it, would compromise independence with regard to publicly held company audit engagements. However, for AICPA members who did not practice before the SEC, the "substantial interest" interpretation continued under the AICPA code. Thus, from 1950 until 1959, when Barr made his comments, a double standard existed. The AICPA leadership decided to address this "schizophrenia" at its September 1960 annual meeting. Carey (1965) described the "donnybrook" that took place when proposals were introduced to establish that

> a member should not express an opinion on financial statements of an enterprise unless he and his firm were in fact independent with respect to such enterprise; that independence was not susceptible of precise definition, but was an expression of the professional integrity of the individual; that the member had the responsibility of assessing his relationships to determine whether he might expect his opinion to be considered independent, objective, and unbiased by one who had knowledge of all the facts; but that a member would not be considered independent with respect to any enterprise if he or any of his partners during the period of the professional engagement or at any time of expressing his opinion had, or was committed to acquire, any direct financial interest or material indirect financial interest in the enterprise or was connected with the enterprise as a promoter, underwriter, voting trustee, director, officer or key employee.

An exception was made in the case of charitable, religious, civic, and similar nonprofit organizations.

Two years of turbulent deferral, debate, and discussion ensued before the AICPA membership voted approval of new Rule No. 13. Finally, for the first time in 1962, the actual word "independence" appeared in the organized profession's code of ethics. There now was substantial semantic conformity between the profession's and the SEC's language (Higgins 1962). The meaning, however, would continue to be debated, since in addition to the issue of the public versus private audit differences, there was a conceptual issue dating back to the 1933 Securities Act's governmental administrative regulations, which established when an accountant would be considered independent. Thus, there was to be a distinction between real independence, or independence in fact—integrity and objectivity—and the appearance of independence. The profession emphasized the fact of independence; the SEC seemed to emphasize appearance, perhaps because the latter was operational and supported prohibitions and/or specific behavioral rules.

The distinction between independence in fact and independence in appearance is illustrated by the comments of Higgins (1962) and Mautz and Sharaf (1961). Higgins (1962) believed that "there are actually two kinds of independence which a CPA must have—independence in fact . . . the quality of not being influenced by regard to personal advantage . . . and independence in appearance . . . freedom from potential conflicts of interest which might tend to shake public confidence in his independence in fact." Mautz and Sharaf (1961) developed a concept of independence with two components, practitioner independence and profession independence. The former was a state of mind relating to the notions of integrity and objectivity; the latter refers to the apparent independence of auditors, as a professional group, in the mind of the public.

Firm Processes

Each major accounting firm that practices before the SEC also maintains a series of self-regulatory processes—systems, policy statements, and practice statements—to insure audit independence. A publicly available compendium of the features of these separate systems, policy statements, and practice statements of the major accounting firms is not known to exist. However, a peer review of major firms affords opportunities for private sharing of best practices. For example, there appears to be an expectation that annual affidavits are required by firms to establish each individual's responsibilities. Further, at least one major firm emphasizes the role of the engagement partner as the sole person responsible for determining independence relating to the engagement. This places both authority and responsibility at the highest engagement-related level.

In the 1980s, however, in at least one notable instance, a firm's internal process approved an activity in uncharted waters. In this instance, a partner secured a loan program with a client bank. Those in charge of the firm's internal processes did not "consult" with the SEC as to its interpretation of the ensuing relationship. Major disagreements and a protracted SEC enforcement action followed. An SEC Accounting and Auditing Enforcement Release and Settlement later effected a revision to AICPA processes (Previts and Merino 1998b, 308). The episode served to point out that firms acting solely on their own internal devices in areas of new opportunities were subject to being second-guessed such that they should view unilateral independence decisions as risky.

The point remains that at least three formal types of independence activity are involved in major public company independence determinations through, respectively, AICPA, SEC, and internal-firm review systems. (One might argue that there are four types of systems if each firm's processes are considered to be peer-reviewed as well as internally reviewed). The value of this redundancy is clearly at issue on grounds of bureaucracy and efficiency, but perhaps less debatable from the public policy perspective of what constitutes "equitable" behavior. If there is a summary thought to all of this, it is that despite all these types of reviews, serious oversight violations can and will occur. One telling example is the case of ESM Government Securities. The case involved the 1985 collapse of a Florida brokerage and the jailing of CPA Jose Gomez, the managing partner of the Miami office of Alexander Grant & Co. (presently Grant Thornton). Gomez was convicted for not challenging the company's false financial statements in exchange for $200,000.

The Politics of Scope of Services: The 1970s and After

It had become commonplace in the professional literature in the 1950s to treat the CPA as a business consultant. In the 1953 edition of the *CPA Handbook*, for instance, Marquis Eaton, a future president of the AICPA, wrote a chapter detailing the types of consulting engagements then performed by CPAs (Mednick and Previts 1987). By the 1970s, consulting engagements had expanded substantially as part of what large accounting firms did, particularly following audit or tax seasons.

The increased level of congressional interest in the role of auditing versus nonauditing services provided by the then Big Eight firms to clients and others was a major focus of *The Accounting Establishment* (United States Senate 1976), an exhaustive 1,760–page Senate staff study widely circulated after hearings on CPA firm consulting services. From this platform, a variety of new market-based initiatives was debated and attempted with long-term and perhaps unintended impact on the scope of CPA services. The scope-of-services debate was focused by two divergent viewpoints. One viewpoint asserted the efficient allocation of professional services through a one-stop-shopping approach to providing corporate support services. This "efficiency," expansionary view of CPA services was countered by those who viewed such expansion as threatening the independence of auditors and creating economic and commercial conflicts of interest, thereby reducing the fairness of the capital market playing field.

There was also the question of the role of the auditor with regard to the detection of fraud. In particular, what did the public expect the audit to do? In 1978, the Commission on Auditor Responsibilities, chaired by former SEC chair Manuel Cohen, concluded that, among other things, many users of financial statements appeared to misunderstand the role of the auditor and the nature of the services offered. The Cohen Commission's identification of this expectations gap has led over time to increased political and popular awareness about the role of the audit and auditor with respect to detecting fraud. Another special commission chaired by James C. Treadway Jr., a former SEC commissioner, concluded its comprehensive program of research and hearings in 1987. While fraudulent financial reporting was its principal concern, the Treadway Commission also looked extensively at other issues, such as audit quality and education, to better establish the community of activities and roles related to the presentation of business and financial information to the investment community and public. The follow-on Committee of Sponsoring Organizations (COSO) currently exists to encourage implementation of the Treadway Commission's recommendations.

During the 1970s, the Federal Trade Commission, in its review of professional service providers, including dentists, physicians, attorneys, and accountants, aggressively imposed competitive solutions in the name of improving consumer choice. Supreme Court chief justice Warren Burger was reported to have opined that, with regard to the advertising of legal services that resulted, one should "never, never, never hire a lawyer who advertises." Indeed, the emotions of traditional professionalism ran deep. The AICPA code of ethics (American Institute of Certified Public Accountants 1978) was eventually dismantled in a similar fashion, in the name of competition. Long-standing CPA prohibitions on advertising and solicitation of another audit firm's clients and personnel all fell to the deregulatory onslaught of the FTC rationale that supported market-based competition as a superior allocating device for professional services. The customer's right to choose among competitive suppliers was becoming attractive as the political mood of the country shifted after 1976, the bicentennial year, which shook off much of the gloom of the first oil embargo and the Vietnam malaise. In addition, professional fee structures were to be modified so that certain forms of nonattest engagements could be based on contingent fees, an arrangement that had previously been considered unethical, even when employed in competition with non-CPA professionals.

Professional moral "software" changed slowly, but by the late 1970s the major firms had begun employing marketing-related personnel and qualifying them as CPA partners. These individuals were to be engaged primarily in assisting the development of proposals for competitive bidding of engagements. Many clients (customers) perceived bidding as an opportunity to reduce audit fees and reap the benefits of efficiency brought about by competition. No one was able to convince either potential corporate clients or accounting firms of any dire consequences regarding the contest between efficiency and fairness. Efficiency arguments and market forces would lead to great changes in firm structure. These in turn favored the provision of nonattest services to the point where these became the dominant focus of audit firms, which used a commodity pricing strategy for audit work that was bid as an entrée for other services. The amount of audit work, as a percent of total revenue, in the large accounting firms began to shift dramatically, and by the early 1990s auditing was no longer a major source of revenue.

The practice and definition of independence that emerged in this market-based era of expansion of public accounting services would differ markedly from the predecessor views of independence. A codification of behavior relating to "appearance rules" was provided in the AICPA *Code of Professional Conduct* (American Institute of Certified Public Accountants 1992) under a structure of principles governing the performance of professional services by its members. Article IV (Objectivity and Independence) now stated, "A member should maintain objectivity and be free of conflict of interests in discharging professional responsibilities. A member in public practice should be independent in fact and appearance when providing auditing and other attestation services."

The code was to be observed by all AICPA members, whether in public practice or corporate or industry practice. The "integrity and independence" section of the code appeared in its restructured form in the late 1980s following action by a special AICPA committee chaired by former board chair George Anderson.

Following the donnybrook of the 1960s, the AICPA code materials on independence applied to publicly and nonpublicly traded companies. At least there would be solidarity as to the fundamental view of CPA independence behavior. In 1992 the AICPA changed the name of its behavioral guidance from *Code of Professional Ethics* to *Code of Professional Conduct*, signaling the beginning of the end of a mandated approach to professional service allocation of the audit function. It also signaled the beginning of a long, deregulatory, competitive period wherein nonattest services became the dominant services provided by CPA firms marketing themselves as professional service firms offering a wide variety of consulting services and an expanded set of tax-planning services.

The 1990s reflected these rapid and unprecedented changes and the paradox of two regulatory agencies, the FTC and the SEC, at cross-purposes. The SEC sought to shore up auditor independence by limiting potential scope-of-services conflicts for the sake of fair markets, whereas the FTC tried to induce a competitive response attuned to the interests of economic efficiency by maximizing outsourcing and reconfiguring knowledge services in a market-driven, customer-based approach. The FTC's one-stop-shopping efficiency arguments prevailed to the point of proposing a broad set of profession-wide changes resulting in a fully multidisciplinary approach to CPA services initially identified by the term "cognitor." This approach had as its goal consolidation of law firms, accounting firms, and consulting firms into market-driven professional services firms. Such firms would be the ultimate one-stop professional providers of external and internal auditing/assurance/attest services; consulting and information systems installation; tax planning and compliance; and legal and advocacy services. The cultures of these service firms would be competitively and economically rational. By virtue of their economic strengths, these firms would be able to overcome traditional concerns about perceived conflicts and similar issues of fairness.

The New Century: Legislation to Restore Investor Confidence

The FTC influences prevailed to shape the new professional services firms that emerged from the cauldron of market forces during the decades preceding the twenty-first century. Yet the SEC's authority and its legislative duty relative to the capital markets, while separate from that of the FTC, was more than equal to any market force influence as far as administration of the audit was concerned. Indeed, the SEC could single-handedly establish the conditions under which audit practice was conducted by using its traditional authority in defining "independence" as the latchkey to lock or unlock access to appropriate nonaudit services offered by those wishing to provide audit services to public companies.

In January 1994, new independence concerns were raised by SEC chief accountant Walter Schuetze. He charged that independent accounting firms served as cheerleaders for their clients in the process of setting accounting standards before the private sector agency recognized by the SEC, the Financial Accounting Standards Board (FASB), and were advocating irresponsible accounting. The Public Oversight Board (POB), another device of the 1970s self-regulatory regime established in response to *The Accounting Es-*

tablishment (United States Senate 1976), reacted promptly to investigate the government's concerns. It appointed a special panel headed by Donald J. Kirk, a former FASB chair and faculty member at Columbia University, and consisting of Ralph Saul, a former president of the American Stock Exchange, and George Andersen, whose special committee in the late 1980s was responsible for reforming the AICPA's *Code of Professional Conduct*. The panel's charge was to assess the working relationships among the profession, the business community, the SEC, and the FASB, and to identify and evaluate steps to support the objectivity, independence, and professionalism of auditing firms.

The Kirk panel, and later the O'Malley panel (also sanctioned by the POB and named after its chair, Shaun O'Malley, retired senior partner at Price Waterhouse), were private sector responses to challenges to the integrity of the auditing process and the auditor expectation gap during the 1990s. Another important development was the formation of the Independence Standards Board (ISB). From its formation in May 1997, through July 31, 2001, when the ISB was dissolved, the SEC partnered with private sector entities, the AICPA, and major professional services firms in a process to establish auditor independence standards. This effort reflected the powerful influence of the 1990s dot-com market on the SEC as a regulatory agency. The ISB was a way of stepping back from governmental regulation to self-regulation of auditor independence. It was developed to mirror the private sector FASB, which the SEC had recognized as authoritative with regard to generally accepted accounting principles (GAAP) since the FASB's inception in 1973.

The Kirk and O'Malley panels, operating under the direction of the POB, sought to improve the effectiveness of corporate governance and auditing by highlighting the relationship of auditing to the overall structure of corporate governance. The Kirk panel pointed out that a key relationship in the effectiveness of the audit process was that between the auditor and a corporate board's audit committee. Highlighting and strengthening that relationship, including a review of the composition and authority of that board committee, was a focus of this panel's efforts. The O'Malley panel on audit effectiveness undertook a more exhaustive and detailed study of a variety of audit service issues and provided its report in August 2000. However, the events surrounding the collapse of the dot-com market and a popular dissatisfaction with auditors in the wake of Enron would mute the effectiveness of the O'Malley panel's efforts in the private sector and leave all its self-regulatory/deregulatory efforts, including the ISB, with no visible means of popular or political support. However, the findings and evidence gathered by the two panels and the recommendations of previous private sector commissions collectively seem to have had an influence, if only obliquely, on the reformations forthcoming in Sarbanes-Oxley in that the self-regulatory organization (SRO) concept traceable to the 1980s recommendations now exists in the private corporate form of the Public Company Accounting Oversight Board (PCAOB).

The events at WorldCom in June 2002 turned out to be a factor determining the conclusion of the lives of the ISB, the POB, and private sector standard-setting for auditing. The allegations of massive fraud at this high-profile telecom, a darling of the dot-com era, made politicians and professional leaders sensitive to the timetable of political accountabilities. The fact that "franchise" would have its say in November 2002 now weighed heavily in the calculus of accountability. Approaches calling for efficient use of process, and sensitive to the power of propertied interests, were no longer given an opportunity to hold political sway in the face of the apparently discredited expectation of a fair market process and assurances that had attracted millions of small 401(k) investors into the equity market.

Now viewed as part of the problem, professional service firms and the accounting industry, its practice units and professional organizations, had become politically radioactive, and their efforts to direct reform became sterile. The allocation of the professional services markets and the independence issues related thereto were resolved by a new social contract, a legislative solution drawing on the National Association of Securities Dealers' (NASD) model to create a separate not-for-profit corporation subject to SEC guidance, while the POB closed its doors in favor of this new superagency, the PCAOB. The Sarbanes-Oxley Act, signed by President George W. Bush in August 2002, was a product of a Democrat-controlled Senate and a Republican-controlled House. It was cobbled together in near record time before the summer congressional recess on the eve of mid-term congressional elections. We now live in the wake of that action, sorting out the flotsam and jetsam of the political compromises and expectations cast in this law.

It is probably far too early to give grades to any of the progeny of this political exercise. The collective political action may have restored public trust in public capital markets, given the stiffer sanctions and increased reporting requirements meant to toughen the processes used to oversee the modern global corporate entity.

Section 201 of Sarbanes-Oxley provides a list of services that the CPA as auditor is prohibited to provide audit clients and requires that other nonaudit services not proscribed by the Act must be preapproved by the public company's audit committee. At the same time, the new law influences audit service markets by establishing the concept of "registered firms," so there are now unprecedented opportunities for an even smaller group of firms to reclaim the economic benefits of their exclusive public company audit franchise in ways that may or may not prove to be sufficient to sustain practice in economic terms.

Most of the major auditing and professional service firms already had chosen, before the passage of Sarbanes-Oxley, to monetize their consulting practices by selling them or through an initial public offering (IPO). Ernst and Young was the first to conclude a sale of its consulting practice to Cap Gemini. IBM's acquisition of PricewaterhouseCooper's similar services followed. Arthur Andersen, prior to its demise, experienced an acrimonious separation that begat Accenture as an ongoing enterprise, and KPMG's IPO for its consulting services is now known as BearingPoint Inc. Only Deloitte retained its view of the eventual benefits of one-stop-shopping, that is, the efficient combination-of-services view of the professional services firm.

Critics observe that Deloitte simply held its view too long to be able to cash in and is now left with the task of rationalizing its knowledge assets to the newly regulated market that proscribes offering many of its service capacities to its own audit clients. But the firm has chosen wisely, it asserts, to view the glass not as half empty, but as half full. That is, since Deloitte will be the only large audit core service firm to offer management consulting services to nonaudit clients, competing with this set of skills may offer nonattest clients a value not provided by other strictly consulting operations.

Multidisciplinary Firms: A Bridge Too Far or the Next Horizon?

What has this journey in words through many eras demonstrated? To begin, one would observe that, politically, the accounting profession became a force in matters of national interest, especially in dealing with tort reform in the 1990s. Its success in that legislation suggests that accountants as a political entity were able to protect their economic interests as well as more established professional groups, such as medicine and law. Overall, however, beginning with the Senate hearings of the 1970s, which were about accounting firms expanding into consulting services, this era has ended in the spinning-off of all such services with the exception of Deloitte, a regression of sorts to the 1970s scope of services. The other insight that the journey affords relates to the term "advocacy," which is a code word for "legal services." Clearly, by the late 1990s, the CPA and professional services firms had plans to extend their one-stop-shopping—efficiency arguments beyond consulting—which at that point had seemed to be a financial success. At a pre–Enron/WorldCom university symposium in the fall of 2001 to discuss the pending assault by accounting firms on the legal establishment, a sense of both disbelief and amazement colored a somewhat fearful outlook by those defending the traditional legal services arrangements (Previts 2002). Litigation and court decisions in the early 1990s had established that, under the provisions of free speech, one could commercially advertise as being both a CPA and a lawyer operating within the same single practice unit. What could be more efficient—two professional services with but one shopping stop? Could it be that by modeling their multidisciplinary practice units to absorb consulting, legal, and accounting services under one roof, the firms would capture and dominate the major corporate outsourcing professional service markets?

The meltdown of public confidence in capital markets in the wake of Enron and WorldCom has rendered the point moot. And the opportunity to establish a market approach that would reduce, if not eliminate, traditional barriers that separated the CPA and the lawyer has been lost, at least for the present. Viewed by the legal establishment as the single most pressing issue it faced, the meltdown of public confidence aroused the organized Bar's effective opposition (e.g., New York State Bar Association 2000).

Among the specifics of the new language regarding legislatively mandated auditor scope of services and independence precepts is the explicit inclusion, among proscribed CPA services to audit clients, of those services relating to "advocacy"—that is, legal services. Perhaps this proscription, along with the increased political acumen achieved by accountants during this period, rounds out the major outcomes of the three decades of contest.

For purposes of this chapter, the allocation of professional services markets is understandable as a negotiation between market forces (property) and political forces (people), not unlike the outline dictated by the Constitution's social contract. At the moment it appears that a politically derived solution has triumphed through Sarbanes-Oxley. However, less than a decade ago it appeared that the allocation was controlled by market forces. Neither the market forces nor the forces of mandate have been exclusively dominant over time. In the future, it is very likely that as competitive forces are enabled with new technologies and accounting firms face new client demands, new ways to redress a market balance will develop as the inefficiencies (excess costs) of the recent legislative mandates and regulations are transferred into operating costs and are seen to restrict companies competitively. In that light, as the recent mandates and regulations become "old mandates and regulations," they may be seen as stifling a "new" economy (Huber 2000). Thus, the final conclusion relating the contests over the proper scope of CPA services and the definition of independent auditor behavior has yet to be determined. Stated simply, "The past is prologue . . . not prediction."

9

System Design

The New Frontier for Ethical Leadership

Marjorie Kelly

MBA students study social responsibility in terms of best practices at good companies. In ethics instruction, the focus is on ethical decision-making skills intended to help managers understand ethics and thus make better ethical decisions. The underlying assumption is that managers have genuine freedom to be ethical and socially responsible, and therefore good companies can be spotted by their exemplary ethics codes, social programs, and environmental sustainability reports. But it is worth remembering that Enron rang all the bells of ethics and corporate social responsibility (CSR). It was designated one of the 100 Best Companies to Work For in America, won many environmental awards, and issued a triple bottom line report. Its CEO gave speeches at ethics conferences and put together a statement of values emphasizing communication, respect, and integrity. The company's stock was in many social investing mutual funds when it went down.

The problem is that our framework for understanding ethics and social responsibility fails to take into account what is really going on inside companies. As Enron, Arthur Andersen, WorldCom, and the rest showed us, what is going on is a single thing—an unremitting pressure to get the numbers, by any means possible.

If we wish to understand why ethical leadership and corporate social responsibility have been pushed aside by so many organizations, we must analyze corporate system design. Assuming that individuals are the nexus of ethics, we too often neglect the overwhelming power of the corporate system design. That design shapes individual behavior toward a single end: maximum shareholder gain. Like a tank, the corporate form is designed to roll over everything that stands in the way of its pursuit of profits and a rising share price. In terms of annual revenue, many corporations are larger than nation-states. If we imagine that individuals wielding Kantian ethics can turn aside this juggernaut, we delude ourselves.

The time has come to take ethical analysis deeper. The new frontier for ethical leadership leads us beyond individual decision making to look at the system design of the corporation, including how to build genuine accountability into that design. This chapter offers a starting system design analysis, examining how the pressure to get the numbers overrides everything else, and how corporate structures create and enforce that pressure. It is offered with the intent of encouraging critical thought about why corporate scandals have become so routine. The chapter suggests that the problem is that structures of corporate power are reserved for the financial elite, and it concludes that the solution is to redesign the corporation to create power for other stakeholders. Much of the content used here has been derived from my book, *The Divine Right of Capital: Dethroning the Corporate Aristocracy* (Kelly 2001), as well as several articles in *Business Ethics* magazine.

Serving the Financial Elite

In a system design analysis, we start by recognizing that in getting "the numbers," companies are not compiling bloodless digits at the bottom of an income statement. They are attempting to boost earnings, which in turn boost stock price, which in turn increases the wealth of those who hold stock or stock options. The excessive pay of chief executives has been singled out for criticism, and that pay has indeed gone from exorbitant to outrageous. But another group that has pocketed unconscionable wealth is the wealthiest 1 percent of the population, who own about half of all stock. In just the waning years of the great bull market, from 1997 to 2000, for example, the wealth of the *Forbes* 400 went up by $1.44 billion each. For every multimillionaire on the list, that was an increase of $1.9 million every day for more than a thousand days. And that represented only the increase in their wealth, not their total wealth.

We are often told that everyone's retirement portfolio shared in the gains. But since 1983, two out of three American households saw no increase in retirement wealth from pensions. Among the wealthiest 5 percent of American households, on the other hand, pension wealth went up 160 percent.

Those who direct the corporate drive to get the numbers, and who profit from it, are the financial elite. They prosper not because they are more productive than everyone else, but because the system design disproportionately favors them. CEOs select their own board members and craft their own pay packages, in the process making themselves inordinately wealthy. Yet they keep their jobs only if they make shareholders wealthy; when they do not, they get fired.

This is a point worth lingering over, for it is often missed. If CEOs are the visible power in corporations, the invisible power behind the throne is Wall Street, particularly the major players on Wall Street. These players demand always to be fed, in amounts that grow larger quarter by quarter. If CEOs allow the feeding frenzy to slow, Wall Street is the power that calls them to account by using tools imbedded in the corporate system design—the lever of stock options, the whip of CEO firing, and the dynamite of the hostile takeover. CEO power may indeed seem enormous, but it is power that can be exercised only in the narrow channel of share price maximization.

It is no accident that corporations have grown more ruthless in recent decades, at precisely the same time as these tools—hostile takeovers, stock options, and CEO firings—have become more common. The firing of CEOs, which today has become routine (and is often disguised as "resignation"), traces its roots to the early 1980s. That was when the stock market languished at levels below those of two decades earlier. Seeing opportunity in that state of affairs, corporate raiders began buying up large holdings and knocking on boardroom doors, using the laws of directors' duties to threaten lawsuits unless boards sold underperforming companies to the highest bidder. This meant companies had to start wringing every dime from operations (sending jobs overseas, closing weak divisions, laying off thousands), or be taken over by someone who would. In 1990, fully one-third of *Fortune* 500 companies were targeted for hostile takeovers. The rest lived in fear of the knock at the door.

If boards had once been sleeping bears, they now began to lumber about and whack CEOs for not being ruthless enough. From 1991 to 1993, activist boards fired CEOs at two dozen behemoth companies, including General Motors, IBM, American Express, Kodak, Westinghouse, and Borden.

The firing of Kodak's CEO, Kay Whitmore, was particularly telling. The company had a long history of social responsibility, tracing back to founder George Eastman. The company ethos was embodied in its long-standing practice of reducing staff only through voluntary early retirements. But in 1993 pressure came from Wall Street, through the Kodak board of directors, to eliminate 10,000 employees. When Whitmore refused, he was fired, and two weeks later the cuts were made. The lesson is painfully clear. Faced with the power of the corporate juggernaut, an individual is often helpless, even when that individual is the CEO.

Still another example of a CEO's powerlessness is seen in the case of Ben Cohen, founder and former CEO of Ben & Jerry's, who in 2000 was forced out of his own company by a hostile takeover from Unilever. Cohen had worked with social investors to put together a group—Hot Fudge Partners—to buy the company at $38 per share, more than double the $17 price of the stock before the takeover battle began. But when Unilever offered $43.60 per share, board members felt they had no choice but to accept. They were unwilling to face the inevitable barrage of derivative lawsuits charging that they had failed to maximize shareholder gains. The end result was predictable. Within three years of the takeover, Unilever had laid off one in five Ben & Jerry's employees, had stopped donating 7.5 percent of profits to the Ben & Jerry's Foundation, and had hired a CEO that Cohen did not approve of, although Unilever had allegedly made a verbal promise never to do so.

In the end, the drive to get the numbers, to boost share price by any means possible, inevitably wins. It wins not because of free-flowing market forces but because of the corporate system design, the laws of directors' duties, the structure of the board, the power to set CEO pay, the ability to bring derivative lawsuits, the power to launch and vote on hostile takeovers, and the power to fire the CEO. These forces give power to the financial elite and to no other stakeholders and create the foundation on which all corporate decisions are made. Even the most powerful CEOs are helpless to change them.

Kay Whitmore and Ben Cohen wanted to make ethical decisions, decisions to avoid layoffs or donate generously to charity, but the system design did not permit them to do so. Instead, it drove relentlessly toward the goals of maximum earnings, maximum share price, and maximum return to Wall Street.

The Role of Shareholders

Simply put, the ultimate nexus of corporate ethics is not the individual but the system design. The problem is not that individuals within corporations lack an understanding of ethics. The problem is that the system itself embraces a single, overarching ethic, that of shareholder primacy.

The Ben & Jerry's case illustrates this ethos particularly clearly, for it shows that it is not simply a sensible ethos about good returns, or healthy returns, but an iron mandate requiring *maximum* returns. If Cohen had succeeded at winning the bid for Hot Fudge Partners, he would have doubled shareholder value in a single year, while also preserving the firm's social mission. But this was not an outcome the system could contemplate or accept. The design demanded absolutely maximum value, even if this meant the abandonment of social mission. As Ben & Jerry's board member Terry Mollner has allegedly noted, legally shareholders are entitled to unlimited profits, and that entitlement is an immoral contract with society. Again, the real ethics problem in corporate America is that maximum gain to speculators trumps all other concerns.

We might ask ourselves what shareholders do to justify the extraordinary allegiance they receive. They invest, we are told. They take the risk to provide capital inputs, so corporations might grow and prosper. Let us test this belief with a little quiz: Shareholders fund major public corporations—true or false? False. Or, actually, a tiny bit true, but for the most part, false.

The truth is, when you invest in AT&T, your dollars do not go to AT&T. They go to other speculators. Equity investments reach a public corporation only when new common stock is sold, which for major corporations is a rare event. Among the Dow Jones industrials, only a few have sold any new common stock in thirty years. Many have sold none in fifty years.

The stock market works like a used car market, as former accounting professor Ralph Estes (1996) observed in *Tyranny of the Bottom Line*. When someone buys a 2000 Ford Escort, the money does not go to Ford but to the previous owner of the car. Ford gets the buyer's money only when it sells a new car. Similarly, companies get shareholders' money only when they sell new common stock. According to figures from the Federal Reserve Bank and the Securities and Exchange Commission (SEC), in any given year about one in one hundred dollars trading on public markets reaches a corporation. In other words, ninety-nine out of one hundred "invested" dollars are purely speculative.[1]

The productive risk in building businesses is borne by entrepreneurs and their initial venture investors, who do contribute real investing dollars to create real wealth. Those who buy stock at sixth or seventh hand, or thousandth hand, also take a risk, but it is a risk speculators take among themselves, trying to outwit one another, like gamblers. It is not about the productive contribution of capital.

Corporations are run to benefit speculators. The reason is that, oddly, we believe shareholders are the corporation. When we say that a corporation did well, we mean that its shareholders had an increase in their stock value. Employees might be shouldering a crushing workload. The company's local community might be devastated by plant closings. Thousands of jobs may have been exported to other countries. Still we will say, "The corporation did well."

To challenge this notion that shareholders matter most puts one at risk of being labeled antibusiness, or anticapitalist. But capitalism itself may not be the problem. Indeed, in any system redesign, there is much wisdom in capitalism that should be preserved. If we go rummaging through its entire basket of economic ideas—supply and demand, competition, profit, self-interest, wealth creation, and so forth—we will find that most of them are sturdy, healthy, and well worth keeping. But we will also find one concept that is inconsistent with the others. This is the concept of shareholder primacy, the idea that the sole purpose of a corporation is to create maximum returns to shareholders.

When we pluck this notion out of our basket and turn it over in our hands, really looking at it, as we so rarely do, we will see that it is out of place. In a competitive free market, it decrees that the interests of one group will be systematically favored over others. In a system devoted to unconscious regulation, it says that corporations will consciously serve one group alone. In a system rewarding hard work, it says that members of that group will be served regardless of their productivity.

Shareholder primacy is a form of entitlement. And entitlement has no place in a free market. It is a form of privilege, and privilege accruing to property ownership is a remnant of the aristocratic past.

That more people own stock today has not changed the market's essentially aristocratic bias. Of the total gain in marketable wealth from 1983 to 1998, more than half went to the richest 1 percent of the population (Wolff 2000). The rest of us may have gotten a few crumbs from this feast, but in pursuing them we are too often led to work against our own interests. Physicians applaud when their portfolios rise in value, yet wonder why insurance companies are ruthlessly holding down medical payments. Employees cheer when their 401(k) plans post gains, yet wonder why layoffs are decimating their firms. Their own portfolios hold the answer.

The Stock Market Plays an Essential Function

Still, decrying shareholder primacy is not the same as saying that the stock market is devoid of value or that it should be eliminated. It is simply saying that shareholder gains should not be the sole value driving the corporation. There is room for other stakeholders to be considered as well.

The stock market does have its worthwhile functions. Stock serves as a kind of currency with which companies can buy other companies. A high share price can also be the basis for a good credit rating, making it easier for firms to borrow at favorable rates. Most vitally, public markets create liquidity, which is what makes genuine investment in companies attractive. Without an aftermarket for share trading, investors could cash out only when a company was sold or liquidated, which would make investing in a company like investing in a house. Money could be tied up for decades.

In making the value of companies liquid, the stock market has the effect of increasing that value. It is in part a function of auction. Because more bidders are available, a stock fetches a higher price, just as a first-edition Hemingway fetches a higher price on eBay than it would at a garage sale. But the auction function can get out of control when new wealth flows primarily to those already possessing substantial wealth. Because the wealth of a multimillionaire can never fully be spent, it can only be reinvested, leaving more and more money to chase essentially the same body of stocks. As we saw in the 1990s, this can cause stocks to artificially inflate in value. When that inflation becomes too large, the bubble bursts, often dragging the real economy down with it.

Thus, while the stock market has its functions, it also has its dysfunctions. Bubbles are one dysfunction. A second is the artificial overvaluation of financial capital and the devaluation of other forms of wealth. Progressive business theorist Paul Hawken (van Gelder 1995, 17–22) described this dysfunction as a "worldwide pattern of decapitalization. . . . Capital, whether it be natural capital in the form of resources, or human capital in the form of low-wage workers, or local capital in the form of functional and healthy local economies, is being extracted and converted to financial capital at an increasingly accelerated rate." This process has sped up dramatically in the last half-century, as the value of the stock market has increased over a hundredfold. In that same period, forests have shrunk, water tables have fallen, wetlands have disappeared, soils have eroded, fisheries have collapsed, rivers have run dry, global temperatures have risen, and countless plant and animal species have disappeared.

This same half-century, not incidentally, is when major public corporations, in cooperation with governments, have come to dominate the world. It is also when the shareholder primacy that drives them has become increasingly out of step with reality, due to a number of massive changes in the nature of major corporations:

- *Increasing size.* Today, among the world's hundred largest economies, fifty-one are corporations. They have revenues larger than nation-states, yet maintain the image of being the "private property" of shareholders.
- *The shrinking of ownership functions.* While we still call shareholders the "owners" of major public firms, they do not, for the most part, manage, fund, or accept liability for "their" companies. The ownership function has shrunk to virtually one dimension, extracting increases in value.
- *The rise of the knowledge economy.* For many companies, knowledge is the new source of competitive advantage. To allow shareholders to claim the corporation's increasing wealth, when employees play a greater role in creating that wealth, is a questionable allocation of resources.
- *The increasing damage to our ecosystem.* The rules of accounting were written in the fifteenth century, when to the Western mind nature seemed an unlimited reservoir of resources and an unlimited sink for wastes. That is no longer true, but the rules of accounting retain fossilized images of those ancient attitudes.

Major public corporations have evolved into something new in civilization, more massive and powerful than our democratic forefathers dreamed possible. Today, as the name itself implies, public corporations are no longer fully private. The major public corporation, as President Franklin D. Roosevelt (Estes 1996, 88) observed, permits "private enterprise to become a kind of private government which is a power unto itself."

The Enron Scandal Provides an Example of Design System Problems

The ultimate example of a company seeking to become a power unto itself was Enron, a company that systematically set out to dismantle its own regulatory structure. It thus took the ethos of our corporate system design to its logical extreme, flattening any and all impediments to maximum share price, even to the extent of damaging the nation itself, so that a tiny elite might prosper. In the process, Enron demonstrated that managing a company solely for maximum share price can destroy both share price and the entire company.

It is tempting to read the Enron saga as a juicy tale of individual villainy. But the deeper issue is why the system lent so much power to villainy and why there were so few checks and balances to stop it. A key reason is that our economic mythology tells us and, more incredibly, we believe, that checks and balances are bad, because free markets are good. Hence, unregulated markets are ideal. Left free to work its magic, self-interest (i.e., greed) ostensibly leads things to work out to the benefit of all, as though guided by an invisible hand. This myth is taught in Economics 101 as gospel truth, trumpeted routinely in the business press, and sold abroad as the cure for what ails all economies.

Enron was a major proponent of the myth of the unregulated market, with chair Kenneth Lay setting out to defeat or undo all regulations for his company. In an extraordinary gesture of hubris, he supplied the White House with his personal list of preferred appointments to the Federal Energy Regulatory Commission, which supposedly oversaw his firm. Enron successfully opposed regulation for derivatives trading, then used such trades to mask debt. To win pipeline, power, and water-privatization contracts overseas, Enron allegedly stepped outside normal procurement procedures by bribing foreign officials, in moves that were later investigated by federal prosecutors. As a result of these and many other moves, Enron was able to operate aggressively in a lightly regulated environment. It created its own regulatory black hole, inside of which it ultimately burned up.

Consider California's experiment with electricity deregulation, which, as Senator Barbara Boxer alleged, left the state "bled dry by price gouging." As CEO of Enron, Jeffrey Skilling had predicted that deregulation would save

California $9 billion a year. But as Boxer noted at a Senate hearing, California's total energy costs soared from $7 billion to $27 billion in a single year. Prices rose a gut-wrenching 266 percent.

Not coincidentally, Enron's stock shot up. Total percentage return to shareholders in 1998 was a remarkable 40 percent. The next year it was a miraculous 58 percent. And in 2000, it was a jaw-dropping 89 percent. Deregulation did indeed work the magic it was designed to work, by turning Skilling's stock options into gold, just before the company was turned into rubble. California was not the only state duped by the magical thinking of deregulation. Enron helped convince Washington state, Massachusetts, New York, and Pennsylvania to deregulate energy markets. And it did the same with government officials in Washington, D.C.

In 1993 Enron persuaded the SEC to grant it an exemption from the Public Utility Holding Company Act (PUHCA), a Depression-era law that prevented utilities from diversifying into unrelated risky businesses. Enron pursued this diversification, to its disaster. As Representative Ed Markey (D-MA) put it, "If Enron had been regulated under PUHCA, I seriously doubt that the types of transactions that brought this company down would have occurred." Another success at defeating regulation came in 1997, when the company won exemption from the Investment Company Act of 1940, allowing it to leave debt from foreign power plants off its books. This led to dubious offshore partnerships, which contributed to the firm's undoing.

Still another deregulatory move came in 1999, when Congress killed the Glass-Steagall Act of 1933, which had separated commercial from investment banking. This allowed J.P. Morgan, for example, to entangle itself with Enron in conflicts of interest. It underwrote bonds for Enron, traded derivatives contracts with the company, bought stock in the firm, and had a research analyst covering the company (who recommended it as a buy until the end), even as the bank risked billions in loans to Enron. Lured by millions in investment banking fees, J.P. Morgan was left with $2.6 billion in Enron debt. Glass-Steagall would have prevented that.

Deregulatory pressures by other firms also helped create the climate that led to Enron's undoing. Accounting firms helped defeat a proposal to separate auditing and consulting practices, leaving firms reluctant to challenge major clients. Businesses opposed truthful accounting for stock options, which led executives to deliberately inflate stock prices.

Piece by piece, system design protections that might have prevented the debacle were defeated. Layer by layer, existing protections were removed. The result was the train wreck of Enron. What is astonishing is not that this wreck occurred, but that we bought the deregulation myth that led inexorably to it. We swallowed this fairy tale about some invisible hand.

Why were there so few checks and balances to stop the greed of Enron executives? It was because the nation had fallen under the spell of the deregulatory myth, which allowed Lay to systematically eliminate oversight mechanisms.

Why did the system design lend so much power to greed? It was because the nation had fallen under the spell of a second myth, that a rising share price is the very definition of corporate success. No one minded that Enron executives were becoming fabulously wealthy, because investors thought they too were becoming wealthy as the price of Enron stock soared. The executives had met the goal they were given; they were being celebrated rather than questioned. So when Enron vice president Sherron Watkins raised questions, she was brushed aside. There were no system mechanisms that allowed her to press her concerns effectively.

In a presentation at the Haas School of Business at the University of California–Berkeley, Watkins (2003) said that when she told Lay that certain transactions might be fraudulent, she expected a thorough investigation and the creation of a crisis management team. "However, no other top executives came forward to back me up," she said, "and Ken Lay gravitated toward good news and didn't quite accept what I was saying." Attorneys decided nothing was amiss, but advised that certain transactions be unwound "because the optics weren't good," she added. "That unwind wiped out $1.2 billion from shareholders' equity and started Enron's free fall, ultimately ending in bankruptcy, roughly six weeks after the press release announcing the unwind."

The house of cards had fallen, but merely from the weight of its own deception, not because the system design had effective mechanisms for reining in greed. Indeed, the system was designed to encourage, reward, and require greed. The public has yet to grasp this. In the wake of Enron, the mantra remains that we must align executive and shareholder interests. But this close alignment was itself the problem. When we define business success as maximum share price, a soaring price makes it impossible to see problems. What could be wrong? The business is succeeding beyond anyone's dreams.

Enron's problem was not a lack of focus on shareholder value. The problem was a lack of accountability to anything except share value. This led to a culture of getting the numbers by any means necessary.

But here is the critical point: the Enron story is really not about Enron. It is about business as usual. If Enron was laser-focused on earnings per share, this was far from unique among public companies. It was what Wall Street demanded and enforced. When firms fell short of earnings projections by just pennies, their stock prices were severely punished. Earnings management, the logical response, was widely practiced. General Electric, known for uncannily smooth earnings growth created through accounting gimmickry, was the most admired corporation in America.

If earnings management was not unique to Enron, neither were its questionable special-purpose entities. After bankers at Citigroup and Credit Suisse First Boston helped Enron create its complex partnerships, they took the idea on the road and sold it to other companies wanting to improve their financial statements. Chief financial officers won awards for devising clever ways to remove debt from balance sheets. WorldCom CFO Scott Sullivan, ultimately indicted for orchestrating the company's $7.2 billion fraud, was earlier celebrated as one of the finest CFOs on Wall Street.

Individual culpability cannot be denied. But the fact that so many executives committed such similar frauds is evidence of system-wide pressures at work. It is easy for investors to single out outrageous stock option packages and complain how executives cashed in and bailed out, leaving shareholders with little or nothing. But this is like dog owners training their dogs to attack, then complaining when they themselves get bitten. CEOs were rewarded for their ruthlessness. And that ruthlessness was accepted—even celebrated—as long as shareholders benefited from the bites taken out of employees through low wages or benefits reductions, or the bites taken out of communities through tax evasion and corporate welfare. But when the bite was turned on shareholders, suddenly there was a crisis. Heaven and earth had to be moved to call the scoundrels to account.

What was exposed was not only the villainy of a few CEOs, but the narrowness of the financial world's sense of ethics. Breaches of loyalty were of little concern when it meant laying off devoted employees after twenty years of service or closing plants and letting company hometowns fall to ruin. That was hard-nosed business. But breaching loyalty to shareholders was a crime.

That is not to say that taking advantage of shareholders is excusable, because it is not. The punishments that executives are receiving serve as a reminder that even the most powerful are not above the law. But to understand the causes and conditions that gave rise to their behavior is to begin the process of system change.

An Opening for Change

If maximum share price is an irresponsible management theory, and deregulation a flawed economic theory, there are better theories already at hand. It is intriguing that the movie *A Beautiful Mind* won an Academy Award during the Enron scandal. The protagonist, John Nash, won a Nobel Prize for proving that Adam Smith's theory was incomplete. Nash demonstrated that self-interest alone can lead to disaster for everyone. Self-interest coupled with concern for the good of the group is most likely to lead to the benefit of all.

Nash's mathematics revolutionized game theory and is now central to evolutionary economics, which emphasizes that cooperation is as vital as competition. It is a more evolved theory than the invisible hand and more appropriate for an economy that has moved beyond Adam Smith's eighteenth-century world.

We might think of Nash's theory, his completion of Adam Smith's theory, as the compass pointing the way toward a new system design. It can empower us to begin imagining a corporate system built to serve not financial elites but all stakeholders.

If Nash provides the theory, the Enron crisis has provided a historic opening. History shows us that it is crisis that cracks open the public's consciousness and creates the space for new ideas to rush in. The year 2002 did in fact see a great flurry of reforms—campaign finance reform, new criminal penalties for CEOs filing false financial statements, a new accounting supervisory board, new stock exchange rules about board independence, and an increased SEC budget. In the wake of a felony conviction, the accounting firm Arthur Andersen disintegrated overnight. Other accounting firms spun off their consulting divisions. Energy firms went under or closed their trading divisions. Many companies began expensing stock options without waiting for a legislative mandate. Countless businesses restated financial statements.

It looked as if massive change was under way. But when the din subsided, almost nothing had really changed. Campaign finance reform proved relatively toothless. The new accounting board likewise was biting gum against gum. As for the "new" penalties for financial statement fraud, filing false financial statements had already been a felony for seventy years.

A program for real economic reform has yet to be found. The public's consciousness has indeed cracked open, but truly new ideas have yet to rush in. Instead, the cracks have been stuffed with old ideas, particularly the single old idea of shareholder primacy.

With the exception of campaign finance reform, the changes thus far have been much ado about a single thing—shareholder protection. When the SEC budget was increased and accounting supervision was improved, it was to protect shareholder interests. When stock exchanges set out to make boards independent, it was for shareholder protection. When CEOs were made more accountable or Arthur Andersen was indicted, it was to safeguard shareholder interests. Shareholder wealth is still the sun around which the economy is believed to revolve.

What is extraordinary is that it was slavish devotion to share price that created the crisis in the first place. By pushing too hard on that one element of the system, executives destabilized the entire system. It is like flying a 747 solely for maximum speed and shaking the plane apart in the process, or taking steroids to pump up muscle mass and destroying the body. A one-dimensional company is not healthy, any more than is a one-dimensional life.

An Agenda for System Redesign

Maximum gain for speculators is unworthy of being the central purpose of a democratic economy. It is time we redefined economic success as something more than a rising stock market. The purpose of our economy is to support life. We need a new vision of a healthy economy, rooted not in the unsustainable wealth of a few, but in the enduring prosperity of the many.

Such a shift is so simple yet so radical that it will take time before a new vision is complete. But pieces of the vision can be sketched. What is offered here is not the last word, but the first word of the new conversation we must begin.

In simplest terms, we must change the corporate design so that the economic rights of employees and the community are as vital as the rights of shareholders. In terms of system dynamics, the existence of such rights would diffuse the laser focus on share price, keeping corporate behavior more in tune with the real economy and less likely to fly off in destructive flights of fantasy.

Getting there means giving parties other than shareholders a chance to have their interests represented and served in integral ways in the system design. This begins with changing corporate purpose, which resides now in the state laws of directors' duties. These laws could be changed state by state or in a single piece of federal corporate chartering legislation. The aim is to shift directors' duties from their existing duty of loyalty to shareholders alone to a broader loyalty to, or a duty not to harm, employees, the community, and the environment. These new rights should be enforced with the right to sue, perhaps buttressed by individual director liability. If directors knew their personal wealth would be at stake when corporations evaded taxes or laid off tens of thousands of employees, business behavior would change quite quickly. One model piece of legislation, known as the Code for Corporate Responsibility, drafted by attorney Robert Hinkley, is already being considered by legislators in Minnesota and California and is being promoted by grassroots citizens' groups.

As purpose shifts, so too must the measurement of success. This means creating supplemental financial statements that measure corporate impact on employees, the community, and the environment. Work on such statements is already far advanced through the Global Reporting Initiative, a coalition of social investors, environmentalists, and mainstream accounting groups.

All that is needed is rule-making by the SEC, which is being sought by the Corporate Sunshine Working Group coalition.

Likewise in need of change are corporate governance structures. Since CEOs today pick their own boards, or have cronies on the board pick them, it is absurd to imagine that those boards can control CEOs. The favored fix is to increase the number of independent directors, but this is as pointless as counting angels on the head of a pin. If independent directors were the solution, then there would have been no problem at Enron, where fifteen of the seventeen directors were independent. It is little wonder that independents are no great help. When directors have no personal knowledge of a company, are selected by insiders, are ratified in uncontested elections, and fly into town once a month to view high-level reports far removed from the daily life of the company, it is fantasy to imagine they can effectively govern.

Far better would be to follow Europeans in creating a system of nonmanagerial worker representatives on corporate boards, as suggested by John Logue of the Ohio Employee Ownership Center. Employees know what is happening in companies, as Sherron Watkins knew what was happening in Enron. If employee board members had the resources to hire financial consultants from company funds, as they do in Europe, worker directors could provide a significant counterweight to managerial abuse of power. He emphasized that in the United States, employee-owned companies with worker directors have financially outperformed those without such directors.

There also needs to be a broad principle that corporations must not harm the public good, returning us to the founding ideals of America, when corporations were chartered only to serve the public good. This might be enforced with a sliding scale of penalties against corporate lawbreakers, from withholding government contracts or increasing taxes to pulling the corporate license to exist.

These are a few of the most fundamental structural reforms that would redesign the corporate system to serve all stakeholders. If these proposals seem unlikely to be enacted, we might recall how far-fetched the conservative agenda appeared before it gained ascendancy. We must recall how that agenda was advanced by a fringe group sustained by the conviction that its ideas would ultimately prevail. In part because of that conviction, over time it was proved right.

Yet we need not create a massive nationwide movement to begin making system change, for change begins in the mind. The American Revolution, the end of apartheid, and the rise of feminism all began as nothing more than ideas. And ideas can arise and spread quite simply, without the aid of massive budgets or armies or laws. They can spread simply from the power of conversation and from the willingness to dream a little wildly and begin asking each other, What if?

We can begin these conversations in our own universities and in our own companies, by dreaming together of new ways that ethics and corporate responsibility can be designed into companies, not as voluntary initiatives tagged on the side, but as fundamental elements of the framework of power. Could we imagine a genuine separation of powers such that an ethics committee would have the power to veto key corporate decisions and override the CEO? What if mergers required an employee vote of approval? What about controlling CEO pay by giving employees the right to impeach, and the right to approve CEO pay? What if a company could not move a plant out of town unless the city council approved? What about making the bulk of bonuses contingent on meeting environmental goals?

Perhaps we need a conference on the topic of corporate purpose. Do companies really exist solely to fuel the stock market? Maybe we need a student essay assignment on imagining the corporation of the future. What are the corporate forms that can hold social mission in place for generations to come? Perhaps managers could start company meetings by asking employees whether they were facing pressures to be unethical. Perhaps ethics officers could institute an audit of ethical complaints in order to begin looking for patterns, trying to discover where system pressures were most problematic at particular companies.

Each of us can begin in our own sphere to explore this new frontier of ethical system design. If we are teachers or students, we can begin with colleagues and fellow students. If we are managers, we can begin with our staff. Regardless of our employment situation, all of us can begin, in our minds, to loosen the constraints on what we dare to imagine is possible. Solutions will not be immediate, because the work we are undertaking is large in significance and far-reaching in impact. Future generations will depend upon it, for what we are undertaking is nothing less than writing a constitution for a just and ethical corporation. This is the future of ethical leadership. And there is only one thing absolutely certain about this work: we will never complete it if we do not begin.

Note

1. According to Federal Reserve Bank figures compiled in the 2000 *Statistical Abstract of the United States*, sales of new common stock in 1999 were $105.7 billion. Also in 1999, the total value of all shares traded was $20.4 trillion. Thus, sales of new common stock represented less than 1 percent of all stock trading. This was typical of the 1990s.

10

Ethical Leadership for Improved Corporate Governance and Better Business Education

Gene R. Laczniak and Patrick E. Murphy

Beginning with the unraveling of Enron's financial position in October 2001, the U.S. marketplace has been stained by a rash of ethical scandals that continues to unfold. The collective fallout from the questionable business behavior that has occurred is enormous. Enron, WorldCom, Tyco, Qwest, and Global Crossing alone have accounted for the loss of approximately one-half trillion dollars in shareholder wealth through their aggregate misdeeds (Horovitz 2002). Between 1997 and 2002, the frequency of earnings restatements dramatically accelerated (approximately one in ten *Fortune* 1000 companies restated), resulting in well over $200 billion in write-downs (Byrnes et al. 2002). Not included among these damages is the pain (both financial and psychological) caused to employees, customers, suppliers, and host communities. In the wake of such incidents, several common queries have been sounded:

- What do these events signify about contemporary business practice?
- What actions can prevent such seemingly widespread business scandal?
- What do business leaders need to do to imbue the system with greater integrity?

The purpose of this chapter is to stimulate a dialogue about the changes that should be considered to strengthen corporate governance and business education in light of the damaging revelations about questionable business conduct. No one has a monopoly on the truth about integrity or even the best

175

any study implications for

solutions for improving ethical corporate behavior. However, factors have
been identified in the business ethics literature and elsewhere that may prove
helpful. These factors and related insights can be used to begin a conversation within the business community (including the voice of business educators) about what needs to happen to improve the climate for ethical decision
making in U.S. corporations.

The chapter consists of four parts. First, propositions about the nature of
the recent business scandals are postulated. Second, possible antecedent causes
of the ethics meltdown are identified and discussed. Third, observations about
the role of business school education in contributing to the "ethics crisis" are
offered along with proposals for enhancing ethics education in business. Finally, additional corporate adjustments and reforms worth exploring, and
perhaps implementing, are suggested.

Propositions About Business Ethics Scandals

Thousands of media reports, newspaper and magazine articles, and editori-
als have appeared about the unfortunate events that have scorched the U.S.
business landscape. Despite all that has been written, several points need to
be more resolutely voiced. Keeping the following four propositions in mind
may help business better understand future epidemics of ethical failure, but
they will not cure them.

Proposition 1: Many of the recent scandals are less about ethical misjudg-
ments and more about patent illegalities and corporate corruption. Ideally,
ethical standards are meant to guide managers who face difficult decisions
involving moral questions not answered by the minimum expectations of
blackletter law. There is a difference between ethical shortcomings in organizations and outright criminality, although the two are related. In particular,
a weak ethical climate will allow criminal behaviors to flourish unchecked.
But certainly, many of the best publicized business abuses were blatantly
illegal. To characterize these events as merely ethical shortcomings obscures
their ugliness.

For example, the Enron partnerships, created to offload debt and inflate
profits, were clearly intended to mislead the markets regarding the firm's
material financial condition (Byrne 2002a). This behavior constituted a direct violation of long-standing Securities and Exchange Commission (SEC)
regulations. Former chief executive L. Dennis Kozlowski of Tyco International allegedly looted at least $170 million of company money, and perhaps
as much as $600 million, through fraudulent security sales and other
unsanctioned actions in order to purchase multiple mansions, buy artwork,
and even throw a multimillion-dollar birthday party for his wife in Sardinia,

Italy (Maremont and Cohen 2002). He is being prosecuted using existing gangster racketeering legislation (McCoy and Strauss 2002). Adelphia Communications founder John Rigas, along with his two sons, also officers of that corporation, are charged with defrauding cable TV investors out of billions of dollars in company funds to purchase condominiums, personal stock, and even a golf course. This was basic embezzlement.

In short, these are all gross illegalities, not merely thorny ethical miscalculations (Stoller 2002). New business regulations are not needed to protect against such misdeeds. Most of the dubious actions taken by those under investigation were clearly understood by business practitioners to be wrong. More elaborate or more visible codes of conduct would likely not have prevented the worst of these abuses, although a more ethical business climate may have impeded the lawlessness by getting knowledgeable parties to speak up sooner.

Proposition 2: Given an economic system that is lubricated by harnessing the self-interest of individuals, a certain threshold of unseemly business behavior should be expected. A review of business history unfortunately suggests that there regularly have been other periods of major business scandals (Rosenstein 2002; Clinard and Yeager 1980). Clusters of ethical failings capture the attention of the broader community and precipitate government actions. For example, the primal industrial development of the 1890s was scarred by monopoly, price fixing, and worker exploitation. Those who study economic history know that the term "robber barons" has its roots in ruthless, heavy-handed profit taking, often at the expense of employees, investors, and other competitors. However, near the turn of the twentieth century, substantial adjustments in the economic system were made through regulatory controls— labor protections and antitrust reforms such as the Sherman Act and the Federal Trade Commission (FTC) Act. The "roaring twenties" also was an extended period of intensive financial investment that stimulated significant economic development and, eventually, unbridled financial speculation.

These events culminated in the Great Depression and subsequent business regulation, such as the Robinson-Patman Act and the Securities Exchange Commission Act, that better monitored competitive practices and established additional protections for workers, investors, and consumers. Then, the much praised post–World War II economic expansion, sometimes called the "nifty fifties," also produced as its by-product social negatives in the form of various product safety scandals as well as measurable damage to the physical environment. Regulatory additions to buffer these and other damaging externalities, such as the Environmental Protection Act and the Consumer Product Safety Act, eventually were instituted.

Now, the decade-long technology boom of the 1990s seems destined to be capped by the reform of accounting practices and corporate financial reporting. An initial step is the Sarbanes-Oxley Act of 2002. A poignant question is, Does Sarbanes-Oxley primarily treat symptoms rather than the root cause of the impropriety of business organizations? Because it does seem clear that since a small percentage of business executives will consider the law as the maximum of their moral obligation, future regulation will have to continue to evolve along with changing business practice.

Proposition 3: Ethical and legal transgressions by business seem to markedly increase in times of extended economic prosperity. There are several discernible reasons why this occurs. For one thing, when financial success is prolonged and widespread, pressure mounts on executive leaders to maintain positive momentum and keep up with their arguably successful competitors, even after business and economic cycles inevitably turn downward. This disposition to extend and replicate economic success at all costs creates a temptation effect that often overrides beneficial corporate value systems. No chief executive wishes to preside over a period of dramatic downturn, even if due to relatively uncontrollable systemic cycles, particularly after a time of prolonged growth and profitability. In their urgency to replicate past financial success, expediency often trumps the ethical judgment of business executives. Relatedly, when times are economically and financially prosperous, there is a tendency for those monitoring the system to become less circumspect. Call this the opportunity effect: regulators, corporate auditors, and boards of directors often doze off in the watchtower. Sated by success, the regulatory system (both internal and external) becomes sleepy, much like a diner after a sumptuous meal. Furthermore, periods of ongoing economic rewards seem to breed unwarranted vanity as well as a sense of entitlement in some top managers. Because of experienced past success, executives predict and expect future success, and, therefore, overconfident managers are willing to take greater risks and possibly unethical actions to attain revenue growth, profit, and continued personal recognition for their leadership. Label this the "risk-reward effect."

According to various behavioral models of ethical decision making (e.g., Ferrell and Gresham 1985; Hunt and Vitell 1986), unethical behavior is a function of a manager's propensity to act unethically (i.e., the managerial value system); the opportunity to engage in unethical behavior; and the expectation of unethically securing reward without the proportionate risk of being caught. Simply put, each factor in this ethical behavior dynamic is pushed in the wrong direction by sustained economic and organizational prosperity. In other words, the pressure on management to continue success at all costs can erode personal and corporate values. Then, as the economic and business expansion crests, managers are reluctant to leave residual "money on the table," even if short cuts are required to achieve announced financial targets. Simultaneously, for the reasons mentioned, the built-in checks and balances of the system become lax, thereby creating seductive possibilities. The upshot of all of this is that the time to be most watchful for business mischief is when things are going well. Another lesson is that while it may be difficult to change managerial value systems, much can be done organizationally and through public policy to reduce the opportunity for ethical transgression and to increase the risk of punishment for business wrong-doers.

Proposition 4: The recent U.S. business scandals are also decidedly different from what went on in past decades. The business community now is questioning the integrity of the system itself. As a point of comparison, many earlier legal and ethical transgressions merely increased the public's skepticism about business. For example, in the 1990s, Firestone's failure to recall faulty tires quickly and AstraZeneca's (the European pharmaceutical company) reluctance to address repeated complaints about sexual harassment of employees at U.S. facilities constituted scandals of significant scope and obvious ethical collapse (Jennings 2000). These events were widely publicized, and the public was outraged. Nevertheless, the typical reaction of the business community to such scandals was that the dubious behavior, while regrettable, was not generalizable beyond one company or at most one industry. In other words, despite public disgust, the confidence in the business system by its architects (i.e., the business community) remained high. However, the current situation has caused an extraordinary erosion of trust among many members of the business community (Wessel 2002). The present scandals have undermined the very credibility of the economic system. These collective misdeeds have had a disturbing impact on financial and corporate veracity, the implications of which are far-reaching and strike to the core of the U.S. economic system. Why is this so?

Within the spate of recent business scandals, we find a welter of troubling financial deception and business miscues:

- Exaggerated profits were made possible by overbooked revenue and off-ledger expenses, all of it certified by reputable public accountants such as Arthur Andersen (Jones and Krantz 2002).
- Stock analysts from major brokerage houses, such as Smith-Barney and Merrill-Lynch, betrayed small investors with inflated stock recommendations to curry investment banking business as well as to "ladder" the near-term prices for their company-sponsored IPOs (Balzar 2002; Backover 2002).
- Executive stock options and deferred compensation were given to top management without being counted against expenses, further under-

mining the likelihood of companies meeting projected financial targets (Morgenson 2002).

- Boards of directors rubber-stamped management initiatives with minimal inquiry. For example, the Enron board twice waived its code of ethics, which explicitly prohibited officer involvement in outside partnerships. These waivers were granted without discussion and without debate (Byrne 2002a). Also, the board of directors of the New York Stock Exchange (including the compensation committee) claimed it had no idea that former chair Richard Grasso's salary and retirement benefits were so lavish (Thomas and Norris 2002).
- Corporate board committees continued signing away shareholder wealth to chief executives based on a shell game of "benchmark compensation" supposedly necessary for the motivation and retention of top executive talent (Farrell 2002). In 2002, according to the *Corporate Library*, as the typical Standard and Poor's 500 stock fell by 24 percent, the compensation of CEOs increased 11 percent on average (May 2003).

These and related practices have made the larger business community wonder if it can believe the information being disseminated from corporations—the very corporations that might be invested in, partnered with, or worked for in some capacity. The net result is a crisis of confidence in the integrity of the business system itself.

Consider some well-publicized quotations about the recent business scandals:

- "There has been a massive failure in corporate governance."
  (Bill W. George, retired chairman and CEO, Medtronic Inc., quoted in the *Wall Street Journal*, February 24, 2003, R1)
- "In their greed and their gluttony, these crooks sacrificed the retirement years of teachers, truck drivers, nurses, and farmers to enrich themselves."
  (Paul O'Neill, former U.S. Treasury Secretary and former CEO of Alcoa, quoted in the *Milwaukee Journal Sentinel*, July 11, 2002, 3D)
- "In my lifetime, American business has never been under such scrutiny. To be blunt, much of it is deserved."
  (Henry M. Paulson Jr., CEO, Goldman Sachs, quoted in the *New York Times*, June 6, 2002)
- "In the midst of great prosperity and the boom of the 1990s, there has been a [clear] erosion of professional, managerial, and ethical standards and safeguards."
  (Paul Volcker, former chair, Federal Reserve Bank, quoted in the *Chicago Tribune*, February 15, 2002, 4A)

- "An infectious greed seems to grip much of our business community." (Alan Greenspan, chair, Federal Reserve Board, quoted in the *South Bend Tribune*, August 15, 2002, C2)

The individuals quoted are not left-wing crackpots, socialist university professors, or third-world antiglobalists seeking to derail capitalism. They are among the most respected captains of the American economic system, and they are shocked, saddened, and growingly disturbed about the practices and veracity of the business and financial system.

Factors Contributing to the Ethics Meltdown

One is certainly left wondering what factors created the environment that encouraged so much questionable behavior by high-level executives. Only in knowing the likely causes can society prescribe effective cures. Clearly, one element was the irrational exuberance of sustained economic prosperity, as Federal Reserve Chair Alan Greenspan repeatedly and memorably characterized it. The late 1990s environment of sustained and rapid growth created both the opportunity and the motivation for some executives to engage in unethical actions so as to maintain profit streams.

A second major factor generating the scandals was the increasing acceptance of aggressive accounting practices and the associated willingness of CFOs and auditors to push the envelope regarding what constitutes appropriate financial disclosure (Nussbaum 2002). Accountants, especially internal and external auditors, are the guardians of the financial system, and small investors have always been their fiduciary wards. What transpired is now clear. Many auditing teams became too cozy with their clients, on whom the auditing firms depended for additional consulting revenue (Byrnes et al. 2002). In the self-regulated environment of the accounting industry, generally accepted accounting principles (GAAP) definitions were stretched to the limit and Financial Accounting Standards Board (FASB) loopholes were exploited to create a misleading picture for the investors of too many corporations (Byrnes et al. 2002). Corporate and outside legal counsel at many of these organizations also aligned with accounting to support the aggressive interpretation of reporting rules. Sarbanes-Oxley only addresses part of the problem. For the most part, the public accounting sector has remained relatively unrepentant. As recently as mid-2002, the chair of Big Four accounting firm Ernst & Young opined that recommended restrictions on consulting income of auditors from their clients and the mandatory rotation of auditors would damage the quality of auditing services and repel qualified students away from accounting careers (Turley 2002). Robert Elliott, former head of the American Institute of

Certified Public Accountants (AICPA), has called Sarbanes-Oxley regulations over financial reporting akin to "the criminalization of risk taking, which is the criminalization of capitalism" (Schroeder 2003).

Some people in the business community believed that Arthur Andersen was driven out of business by overzealous federal government prosecutors looking for a scapegoat. Television journalist Lou Dobbs (who for a short time served as an Arthur Andersen consultant) used substantial portions of his nightly *Moneyline* TV show on CNN in 2002 to portray Arthur Andersen as the hapless victim of a federal government witch hunt. Yes, it seems true that the shredding of Enron audit materials was limited to Arthur Andersen offices in Houston, Texas, and only linked back to the oversight field office in Chicago (Byrne 2002b). However, Arthur Andersen's honesty and auditing objectivity had been persistently and deeply questioned in various governmental investigations nationally and internationally due to its dubious certification of financial malfeasance at Sunbeam, Waste Management, Arizona Baptist Foundation, Global Crossing, HIH (Australia), and WorldCom (Toffler and Reingold 2003). Joseph Bernardino, the Arthur Andersen CEO, seemed to seriously fail the leadership test. Instead of declaring a crisis in the "culture of honesty" cherished by the firm's founder, Andersen instead, when faced with repeated audit failures, adopted a "deny, deny, then settle without admitting guilt" mentality (*USA Today* 2002a). Ironically, Bernardino, who presided over this supreme integrity meltdown at Arthur Andersen, is now on the business ethics lecture circuit, addressing how organizations can manage corporate scandals (Gores 2002).

The third, and possibly main, factor contributing to the scandals was the emergence of the CEO as media star. Trouble was probably inevitable when celebrity CEOs like Martha Stewart, Dennis Kozlowski, Jack Welch, and Kenneth Lay began appearing on mainstream magazine covers, TV talk shows, and the cocktail circuit of Washington, D.C., and New York City. CEOs' salaries, as well as their power over boards of directors, had become unhealthy (Weintraub, Grover, and Gogoi 2002). In too many questionable incidents of business behavior, CEO-controlled boards of directors remained passive and unquestioning about what many observers perceived as dubious schemes (Strauss 2002b). Exorbitant CEO compensation, along with growing directors' fees, seemed contributory to the problem (Fabrickant 2002).

Let us briefly examine CEO compensation. In these comparisons, the figures used are conservative as compared to numbers reported in other published sources (Knight 2002). With regard to chief executive pay, in Europe, the ratio of the top executive salary to the average rank-and-file worker is about 40 to 1. So, if a typical worker position is remunerated at $20,000 or 20,000 euros (assuming a one-for-one par value), the managing director (or

CEO) of the organization would receive a salary of about $800,000 (placing him or her in the top 1 percent of all U.S. salaried employees). Among the top 500 or so corporations in the United States, the ratio of top executive salary to the average worker salary is more than 400 to 1 (*USA Today* 2002b; Farrell 2002). Thus, if the average worker salary is about $20,000, then the remuneration for the typical top U.S. executive (including annual deferred monies and stock options but not benefits) would be $8 million. Krugman (2002) reported that the salary plus benefits of the average U.S. worker increased 10 percent to $36,000 per annum from 1980 to 2000, whereas the top 100 chief executives' average (total) compensation over the same period increased from $1.3 million to $37 million or 1,000 times that of the average worker. Are such high levels of recompense necessary to motivate CEOs to discharge their occupational responsibilities? Are board compensation committees credible when they imply that qualified top executives cannot be hired and retained for a mere $3 million or so per year? It is notable that when Daimler-Benz took over Chrysler Corporation, German managers were shocked to find out that the comparable salaries of their executive counterparts at Chrysler were frequently ten times what the German executives were being paid by the German company. Because a large proportion of CEO and other top executive bonuses were linked to short-run share prices, in the late 1990s some, if not many, chief executives took actions that were not in the best long-run interests of their company in order to lock in their high rates. A few, their egos inflated by personal success, crossed the line and treated their companies like personal piggy banks (McCoy and Strauss 2002).

Ethical Decision Making and Business Schools

Did business schools contribute to the breakdown in ethical decision making? The answer is regrettably yes. Many of the key participants in the recent scandals were business school graduates. For example, Jeffrey Skilling, the Enron CEO, had a master's in business administration (MBA) from Harvard. Andrew Fastow, the CFO of Enron, had an MBA from Northwestern; Kenneth Lay, former Enron chair, graduated from Oklahoma State University with a business degree. Koehn (2003) believes that business schools instill in our future managers the wrong values or ignore issues critical to developing integrity in the next generation of corporate leaders. This viewpoint is gaining momentum.

Jeffrey Garten, dean of the Yale School of Management, suggested that business school education requires careful reexamination. He contended that broad social dimensions of business operations, such as environmental protection, globalization, public policy, and management integrity, need far better coverage and integration into existing business school curricula. Garten stated that business school education effectively addresses the factors required for success at the firm level but does not deal with the questions of what society requires of its business leaders (Garten 2002).

The evidence supporting such opinions is attention-getting. For example, a 2002 Aspen Institute survey of 2,200 MBA students at thirteen major business schools (nine in the United States, including Wharton, Darden, Berkeley, and Columbia) seemed to suggest that financial imperatives become more important to students over the course of their MBA education (Mangan 2002b). When the respondents started business school, they thought that company priorities should be customer satisfaction and product quality. Certainly, such priorities should be at the heart of any successful business enterprise. By the time the students finished their MBA education, they understood the top company concern to be shareholder value. In other words, their dispositions had demonstrably shifted toward a financial preoccupation. Furthermore, the study's MBA respondents indicated that if they were to face an ethical conflict due to disagreements with extant corporate values and policies, they would leave their company rather than fight for change (Mangan 2002a). One wonders if such managerial capitulation is the sort of business leadership that an MBA education ought to instill.

The Association to Advance Collegiate Schools of Business (AACSB), a prominent accreditation body of business schools worldwide, requires that ethics and corporate social responsibility be a part of the business curriculum for a program to be certified for accreditation. Moreover, it has strongly encouraged a reexamination of ethics education by business schools (Mangan 2003). In the wake of the ethics scandals, President George W. Bush, himself a Harvard MBA, noted that business schools should be "principled teachers of right and wrong and not surrender to moral confusion and relativism" (Alsop 2003). However, AACSB does not specify the way in which ethics information should be delivered as part of MBA training. For example, faculty members could teach a required course on business ethics and social responsibility or they could integrate relevant ethics information throughout various business course offerings. There are major benefits (as well as disadvantages) to both approaches (Singer 2002). The "defined class" approach is easier to implement and makes clear to all that some ethics education is being covered. However, the risk is that the specified class becomes an ethics ghetto, a do-good course viewed by many students as a hurdle necessary to secure the business degree, especially if it constitutes the only ethics training in the curriculum.

The second approach, incorporating ethics into all courses, is potentially more effective because it allows for integrated, class-specific applications.

However, this strategy risks being undermined by professorial neglect. Substantive common-body-of-knowledge requirements in basic classes (due to the importance of covering essential disciplinary material) will regularly displace ethics and values discussions. Furthermore, many faculty members feel untrained or uncomfortable condemning strategic behavior that is not legally prohibited. Or they believe that they ought not advocate the moral superiority of taking actions that are not required by law. Put another way, faculty members may see staking out values and ethical positions in the classroom as proselytizing an arbitrary standard. Ironically, the strongest values-based training in business schools is often provided at institutions that some might view as the most doctrinaire. For example, at religious-based institutions, including Brigham Young University, Pepperdine, Texas Christian University, and various Catholic universities, including Marquette and Notre Dame, strong normative philosophical views, often grounded in religious tradition, are unapologetically stated. However, the fact that the injection of some ethics training is required for accreditation of business schools may push the "b-school and ethics" debate more toward *how* ethics education might be best delivered rather than *what* needs to be better addressed.

The root problem of decaying business ethics could well lie in what business schools are currently teaching. Recently, some of the sharpest criticisms of business school training have come from within the academy. For example, Sumantra Ghoshal, a professor of business strategy at the London Business School, suggested that the sort of competitive strategy frameworks taught as part of the MBA curriculum might impart values that are in opposition to good business ethics (Ghoshal 2003). Specifically:

- Agency theory reinforces the idea that managers are primarily economic agents of their employing organization. According to this view, the overriding goal of management should be to maximize shareholder value. In order to better align management with investors, top managers should be granted substantial stock options so that they also become significant shareholders. However, such investiture has become quite problematic and actually may be counter to stockholder interests. A recent analysis of 584 firms found that companies with high levels of CEO compensation in the form of options were significantly more likely to have accounting restatements (Harris and Bromiley 2003). And a study of 1,500 large U.S. companies over a ten-year period, conducted by two Rutgers University academics, concluded that firms dispensing larger than average option grants to their top five executives delivered lower than average total returns to their shareholders (Morgenson 2002).

- Transaction cost-analysis underscores the view that one of the primary roles of management is to rigidly control process and thereby tightly monitor employees in order to reduce costs and ensure they stay on task. Arguably, such a philosophy fosters antipathy, if not hostility, among manageers and employees.
- Competitive strategy theory implies that competitive advantage derives from creating points of leverage (via quasi-monopolies) in order to extract maximum gain from suppliers, customers, regulators and, of course, competition. This perspective surely mitigates stakeholder voice over business actions.

The influence of such thinking in business schools is so strong that contemporary U.S. corporations have evolved a form of capitalism that elevates the priorities of big investors and suppresses the claims of other stakeholders, even when compared with business practice just twenty or so years ago (Nielsen and Leigh 2003). Back then, CEO salaries were small compared with current pay packages; most executives were not as single-minded about return-on-investment (ROI) and tried to forge long-term partnerships with employees and suppliers; and workers had a better safety net of benefits and imagined working for one organization for their entire career (Krugman 2002). Ronald Duska, a professor of ethics at the American College, contends that today's MBA students have been "Whartonized"—that is, corrupted by bad ethics. He believes far too many MBAs hold a hierarchy of values that elevates firm growth and profitability as supreme above all other possible company goals; performance is judged exclusively by the utilitarianism (if not egoism) of financial indicators (Duska 2003).

It may even be that the time-tested case method so dear to many MBA programs is partially to blame (Harris and Bromiley 2003). Future managers are taught to be can-do decision makers who are responsible for achieving specific financial targets. The case approach conditions managers to rapidly isolate the issue at the root of problems and generate quick solutions or fast fixes, always with an eye toward the maintenance or improvement of profitability. The protocol is short-run and driven by the bottom line. The end result could be an implicit ethical assumption reinforced in many decision-making models central to MBA programs.

This unspoken ethic of MBA education might best be described as a form of restricted economic utilitarianism. In the absence of other articulated values, MBAs gravitate to using cost-benefit analysis with utility measured in dollars (mostly calculated in the short run since the long term usually cannot be reliably estimated) and oriented toward large shareholders (the primary stakeholder group whose good is being evaluated and maximized).

This MBA philosophy is played out by managers, who accept that business is a game conducted on behalf of big investors. Executives who oversee companies with below average profits in their industry sector are perceived as losers. What matters most is the bottom line. Consistent with utilitarian thinking, the means to achieve that end can include any legal tactics; illegal approaches are sometimes used as well if they cannot be easily detected. Personal ethical values are perceived as limited to one's home life and are too regularly left at the door when the executive enters the workplace. Amitai Etzioni, the eminent George Washington University sociologist who taught business ethics at the Harvard Business School in the 1980s, has become so disgusted by the profit mania of business schools that he wants the U.S. Congress to haul business school deans into a congressional hearing to explain to the American public what they have been doing and what they plan to do differently in order to improve the ethical sensitivity of future business managers (Etzioni 2002).

What should be done? A number of positive recommendations for enhancing business ethics education have been put forward over the years. It probably should fall to a national commission composed of recognized business leaders and seasoned business educators to evaluate the efficacy of these various possibilities (Garten 2002). However, in an effort to build the agenda, the following steps deserve discussion and possible consideration:

- Applicants to business schools should have their credentials checked. No convicted felons need apply. Those who materially misrepresent their background on submitted resumés should also be excluded from matriculation (Merritt 2003).
- Ethics should be integrated into functional business school classes such as marketing, finance, and operations. This integrated approach of having some ethics discussions in all classes is potentially quite effective because it allows for cross-curricular and subject-specific application of ethics to the tools and theories being discussed (Samuelson 2002).
- More business case studies that raise ethical issues should be incorporated into the curriculum (Mangan 2002b). Virtually all business school cases could incorporate an ethical twist, with proper discussion guidance provided by expert case writers.
- MBA education should include a class or module on ethical theory so that students understand the basic ethical philosophies that might be operating in a specific situation (Koehn 2003). At a minimum, MBAs should be sufficiently morally literate to comprehend that economic utilitarianism underlies many business decision models embraced by the business community.

- Professional ethical norms (i.e., codes of conduct) for each subdiscipline of business (e.g., finance, marketing, statistics, and human resources) should be delivered by academic departments to their majors. For example, advertising and public relations majors should be conversant with the codes of ethics of the American Association of Advertising Agencies, and accounting majors should be made aware of the many standards promulgated by the AICPA and other accounting groups.
- As part of the training and development of future business leaders, values (i.e., meaning morals) assertiveness should be taught so that future managers are willing to challenge wrongful behavior that they witness in their organizations rather than quit their jobs (Samuelson 2002).
- MBA graduates should take an ethics oath upon graduation similar to the Hippocratic oath taken by medical doctors. This approach is seriously being discussed for MBA graduates of the Institute de Empresa in Madrid. The precise form of this oath needs to be crafted, but it should affirm the ideal that managers are not only economic agents of their organization but caretakers of the economic resources of society (Alsop 2003).
- Corporate recruiters should be encouraged to test and interview for ethical sensitivity in the students they hire (Garten 2002). If firms like Goldman Sachs included an ethics test in their interviewing processes, the study of morals would be in such demand by MBAs that its status would be sacramental.
- Business students should be taught to measure and appreciate business success more broadly than with only financial metrics (Etzioni 2002). The balanced scorecard approach to assessing organizational performance as well as the social audit would be useful tools in this vein (Paine 2003).
- Corporations should support the establishment of ethics professorships in every business school (Merritt 2003).
- Business professors should avoid defining social responsibility as consisting solely of philanthropy and volunteerism (Samuelson 2002).
- Business faculty should refrain from celebrating the hardball or cowboy culture of business strategy (Samuelson 2002). Despite the popular metaphors, business is not like war. Its purpose is not to annihilate competitors but rather to serve buyers and, in doing so, serve the economic needs of a broader society.

Without the willingness to embrace and implement ideas such as those mentioned above, business schools will be left with the status quo and will remain part of the ethics problem. Richard Ellsworth, a management professor at the Claremont Graduate University, aptly characterized the current situation as follows: "The idea that the most important goal is to maximize shareholder wealth has permeated the entire curriculum of many business schools; that notion establishes a foundation that builds upon greed. It can prompt people to put their own financial interests ahead of the general good" (Mangan 2003).

Changes Necessary for Better Business Ethics and Corporate Governance

The Sarbanes-Oxley Act outlawed some misleading financial practices and codified public expectations about the transparency of financial instruments and the behavior of top managers with regard to financial reporting. For instance, the requirement that CEOs and CFOs certify their financial reports for accuracy, that executive bonuses must be returned if company earnings are restated, and that companies must disclose any board waivers to company codes of ethics will restore some public confidence in the veracity of business operations. Also, the accelerated prosecution of executives who engaged in financial improprieties sends a jarring, attention-getting message to the business community. Since July 2002, the U.S. Justice Department has initiated 320 investigations against more than 500 persons, most of them high-ranking executives (Byrnes et al. 2003). Because proving financial fraud or obstruction of justice is very complex, many of these investigations and prosecutions are still ongoing. Nevertheless, the possibility of criminal conviction and jail time for CFOs and CEOs should suppress the more blatant cases of financial fraud and business malfeasance.

Despite the existence of Sarbanes-Oxley (and earlier legislation), we are likely to continue to see periodic waves of business ethics scandals in the future. One reason is that the regulation of morality by law has never been the most efficient or effective solution for handling business wrongdoing (Pinkerton 2003). Stronger locks may guard the vaults of corporations, but if the executive ranks are populated by a disproportionate number of crooks, they will find ways to game the system (Fass 2003). The oversight of business behavior by extended regulation has been labeled compliance-based corporate social responsibility (CSR). Compliance is driven by external expectations and reporting pressures; it breeds a legalistic and "checkbox" mentality among business organizations (Donaldson 2000). Enron, for example, was perceived to have an outstanding corporate compliance process. Other corporations that have been involved with infamous ethical controversies over the years, such as Philip Morris (now called Altria Corporation) and Dow Chemical, are also known for their efficient, compliance mentality. Of more long-term value to society is a conviction-based philosophy of CSR. Conviction-based CSR is inspired by a company's vision and the ethical and professional values inherent in its corporate culture. It is both more flexible and more easily internalized by the organization than a legalistic type of compliance. But for conviction-based CSR to be effective, a modified vision of business purpose must be accepted.

Conviction-based CSR implies fundamental changes in corporate governance and executive development and seems to be what is required to meaningfully improve business ethics. Such radical adjustments are not likely to be warmly embraced by many corporations. And without a major change in business perspective, significant evolution in the ethical climate of business will probably not occur. Consider the following recommendations for making major, lasting improvements in business ethics. These recommendations are consistent with conviction-based CSR.

Recommendation 1: The business and financial system must place significantly less weight on corporations hitting the numbers on a quarterly and perhaps even on an annual basis. Case studies of ethical violations by business executives suggest that a short-run orientation often impels ethical abuse (Paine 1997). When executive bonuses and stock options are linked to hitting short-term financial targets, is it surprising that corporate integrity is sometimes sacrificed to reach personally lucrative goals? The prevailing short horizon obsession of managers and financial analysts must give way to a preference for long-run strategic achievement and an orderly progression toward the attainment of company objectives specified in its long-range plan (George 2003). Dispensing with the quarterly mentality of American business is not a new idea.

In 1980, and partly as a response to the growing inroads of Japanese companies, a Harvard professor and a McKinsey consultant coauthored an article in the *Harvard Business Review* titled "Managing Our Way to Economic Decline" (Hayes and Abernathy 1980). They eloquently made the argument for adopting a broader, long-term perspective. These authors lamented the predominant focus on short-term financials to the exclusion of long-term investments in meaningful, innovative new products and services. Collins and Porras's (1994) *Built to Last*, a business best seller, is another well-known book stressing a similar message. There is some hope of change: for example, Coca Cola Corporation announced in 2003 that it will no longer provide quarterly earnings estimates to financial analysts. However, the logic of the long-run approach has since been mostly forgotten by the financial community.

Recommendation 2: Organizational success must be measured in a balanced fashion. Executives should be rewarded and promoted for their accomplishments in areas other than financial performance (Covey 2002). These success metrics might include avoiding lawsuits, receiving environmental protection awards, registering high rates of customer satisfaction, achieving high product reliability and durability ratings, and being ranked as a desirable organization for employees to work for.

In a classic piece of business analysis, Kaplan and Norton (1996) articulated the balanced scorecard approach, laying out how nonfinancial objectives can be identified and integrated into the formulation and implementation of corporate strategy. Such thinking has been extended in the development of paradigms that elaborate in considerable detail how various corporate and social responsibilities incumbent on business organizations can be measured and reported on as part of the strategic planning process (Gardiner 2002). For example, Royal Dutch Shell utilizes a triple bottom line approach that reports social and ecological initiatives as well as financial results. This broadened perspective is a beginning step for corporations serious about explicitly recognizing the ethical obligations inherent in practicing a higher standard of business. An excellently articulated blueprint for meshing a balanced approach with the realities of strategy formulation can be found in Lynn Sharp Paine's book, *Value Shift* (2003).

Recommendation 3: The reign of the imperial CEOs should be tempered. William McDonough, past president of the New York Federal Reserve and chair of the Accounting Oversight Board, believes that the growing disparity between CEO and average worker salaries in the United States has become a grave moral concern (Byrnes et al. 2003). In the future, CEO pay must be better linked to overall company performance; various bonuses and deferred compensation packages should not be handed out without risk for the CEO, as they often are (Strauss 2003). Chief executive officers should not be allowed to also hold the position of chairman of the board, because the dual offices concentrate too much power. CEOs without exemplary performance (measured in a balanced fashion) that puts them in the top third of their industry peer group perhaps should be restricted by their board from serving as a director for other companies (Luke 2002). Consistent with the recommendations of retired Medtronic CEO Bill George (2003), as articulated in his insightful book, *Authentic Leadership*, boards should select CEOs based on their character and their values rather than on their ability to create short-term improvements in company financials. For example, as a point of contrast, "Chainsaw Al" Dunlap (former CEO of Sunbeam and other companies) could hit the numbers. For several years, Chainsaw Al was the darling of both the business community and media. Dunlap made his reputation by being able to eke out profits from seemingly doomed organizations. Eventually, Dunlap was shown to be as false as the Wizard of Oz, when closer examination of his record indicated that company financials were improved through a combination of accounting tricks, asset stripping, and cruelty to employees by means of wholesale downsizing. Sadly, there is evidence that CEO compensation continues to escalate unabated (Lublin 2002a), and the reign of overly powerful CEOs remains. Moreover, departing CEOs, even if they resign, are often guaranteed a lifetime of riches in their severance packages (Joyner 2003). At the same time, the general public remains furious over such packages (Jones 2003).

Recommendation 4: Boards of directors require drastic reform. Boards must become truly independent overseers of company management. As of 2002, 13 percent of the companies listed on the New York Stock Exchange still did not have a majority of outside directors, effectively eliminating any meaningful controls on top management (Hymowitz 2003). Minimal reform would seem to require the following. Companies should develop principles of corporate governance, publish them, and report annually on conformance; require outside directors to always be in the majority and to meet regularly without the presence of internal directors; require that audit, compensation, and nominating committees be composed of solely outside directors; require that no more than three members of the board be top executives of the corporation; require that directors be annually evaluated and attend at least 75 percent of all scheduled meetings in order to continue their service as director; ensure that the nature and level of director's fees be transparent to stockholders and the public; and require that directors never sit on more than three other corporate boards.

Recommendation 5: Business firms ought to be more wary of managerial fads. Techniques such as reengineering, right-sizing, responsibility-centered management, pro forma accounting, and "rank or yank" evaluation of employees all have their role and typically speak to some dimension of the organization that could benefit from improvement. Too often, however, such one-trick applications are force-fitted to an organization because they are the pet project of the CEO or another top-level executive. These techniques are sometimes tools of desperation adopted to quickly improve a firm's financial picture. If the elevation of a particular technique in an organization becomes a mania, it usually causes unexpected repercussions and quite commonly becomes an ethical problem as well for both middle managers and lower-level employees. Frankly, one would expect a higher level of thinking from seven-figure CEOs than commanding that all employees understand and adjust when their "cheese has been moved."

Recommendation 6: Companies must commit to developing a culture of integrity. Integrity involves having high ethical standards and adhering to them no matter what the pressures. The elements of successfully implementing ethics in a company are the same ones that have been articulated for the past twenty-five years or more (Ottoson 1982; Laczniak and Murphy 1985, 97–105). Successful implementation begins with a CEO who must not only publicly embrace core ethical values, but live them (Laczniak 1983). It involves espousing these values in a corporate mission statement and articulating them further in an ethics statement that specifically addresses the knotty ethical issues common to a particular company or industry sector (Murphy 1998, 1–11). The code should be dynamic and therefore periodically revised (Laczniak and Murphy 1993). The basics of a company's values statement and code should be so prominently communicated that every employee knows and can verbalize the essentials (Murphy 1989). Management behavior should be monitored, including that of the CEO, whose actions should be checked by the board of directors. When ethical violations occur, proportionate punishments must be meted out. Because the fundamental purpose of codes is not to punish but to guide the actions of all managers and employees, creative applications of a company's ethical values, acts of moral imagination so to speak, also should be meaningfully rewarded (Hayes 2002). The details of executing all of these steps have been extensively treated in the ethics literature (e.g., Laczniak and Murphy 1993). The most vexing ingredient in the recipe for better ethical behavior is the force of will to always keep ethics at the heart of a company's purpose. This is exceedingly difficult given the constant pressure on managers to be economically successful.

Recommendation 7: Powerful corporations should assume their ethical and moral responsibility. The power-responsibility equilibrium basically states that if an economically powerful organization does not willingly undertake its corresponding social and ethical responsibility, it will lose power. This is what happened with the passage of the Sarbanes-Oxley Act.

The power-responsibility equilibrium can also serve as a positive force when highly ethical corporations that are also large and influential exert peer pressure over other companies. An excellent example occurred when Vanguard, the mutual fund giant, took a strong stance on key proxy issues. In 2003, Vanguard approved of just 29 percent of the full slates of directors proposed by companies in which it invests (versus 90 percent in 2002). Corporate governance experts said that these actions by Vanguard will influence management and embolden stakeholder resolutions. This position by Vanguard, an industry leader, should make other funds more willing to stand up to management in the future (Brown 2003).

Recommendation 8: Corporations, business schools, and professional associations ought to accept, teach, and testify that executive-level management is a vocation. A vocation is a special calling to accept the responsibilities of a critical position, such as that of a teacher, priest, counselor, or doctor. Management should be viewed as a calling because the position of a high-level executive involves stewardship over organizational resources that are also part of society's economic infrastructure (Novak 1996). Put another way, the elite role of top managers in corporations involves a sacred trust of responsibility not just to owners or shareholders, but to society. Again, we need to ask ourselves: Why is deviant corporate behavior perceived by so many to be such a serious failing? The answer lies partly in the notion of business leaders as economic caretakers.

Corporate executives have been given temporary custody over resources of enormous scope. Seen this way, high-level management may be the ultimate helping profession. Surely, any dishonest act by an employee is unfortunate, whether it is a retail clerk who pilfers products off the shelf or an executive assistant who liberates pens, envelopes, and paper clips for home use. But the stakes are much greater when a top-level corporate executive unethically squanders the economic resources that could potentially benefit a multitude of stakeholders. Because their ethical and legal malfeasance can cripple the pension funds of many thousands of employees, the planned-for dividends essential to the financial well-being of numerous small stockholders, or the economic livelihood of a community where the organization's key operations are located or headquartered, the ethical failings of a few top managers become the despair of the many.

If high-level business management is more purely seen as a vocation involving economic stewardship, that perspective implies superordinate duties and obligations that managers owe to society, even as they serve their employer (Laczniak 1998). Without doubt, a major purpose of business is to increase long-term shareholder value through profitability. Ideally, that profit level should be consistent and improving. This purpose, though, raises the question. Why is profit important? The short answer is that profit serves as a reward for risk. Further, profit creates an incentive for business organizations to provide the desired and required commercial services needed by society. Looked at this way, profit and its associated financial measures are a means to an end, not an end itself. And consistent with this view, business leaders are the de facto designated guardians of the commercial system on behalf of society.

Ultimately, we must live with the fact that the enlightened self-interest of profit possibilities drives our economic system (a very good thing) but that there also exists the likelihood of ill-gotten, inordinate profit (a bad thing). Some executives will succumb to their darker side, for a certain level of ethical abuse is inevitably part of the business terrain we are destined to inhabit. But when the level of questionable management behavior becomes too excessive or too prevalent, it is the responsibility of the broader community to restore balance (Vogel 2002). The challenge is to devise mechanisms that will inspire business to choose the higher road and also will channel the personal self-interest essential to the system so that corporate behaviors are constrained in a socially responsible direction.

Why Ethics and Profits Can and Must Work Together in Business

Donald P. Robin

Building on the premise that ethics is important in all societies, this chapter develops expectations for business in an ethical society. The discussion accepts capitalism as the best economic system but also recognizes its potential for abusing stakeholders. The chapter then describes an approach to business that maintains and improves profitability while also protecting and integrating stakeholders. Hopefully this approach can provide an important future direction for business ethicists working within the capitalistic system to uncover strategies that can achieve both the mission of ethics and the mission of profits.

The Purpose of Ethics

The majority of people in ethical societies are better off than the people in less ethical societies. People in an ethical society gain the ability to trust that others will respect them as individuals, deal with them honestly and openly, treat them fairly, and provide them with an equal opportunity. In short, people in an ethical society have a decent chance, though not a guarantee, to live well-measured, happy lives.

In an unethical society, power and chance dominate what happens to people. There is no reason to expect others to be honest, fair, open, and respectful. Comparative power defines relationships, and trust is limited to what power can enforce. Chance also plays an important role. Being in the wrong place at the wrong time, figuratively or literally, can offset existing power and produce harmful outcomes. This law of the jungle defines the environment of an unethical society. Life in gangs and crime families, for example, gives us a glimpse into life in an unethical society.

Justification for a Purpose of Ethics

Most of us recognize the tendency for things to go wrong occasionally in our daily lives. Warnock, in *The Object of Morality* (1971), argued that the existence of ethics helps to ameliorate this tendency. In explaining this tendency toward negative events in our lives, he identified the limited rationality and limited sympathies of human beings as primary causes. People of limited rationality are not naturally disposed to always do what would be best for them and for others in the long-run. Instead, people often focus on short-run, blatant, and obtrusive satisfactions. In his definition of limited sympathies, Warnock noted that most people are more concerned about their own wants and needs than those of others. Further, even when people focus on the needs of others, "it is quite likely to be only about *some* others—family, friends, class, tribe, country, or 'race.'" In addition to this comparative indifference toward others, people cannot even expect that "active malevolence will not be forthcoming" from their fellow human beings (17).

Sometimes dependent and vulnerable, people often need the help, or at least the cooperation, of others to complete tasks and to protect themselves. Further, people are often in competition with others, and in a world of limited rationality and limited sympathy, resources, knowledge, skills, information, and intelligence are also limited, further contributing to the tendency of things to go wrong. Warnock summarized his views by stating that "the 'general object' of morality . . . is to contribute to betterment—or non-deterioration—of the human predicament, primarily and essentially by seeking to countervail 'limited sympathies' and their potentially most damaging effects" (26).

Philosopher Thomas Hobbes, in *Leviathan* (1651/1991), went further than Warnock in describing the human condition without some form of morality. Hobbes believed that a natural state of war, broadly defined, exists among humans. This condition creates anxiety, violence, and constant danger, which in turn produce a life that is "solitary, poor, nasty, brutish, and short." Hobbes described his view of humans as follows: "in the first place, I put for a general inclination of all mankind, a perpetual and restless desire of power after power, that ceased only in death" (89). Hobbes believed that only through an enforced social order, as in the legal structure of society, could human beings find peace.

In Warnock's view, the propensity for things to go wrong exists, but life is not nearly as hopeless as Hobbes thought it was. Warnock noted that this propensity is much lessened when ethical behavior is adopted by the citizens of a society. Other philosophers seem to have a view similar to Warnock's. Both Aristotle and John Stuart Mill believed that the purpose of ethics is to create conditions that allow individuals the opportunity to pursue a well-structured and happy life. Mill, like Hobbes, was especially concerned about the abusive use of power: "The sole end for which mankind are warranted individually or collectively in interfering with the liberty of action of any of their number is self-protection. . . . The only purpose for which power can be rightfully exercised over any member of a civilized community, against his will, is to prevent harm to others" (1859/1956, 13). Mill's view can be used to justify an ethical standard that represents protection against the abusive use of power. The purpose of ethics is to reduce the impact of the law of the jungle.

The Role of Business in Achieving the Purpose of Ethics

A world without ethics, as described by Warnock and Hobbes, makes trust impossible, a particularly damning conclusion for the conduct of business. Without trust at any level, business would be impossible, and the more trust that business can develop with each of its stakeholder groups (employees, customers, suppliers, etc.), the more efficient and effective business dealings with those stakeholders become. Further, business in capitalistic democracies, with the profit motive and its limited, although often positive, focus on selected stakeholders, can be described using the language of Warnock. That is, without morality, business is much less likely to contribute to the betterment—or the nondeterioration—of the human predicament. In this scenario, society, through its government, is much more likely to constrain and direct the activities of those businesses operating within its borders. To prevent this outcome, business must behave within society's ethical expectations.

Comparing the ethical society and the unethical society, it is easy to conclude that ethics provides a significant advantage that is worth pursuing. As an alternative, the unethical environment is a natural outcome of an unethical society. It should be noted that an ethical or unethical society can be a community of nations, the society of a single nation, the society of business firms within a nation, or the society within a single business firm.

An Ethical Society's Expectations for Business

The concept of an ethical society is important because it provides a benchmark or exemplar from which deviations can be treated. It also allows us to ask if these deviations, or ethical problem areas, are due to the problems of a society, the problems of businesses in that society, or some combination of these. If a business is meeting the expectations of an ethical society, then it is behaving ethically. However, it is possible for society to deviate from its ethical exemplar and demand something unethical from business. When that occurs, business suffers, since society determines the nature of, and rules for, the businesses operating within it. The unethical actions foisted on business by such a society must be dealt with differently from the case where business is the source of the problem. Using the ethical society as a model, we can define exemplary behaviors for business firms. Then, even if the society in which businesses operate deviates from the ethical norm, a standard still exists to guide behavior.

Value and Mission of an Ethical Society

What are the values and goals of an ethical society? One concept of an ethical society is based on the ideas of the social contract theorists. These theorists believe that everyone has a duty to abide by certain natural or reasoned rules of a society. John Locke's arguments favoring "natural rights" (Hunt 2003, 29) and John Rawls's (1971) "veil of ignorance" mechanism can be used to discover the rules of an ethical society. Further, one of Immanuel Kant's (1785/1964) formulations of his "categorical imperative" describes an ethical society. Unfortunately, each of these theorists came to somewhat different conclusions about the specific rules that an ethical society should adopt.

It could be argued, however, that each formulation represented an attempt to satisfy the purpose of ethics, and that is the approach adopted here. Thus, rather than attempting to establish specific rules for an ethical society, the approach suggested here is to allow the agents of society to determine what is appropriate, given the history, time, and context of the situation in which they find themselves. However, agents of society must be guided by the mission of ethics, and business decision makers must be guided by the mission of an ethical society.

The general mission or purpose of ethics must be accommodated by the mission of an ethical society. That is, a society cannot be ethical unless it makes its best effort to satisfy the general purpose of ethics. Recall that this purpose is described as moving society away from an environment where chance and the abusive use of power can dominate relations between people. Instead, agents of society must move toward an environment that supports a more structured, happy life for society members. Thus, an ethical society provides an environment for its people that facilitates (but does not guarantee) a well-structured, happy life for its citizens. Society's efforts may not produce perfection, but its mission is a target that it must constantly strive to attain.

Expectations of an Ethical Society for Business

What, then, would an ethical society expect from business? The mission of an ethical society is certainly much broader and encompasses more than its charge to business. However, one of the most important components of an ethical society's mission is to find an efficient and effective way to fulfill the economic function. Thus, one of the expectations of an ethical society for its businesses is that they operate in an efficient manner. It is incumbent on an ethical society to create a type of economic system that allows businesses to best achieve this expectation.

An ethical society would expect the businesses that operate under its auspices to understand the broader ethical mission and operate in a manner that satisfies it. Thus, being an efficient and effective provider of goods and services is not enough; businesses must attempt to do so in a manner that does not conflict with society's mission for its citizens. When natural conflicts do occur, society expects businesses to make a legitimate effort to reduce their negative impacts.

What are the options for an ethical society that is trying to establish a role and structure for businesses? Capitalism seems to be the clear winner in the search for the best option. In *The End of History and the Last Man*, Fukuyama (1992) argued that a great number of the advanced countries of the world have adopted or are moving toward capitalistic economies. His "end of history" simply means that there is a broad evolution of societies worldwide toward a final point of agreement, and, economically at least, that point is capitalism. Capitalism clearly provides the most efficient and effective structure for performing the economic function, but capitalism can also produce some effects that are negative with respect to the broad mission of an ethical society. For that reason, no industrially advanced country has a system of totally unfettered capitalism.

Based on the preceding discussion, it is reasonable to expect that an ethical society would create a business structure based on capitalism but tempered to ameliorate the law-of-the-jungle impacts on the stakeholders of business. In creating this structure, society must weigh the benefits of capitalistic freedoms against the potential harms to employees, buyers, suppliers, and communities for many specific cases. The role of businesses in this process is to find alternative strategies and tactics for advancing their shareholders' wealth that also minimize harm and/or maximize benefits to other stakeholders.

Stakeholder Considerations

Many moral philosophers believe that an organization has a moral obligation to stakeholder groups that are subject to an important impact from the organization's actions. If businesses abuse their relations with their stakeholder groups, then society, acting through its agents in government, must create constraints and directives to prevent future abuses. For example, as the United States moved into the twentieth century, few restrictions or directives existed to control business behavior, but throughout the century, the business regulatory environment changed. Substantial legislation now exists to control and direct businesses. However, the inefficiency, and even the ineffectiveness, of a legislative approach can produce less desirable outcomes for both business and society than an ethics-based approach. A good exposition of the problems with a legislative approach appears in Philip Howard's book, *The Death of Common Sense: How Law Is Suffocating America* (1994). The book explains why rules cannot effectively replace ethical thinking and goodwill.

To avoid the problems of massive regulations, it is incumbent on businesses to search for methods of operation that protect their shareholders while increasing their wealth. Are there better ways to achieve the goal of increased wealth? Compared to the approaches that many businesses use, the answer certainly seems to be yes. There are many reasons why ethical organizations are more profitable in the long run, and the discussion now turns to one approach for achieving this goal.

A Profitable and Ethical Approach to Business

This section suggests a productive, synergistic approach for satisfying both the profit and ethics objectives. The approach is to build links of trust between a company and each of its stakeholder groups. These trust links focus on fair treatment and mutual respect.

Defining Trust

Following his review of the literature, Hosmer (1995) suggested a definition of trust that is adapted here for the purpose of building trust links with stakeholders. Specifically, trust is defined here as reliance by stakeholder groups on a voluntarily accepted duty of a company to treat them fairly and with respect in an economic exchange. (See Hosmer [1995, 399] for a comparison definition.)

Trust must have a focus. We could, for example, trust homicidal maniacs to continue killing innocent victims, or alternatively, trust a doctor not to do any unnecessary harm to us. Because the interests of stakeholders depend on the situation surrounding economic exchanges, companies should inquire about the harm and benefits that could accrue to each stakeholder group from an exchange. The company has a fiduciary duty to sharehold-ers, as a special stakeholder group, to provide maximum long-term profits, subject to being a good citizen. It is comforting to note that this approach also satisfies what an ethical society would expect from businesses, in that it supports the capitalistic objective and reduces the impact of the law of the jungle on stakeholders.

A second issue related to the definition is reciprocal trust. The focus of the definition is on stakeholder trust in the company to behave with fair-ness and respect. The definition could be rewritten to focus on stakeholder behavior toward the company—stakeholders certainly should behave with fairness and respect toward the company. However, the company typically has little control over the stakeholders and must generally make its own decision about whether to trust them. Since it can control its own behavior toward the stakeholders, the working definition presented previously will guide this decision.

Characteristics of a Trusting Relationship

A trusting relationship has several characteristics. The first is optimism in the trusting party that the other person or group will fulfill its expectations. This characteristic is corroborated by Bhide and Stevenson (1990, 124) in a *Harvard Business Review* article that discusses honesty and trust in business: "Even with a fully disclosed public record of bad faith, hard-nosed businesspeople will still try to find reasons to trust." Trust also includes vul-nerability on the part of the trusting party. Hosmer (1995, 390) noted "the expectation that the loss, if trust is broken, will be much greater than the gain if trust is maintained." For this reason, trust requires some knowledge of the person, organization, or society in which people are placing their trust. Handy (1995, 44) supported this idea by noting that "trust is not blind. It is unwise to trust people . . . you do not know well." He also believed that a shared commitment among individuals, requiring mutual trust, works better with personal contact, and that trust has boundaries. In business, trust is frequently bound to the achievement of a specific goal and is limited by beliefs about the factors that build it.

Trust involves a free and willing commitment by the trusting party that it will improve cooperation. Fukuyama (1995, 27) echoed this point when he wrote:

> If people who have to work together in an enterprise trust one another . . .
> doing business costs less. . . . By contrast, people who do not trust one
> another will end up cooperating only under a system of formal rules and
> regulations, which have to be negotiated, agreed to, litigated, and enforced,
> sometimes by coercive means.

Thus, there is a rational reason for business people to participate in trusting
relationships.

Fukuyama (1995) also suggested that there is a national or societal tendency toward trust. Some societies are more prone to trust than others, and
according to Fukuyama, this one tendency greatly influences a nation's economic success. Specifically, "a nation's well-being, as well as its ability to
compete, is conditioned by a single, pervasive cultural characteristic: the
level of trust inherent in the society" (7).

Trust also seems to have three dimensions, each of which can vary from
trust link to trust link. One of these dimensions is "affective." Trust often
includes positive emotional feelings toward the object (person, organization,
society) of trust (Lewis and Weigert 1985). Affect is one of the reasons that
trust is increased by personal contact, which makes it easier to like (or dis-
like) someone. Another dimension is "cognitive." People use rational analysis to determine the trustworthiness of an object. The third dimension is
"connotative," or behavior. Trustworthy behavior in the past leads to trusting
behavior in the present.

Finally, it should be noted that there is a hierarchy of trust. Trust can be
given or received by individuals, organizations, and societies. As the final
arbiter of laws and contracts, society represents a trust base of last resort.
However, if society is the sole basis for trust, business becomes very inefficient and expensive. Businesses place trust in other businesses (e.g., suppliers and joint ventures), in society or government, and in individuals (e.g.,
employees and customers). Individuals trust businesses that they work for
and companies from which they buy products and services. Individuals also
trust society through government to rectify the serious problems they have
with businesses.

Requirements for Building Trust

In addition to understanding the nature and characteristics of trust relationships, any manager hoping to use the concept must be aware of how to
build trust links with stakeholders and how to avoid destroying them once
they are built. There are six trust-building factors, five of which are ethical
factors, that have been supported by research. They are equity of treat-

ment, respect for others, honesty in dealings with others, openness, promise-keeping, and competence.

Treating stakeholders equitably or fairly seems to be exceptionally important in building relationships based on trust. In a *Fortune* article, Farnham (1989) noted a trust gap between employees and management, and he suggested that an important reason for this gap is a perceived lack of fairness or equity. The article supports a concern for fairness in everything from the CEO's salary to the office layout. Bartolome (1989, 139) defined fairness in a business setting by stating, "Fairness means giving credit where it's due, being objective and impartial in performance appraisals, (and) giving praise liberally." He also noted that every act of fair play builds and supports trust links. Bromiley and Cummings (1996) found that building trust requires that one person or group not take excessive advantage of others. In brief, trust in business requires recognizing and protecting the rights and interests of all stakeholders.

The focus on concern and respect for stakeholders is another factor necessary for trust-building. This theme was voiced by Butler and Cantrell (1984) when they cited the need for loyalty, described as the willingness to protect, support, and encourage others, as an important factor in trust-building. Bartolome (1989) also noted the importance of concern for others as people: "being available and approachable . . . helping people, coaching them, encouraging their ideas, and defending their positions. . . . It certainly means taking an interest in their lives and careers" (138). Respect by management was also the factor most important to employees as reported in a study by Louis Harris and Associates cited in Farnham (1989). Respect for individuals builds trust whereas a lack of respect destroys it.

Honesty and truthfulness also build trust. Paine reported on the impact of honesty by Wetherill Associates Inc. (WAI), a company that supplies electrical parts to the automotive industry and has a strong commitment to honesty. Paine (1994, 117) wrote, "WAI is known for informing suppliers of over shipments as well as under shipments and for scrupulous honesty in the sale of parts, even when deception cannot be readily detected." The firm has been extremely successful in a market that has shown little growth. Undoubtedly, the trust links it built with suppliers and customers due to its honesty policy played an important role in its success. Butler and Cantrell (1984, 19–28) also identified integrity, which they defined as "the reputation for honesty and truthfulness on the part of the trusted individual," as an important component of building trust. Honesty in negotiations was also cited by Bromiley and Cummings (1996) as important to building trust.

Building trust is also facilitated through the openness of management. Openness means the sharing of ideas and information with others. Bartolome

(1989, 138) described openness as "a matter of keeping subordinates informed, providing accurate feedback, explaining decisions and policies, being candid about one's own problems, and resisting the temptation to hoard information for use as a tool or a reward." He believed the practice increases trust substantially. Farnham (1989, 57) cited "closer, more honest communications between employees and senior management" as one of four things that are very important to workers. Openness was also mentioned by Butler and Cantrell (1984) as a major component of trust-building. Furthermore, openness works with more than employees in building trust. Other stakeholders, such as customers and suppliers, use openness to judge trustworthiness.

Sells (1994) reported the response of management at Manville after concerns were beginning to develop about the harmful effects of its fiberglass insulation: "Our best weapon was our communication policy itself, because most customers understood that we were telling them everything we knew. . . . We also learned that a consistent, conscientious commitment to the truth is a weapon powerful enough to overcome relativity, cynicism, and a great deal of fear" (88).

Promise-keeping and consistency are also required to build trust. Part of the definition of trust by Bromiley and Cummings (1996) involves good faith efforts to behave in accordance with both explicit and implicit commitments. Butler and Cantrell (1984) described consistency as being reliable and predictable and indicated that it is a necessary ingredient for building trust. Granovetter (1985) suggested that being trustworthy in the past leads to trusting behavior in the future. According to Bartolome (1989), behaving consistently and dependably as well as keeping both explicit and implicit promises produces a consistency of character that is important to fostering trust.

Competent, good business sense combined with demonstrated technical or professional ability, seems also to be required to foster trust (Bartolome 1989; Butler and Cantrell 1984). Even if managers are perceived to be decent, honest, and open, stakeholders may not believe they can provide the outcomes that foster trust if they believe the managers are not competent. Perhaps even more importantly, competence breeds admiration and respect, essential ingredients for the leader who uses a trust-based managerial approach.

Factors That Destroy Trust

The most obvious destroyers of trust are failures in any of the six trust-building factors. Lack of fairness, respect, honesty, openness, promise-keeping, or competence can destroy trust links. But, just as it usually takes a while to build trust, it often takes more than one incident to destroy it. Occasional small indiscretions may be overlooked. Most people understand that no one is perfect and are willing to accept that fact in judging the trustworthiness of others. Further, there may be few real alternatives except to trust another party simply because of a need to work together (Bhide and Stevenson 1990). Some level of trust is required for business transactions, or the transactions will not occur. In this type of situation, trust is "sticky" or difficult to destroy.

Other trust destroyers include politics, personality conflicts, ambiguous situations, authority as a judge, denial, fear, and arrogance. Political rather than merit-based decisions are a fairly obvious destroyer of trust (Bartolome 1989). Office politics usually involves a breach of fairness, openness, and honesty. Unfortunately, such politics exist far too often in American business (Jackall 1983). Personality conflict is another fairly obvious trust destroyer. It is represented by the affect dimension of trust and influences the willingness of a party to be open and share information. Further, personality conflict often negatively influences the respect and fair treatment of others.

The ambiguity and complexity of a situation can either increase or decrease the probability of trusting behavior. The less a person actually knows, or can know, about a situation, the more important trust becomes in helping the person cope (Bhide and Stevenson 1990). However, ambiguity can also create doubt about honesty, fairness, respect, promise-keeping, and even competence. Business situations are often ambiguous and complex, and because openness reduces ambiguity and helps remove the doubt about the situation, it is important for building trust.

As Bartolome (1989, 135) noted, "Trust flees authority, and above all, trust flees a judge." Judgment can cause special problems with some stakeholders. In an employer-employee situation, there is no way a manager can avoid all judgment of subordinates. Managers can attempt to be less judgmental in their approach, but some judgment is necessary. W. Edwards Deming's fourteen famous directives for improving quality include the elimination of several points that normally exist for judging employees (see Gabor 1990, 17–30). For example, he suggested that companies eliminate numerical goals, work standards or quotas, management by objectives, and management by numbers. In their stead, he recommended that managers become leaders. Johnson & Johnson is a very successful company that reduces the concerns connected with the judging process. It is known for its tolerance of failure and often retains employees, including managers, who fail in their jobs (O'Reilly 1994). However, one characteristic it does not tolerate is ethical failure. Managers "use ethics to weed out bad managers early; [and] put trust in those who remain" (O'Reilly 1994, 180). Consequently, the company culture at Johnson & Johnson is remarkably different from that at many other companies, and it is also remarkable in achieving profit objectives.

Shortsightedness and/or denial of a problem can cause a loss of trust. Bartolome (1989, 136) observed, "At one time or another, most of us have chosen an uncertain future calamity over today's immediate unpleasantness." This approach can have a significant impact on how a manager's competence and fairness to others are judged.

Other destroyers of trust are fear and arrogance. Fear works against trust; something that is both important and worrisome enough to produce fear in an individual is also likely to produce caution in granting trust. Employees' fear can reduce the efficiency and effectiveness of their work. It can cause them to hide information and problems from people who could help solve them (Bartolome 1989). Another of Deming's fourteen directives is to "drive out fear so that everyone may work effectively for the company" (Gabor 1990, 17). Arrogance comprises a lack of respect for others and often a lack of fairness. Arrogance announces that a person feels somehow superior to others, and that pronouncement destroys trust.

Conditions Necessary for Operating a Trust-Link Approach in Business

Building a trust-based organization begins with the managers and employees of the business. These are the people who interact with other stakeholders. If midlevel managers and employees do not trust top management, then building trust links with other groups becomes very difficult, and probably impossible. The bureaucratic, power-based, command-and-control approach to business is not conducive to building trust in top management. Instead, a people-oriented organization works best. Developing that kind of organization, and building trust links with managers and employees, requires business to establish and maintain three different characteristics— leadership throughout the organization, core values and integrated goals, and fair processes.

Leadership

There are many books and articles on leadership, but the focus here is on the link between leadership and trust. Leadership and trust have a unique dual relationship. Trust is necessary for becoming a successful leader, and leadership is necessary to build and maintain trust. Noting that a leader must work with people to solve problems and discover and take advantage of opportunities, Zand stated that "whether leaders gain access to the knowledge and creative thinking they need . . . depends on how much people trust them" (1997, 89). The lack of two-way trust is corrosive to leadership and diminishes effectiveness.

Handy noted, "At their best, the units in good trust-based organizations hardly have to be managed, but they do need a *multiplicity of leaders*" (1995, 47, emphasis added). The need for a multiplicity of leaders becomes apparent when it is understood that trust-based organizations are people-centered and often entrepreneurial in nature, like 3M (Bartlett and Ghoshal 1995). In that kind of organization, leaders are necessary at all levels, and the real leader may shift with changing situations.

Handy's discussion of the leadership of a rowing team provides insight. A former Olympic oarsman is quoted as saying, "How do you think we could go backward so fast without communication, steered by this little fellow in the stern, if we didn't know each other very well, didn't have total confidence to do our jobs, and a shared commitment—almost a passion—for the same goal?" This same person said:

> Manager . . . is a low status title in organizations of colleagues. [The leader] depends [on the situation]. . . . When we are racing, it is the little chap who is steering . . . and the stroke, who sets the standard for all of us . . . [and] off the river, it's the captain of the crew, who selects us, bonds us together, builds our commitment to our goal and our dedication. Lastly, in training there is our coach, who is undoubtedly the main influence on our work. (1995, 47–48)

Handy concluded, "A rowing crew . . . has to be based on trust if it is to have any chance of success" (48). It is also obvious from this example that even this small organization has several people who fit the label of "leader," depending on the situation.

This ideal, of a group working together, attempting to achieve a common goal, with different individuals taking charge as their characteristics best fit them to leadership of changing situations, can only occur when trust exists. Empowering employees who mistrust their boss or the people with whom they work is a waste of time and resources. But empowered employees who have a common set of values, a common goal, and who trust the people around them can become a powerful force for a company.

Businesses in the industrialized world are moving toward the development of knowledge-based learning organizations (Bartlett and Ghoshal 1995; Senge 1990; Zand 1997). Firms like GE and Motorola operate educational facilities that rival those of some universities. Diminishing in importance are the companies that treat employees as machine-like factors of production, with their predictable, controllable "organization man" (Whyte 1956) as the prototypical employee. "The new deal" between businesses and their employees requires participation and creativity at all levels (O'Reilly and Wyatt 1994). The new organization requires a leader, not just a manager.

The knowledge- and learning-based company must tap the creativity and intelligence of all employees and managers. A major problem in achieving this goal lies in the very nature of knowledge and creativity. Unlike capital assets, knowledge and creativity are intangible, unobservable, and unique to individuals. They can be withheld by people who appear to be actively participating in a task and diligently performing their job. Fear, frustration with bureaucracy, or the smallest emotional reaction to a perceived slight by management or by fellow employees can cause the withholding of employee contributions. Leadership, not power-based bureaucracy, is needed to release individuals' creativity and apply their knowledge. Mutual trust is clearly necessary to reduce fear, remove bureaucratic frustrations, and energize employees to fulfill the organization's purpose.

How do the five ethical factors needed for trust-building influence the leader's task? Through behavior exhibiting these five factors, a leader can unleash employees' potential. Fairness and respect require the leader to be empathetic. An empathetic leader considers the impact of an action on others (Goleman 1998). Only by exhibiting respect for other individuals can a leader adequately apply the tenets of fairness and justice to the situation. Honesty and openness are necessary for employees to capture the information they need and to apply their knowledge and creativity. Bartlett and Ghoshal (1995, 140) concluded that "top management's principal challenge is . . . to create an environment in which people can exploit information more effectively." That challenge cannot be met without the open and honest availability of information. Finally, consistent promise-keeping produces trust, decreases fear, and increases the likelihood that employees will use their knowledge and creativity to help the company.

Core Values and Integrated Goals

A people-oriented leadership philosophy lacks the structure and formal controls prevalent in a bureaucratic, hierarchical, power-based approach to governance. As with the rowing team example, all the employees in a people-oriented company must have the same clear, detailed understanding of its goals in order to work toward them in a fully integrated manner. Further, employees must understand why those goals are important; goals give employees a focus for applying their knowledge and creativity, thus maximizing the impact of the work. Bartlett and Ghoshal (1995, 138) stated, "Corporate leaders found that when people in the organization clearly understand corporate objectives, they measure their own performance against those objectives." Freeing empowered employees, who clearly understand what they are being asked to achieve to do their job, can be more effective than demanding that the same individuals carry out the plans of managers who are not on the front lines.

People-oriented leadership requires constant attention to the communication of business goals in order to present an integrated picture to employees. A personal approach seems to work best in achieving this end. GE's Jack Welch stated in an interview, "Above all else . . . good leaders are open. They go up, down, and around the organization to reach people. . . . They're informal. They're straight with people. They make a religion out of being accessible. They never get bored telling their story. Real communication takes countless hours of eyeball-to-eyeball, back and forth. It means more listening than talking. . . . It must be absolutely relentless" (Tichy and Charan 1989, 113). Of course, effective open and personal communications of this type require trust.

Core values operate as a primary guide and control for the process. These values give definition to a business, and what they define is the very ethos or character of the business. In a people-oriented business, top leaders must create an environment or culture in which all managers and employees understand their role and are self-monitoring. These leaders must constantly work to understand and manage the corporate value system.

What is required to achieve such an acculturation of norms and core values? Certainly, initial indoctrination into the firm's history, culture, and values is needed, but indoctrination and training must be believable when the employee is on the job. All the words and actions of such programs mean little if the words do not match the observed behavior found in the workplace. It is important to hire people who exhibit ethical values in their relations with others.

Another issue important to managing the values and culture of a people-oriented, learning organization concerns failure and punishment. Failure can, and must be allowed to, occur in people-oriented companies. If creative risk-taking is desired from employees, they will undoubtedly fail on occasion. The reaction to failure must not be punishment, but should be learning. An overt effort must be made to understand the causes of a failure and how it could have been prevented. That approach allows employees to learn and grow. Punishment is restricted to breaches of trust—a failure to uphold company values. Then, the message ought to be loud, clear, and severe, so that the company's employees understand that breaking trust is not tolerated. It is even desirable that the severe treatment of those who break trust become part of the company's folklore.

Fair Process

Moral philosophers have debated and explicated many concepts of justice, usually defined in terms of fairness. (For a more detailed philosophical discussion of justice, see Beauchamp 1991, 340–382.) These concepts can be split into two classifications—distributive justice and procedural justice. Distributive justice is consequential, or outcome-related, while procedural justice is focused on fair process. This discussion is limited to the ideas of procedural justice because of its particular relevance to building trust. The most relevant form of procedural justice in business is "imperfect procedural justice" (Rawls 1971, 84–86).

Imperfect procedural justice occurs when every reasonable attempt is made to design procedures that will produce a fair outcome, but the goal is impossible to achieve. The U.S. criminal justice system is an example of this form. The system is an attempt to produce fair outcomes, but published cases in which the system fails are easy to find. Management practices and the company's policies, procedures, and rules cannot always be expected to produce fair outcomes. The occasional unfair outcome is received more willingly by employees when they are involved in the process. When employees are not involved, they feel that "the system" has made them a victim, and in those cases, trust becomes a victim as well.

The emotional reaction to perceived unfairness can be powerful. A substantial amount of research suggests that most people use fairness and justice to judge whether an action is ethical (Robin, Reidenbach, and Babin 1997). In a person-oriented, knowledge-based business, both fair process and fair outcome are important, but of the two, fair process may be somewhat more important to trust-building when employees are involved. Further, the perception, as well as the reality, of fairness must be addressed by leaders at all levels of an organization in order to maintain trust. Trust is particularly fragile in periods of change, so attention to the perception and reality of fair process must be given special attention during these periods.

Beyond Employees to Other Stakeholders

Thus far, the thrust of the discussion has focused on trust links with employees. But, as noted earlier, if employees do not trust the company, it would be very difficult to build trust links with any of the other stakeholder groups.

Fortunately, building and maintaining trust links with other stakeholders also requires the same characteristics of leadership, commitment to core values, and fair processes. An empathic understanding of each group of stakeholders is necessary for respect and for fair treatment of the group; values of honesty, openness, and promise-keeping make company representatives believable; and all of these characteristics build trust. Trust, in turn, makes the company more effective and efficient in its interactions with any of the stakeholder groups. It is perhaps important to note that while trust is required in people-oriented organizations, leaders need not be "liked" by those who work for them (Zand 1997; O'Reilly 1994).

The example of buyers can be used to illustrate how leadership, core values, and fair processes are needed to build trust with other stakeholders. More than typical marketing research is necessary to fully understand what buyers expect from an exchange with the company. Studying buyers at the point of exchange, or even questioning them about their preferences, may not produce an adequate understanding about important features that are difficult for the purchaser to evaluate. Understanding and creative leadership are necessary to discover buyer expectations that they themselves may not even be able to vocalize. Digging deeper for such understanding shows respect for the buyer. Only with that understanding can a mix of products, services, distribution, and promotion be created and priced that produces fair outcomes for both buyer and seller. And since buyers desire change, the task is never-ending.

The core values of many companies contain a concern for the customer (Robin et al. 1989). For Johnson & Johnson, customers come first in its famous hierarchical credo: "We believe our first responsibility is to the doctors, nurses and patients, to mothers and fathers and all others who use our products and services. In meeting their needs everything we do must be of high quality. We must constantly strive to reduce our costs in order to maintain reasonable prices. Customers' orders must be serviced promptly and accurately. Our suppliers and distributors must have an opportunity to make a fair profit" (the Johnson & Johnson credo can be found at www.jnj.com). Very few companies actually follow the core values that are stated in their credo as Johnson & Johnson does. These core values provide real and substantial guidance for the distant subsidiaries of this highly decentralized company, and the approach seems to be very successful (O'Reilly 1994).

When problems arise with customers, fair processes must be in place to deal with their concerns. Those processes must include an opportunity for customers to be heard. Fair outcomes are not always enough to satisfy customers who believe they have been treated unfairly; allowing customers to present their case usually helps.

As with employees and customers, leadership, core values, and fair processes are useful for building trust links with other stakeholder groups. Building trust with stakeholders is possible without these factors, but without them the results are not likely to be consistent.

Trust-Building and Ethics

The five ethical trust-building factors would certainly be considered components of goodwill toward stakeholders. Indeed, these five factors are ethical requirements and are a necessary part of the trust-building process. However, a question remains as to whether the application of these five factors to stakeholder relations is sufficient for a company to be considered ethical. Is a company required to do more to be considered ethical? Certainly, a company behaving according to those five factors with all of the groups it interacts with would be considered more ethical than one that does not behave according to the factors. But is that behavior enough?

Behavior of an Ethical Company

The earlier discussion of society's ethical expectations for business can aid in understanding the meaning of an "ethical company." The discussion explained that an ethical society wants business to pursue its capitalistic objectives, subject to satisfying society's broader ethical objectives. Those broader objectives are intended to provide an environment where members of society have an opportunity (not a guarantee) to live well-measured and happy lives.

One function the ethical society must provide is economic, and the appropriate model is capitalism. Thus, an ethical company is one that efficiently and effectively fulfills its capitalistic objectives in a manner that does not abuse the broader objectives of an ethical society. If this goal is accomplished, the company has achieved sufficiency in ethical behavior. Additional ethical acts may be possible, and they should be applauded when they occur, but the requirements for sufficiency provide the minimum baseline for an ethical company.

The concept of "stakeholders" has evolved to mean any individual or group that has a stake in the company's actions. Stakeholders can benefit or be harmed by those actions. Ethical concerns develop when a company's interaction with its stakeholders produces harm for them. This does not mean that any company's action producing harm for a stakeholder is unethical. It simply means that when unethical action by a company occurs, it involves harm to a stakeholder. Thus, it may be ethically acceptable to close a plant, putting many employees out of work, if the vagaries of business demand it. However, it would be unethical not to treat those same employees with respect throughout the closing process.

Trust-Building and Ethical Relations with Society and Organizations

Society benefits when companies efficiently and effectively perform the economic function in a capitalistic setting since economic prosperity follows such behavior. However, society can also be harmed, for example, when companies pollute the environment excessively. Similarly, other organizations and individuals can benefit, or be harmed, by a company's actions.

There is a hierarchy that, in addition to helping organize discussions about a company's relationships with its stakeholders, defines levels of power. At the top, society defines, directs, and constrains business behavior through laws and regulations, and it is in the primary power position. Of course, an abusive use of this power by society is just as unethical as is an abuse of power by a company. However, as noted earlier, a company's ethical relationship with society is substantially determined by what an ethical society expects from business.

Relationships with other organizations can vary in power differentials, but one of the most important of these relationships is that which exists with competitors. The role of an ethical company with respect to its competitors is to compete in the most efficient and effective manner that it can, thus maintaining the competitiveness of the market. That is, it would be unethical for a company to seriously reduce the competitiveness of the market by attempting to create a monopoly or by any other artificial means (Robin and Sawyer 1998). Within that charge, the five ethical factors apply. Competitors should be able to trust the ethical company to compete fairly, provide the respect due all humans, be honest, truthful, and open without giving away any trade secrets, and consistently keep promises and contracts. However, there is nothing unethical about being a tough competitor. Indeed, that type of behavior is necessary to maintain the efficiency and effectiveness of the capitalistic system.

Suppliers and channel members are stakeholders that are organizations. Trust is particularly important for relationships with these stakeholders. For that reason, a company must carefully behave according to the five ethical factors when interacting with them. But once again, being a tough, efficient, and effective competitor is not unethical, per se.

The most vulnerable stakeholders are individuals—singularly or artificially grouped. While individuals are not powerless, they are often in the most vulnerable position to become victims of unethical behavior.

Trust-Building and Ethical Relationships with Individual Stakeholders

Two groups of individual stakeholders are of special importance—customers and employees. Each group must trust a company to behave fairly on issues important to it because it often has little or no information about those issues. In addition, these stakeholder groups may also lack the desire, expertise, or capacity to adequately evaluate available important information and instead place their trust in the company to treat them fairly.

Customers

There is often a substantial difference between the knowledge about product or service characteristics that customers possess compared to the knowledge possessed by a providing company. The company typically lacks complete information but is much closer to the total knowledge end of the continuum than are customers. Customers are seldom totally ignorant about product or service characteristics potentially important to them, but decisions on many purchases are made with much less than complete information. Customers may have relatively more information about regularly purchased products and services, but even then, information is less than complete. For example, many consumers understand that fluoride is the primary decay preventative in toothpaste, but they may not understand how it works, how well it works, or how it interacts with other ingredients like whitening agents. Similarly, most consumers will have some information about food nutrition but far less than is necessary to plan truly balanced nutritional meals.

It is difficult to fault customers for not seeking such information and applying it judiciously, given their time and energy constraints. A weekly shopping trip for groceries could be extended by several hours if a consumer attempted to apply full nutritional information and plan meals accordingly. Few families today have the time or energy to perform complete nutritional shopping and full planning of meals.

The problem is greatly exacerbated when the product or service is complex and/or infrequently purchased. Thus, customers who purchase an automobile, computer, or financial service may be much closer to total ignorance than when they buy toothpaste or food products. Since a company's knowledge of complex products and services is still likely to be high, the knowledge gap is larger than for less-complex products and services.

How do customers handle the knowledge gap? Many customers give little or no thought to important issues, unless and until a problem occurs. In a very important sense, they trust companies to do them no harm. That expectation does not mean they expect supererogatory behavior from companies. For example, they may understand that hot dogs contain a lot of fat. However, customers would not expect rat droppings in their hot dogs (as occurred in one company's product), even if they could not detect this contamination through personal examination. They trust hot dog manufacturers to prevent such contaminants from occurring, and if they discover a breach of trust, the reaction is usually disastrous for the manufacturer.

Similarly, customers do not expect automobiles to be totally safe in all circumstances (whatever that might mean), but they definitely do not expect cars to burst into flames when hit from the rear at relatively low speeds. That situation would be considered a breach of trust as well as unethical. An even stronger negative reaction from customers can be expected if they discover that this problem could be fixed with a comparatively small expenditure, as in the case of the Ford Pinto (cf. Gioia 1992).

Maintaining trust links with customers requires that a company satisfy the five ethical factors. Abuse of the knowledge gap and concomitant trust that exists between the company and its customers frequently offers the opportunity for short-term company gains. Cases even exist where breaking trust with customers has produced profitable outcomes for comparatively long periods of time. However, the ethical company must honor that trust and act accordingly. As noted, fair and just treatment of the customer does not require supererogatory acts. It does, however, require caring about the customer in a manner that would satisfy most reasonable people. Further, ethical behavior requires respecting customers as individuals, being honest and truthful, being open, and keeping promises. Of course, these are the same requirements for building and maintaining trust links with customers, so trust-building and ethics in relations with customers are a good match.

Employees

Employees represent another vulnerable stakeholder group because they also experience a knowledge gap. This gap has two facets. One facet consists of activities occurring within or to a company that can have an impact on an employee's job. The second consists of the complex, ambiguous, poorly defined situations in which employees find themselves without knowing what the company expects from them. While employees want a reasonable level of information, they do not usually want full and complete disclosure of company actions, because the details would overwhelm them. Like customers, employees must trust employers not to take advantage of them when they do not have complete information. Unfortunately, even the information employees do desire is often not available.

With respect to the first facet of the employee knowledge gap, there is ample evidence that employees become frustrated and suspicious of company motives if there is a lack of information from top management. For example, one of the most important issues to workers who were polled by Louis Harris and Associates and reported by Farnham (1989, 57) was the need for "closer, more honest, communications between employees and senior management." Farnham suggested that top management "explain things— personally . . . 97 percent of the CEO's surveyed believed communicating with employees has a positive impact on job satisfaction, and 79 percent think it benefits the bottom line, [but] only 22 percent do it weekly or more often." Farnham concluded, "When in doubt, be open," (70) and pointed to a situation at DuPont to illustrate the point. DuPont reduced its work force by 37,000 employees from 1982 to 1989, but continued to receive considerable loyalty and commitment by being open with its employees. The company provided bad news as well as good news and gave as much advance notice to its employees as possible.

The second facet of the employee knowledge gap exists when complex, ambiguous, and poorly defined ethical situations occur. Faced with such situations, employees must decide what action the company expects from them. While very few managers would overtly tell their employees to behave illegally or unethically, one approach for encouraging unethical behavior, whether intended or not, is to apply pressure for short-run performance in an environment where there is little opportunity to achieve those goals in an ethical manner (Gellerman 1986, 87–88; Paine 1994, 107–108). Without specific ethical guidance, some employees are likely to behave unethically. Ideally, ethical guidance should be part of the core values of the company's culture and part of employees' jobs. Without guidance, and particularly if the company is seen rewarding unethical behavior, trust in the company's willingness to treat employees fairly and with respect is diminished.

Will a reasonable, continuous attempt by a company to build trust links with its stakeholders be sufficient to meet its ethical obligations to society? The evidence seems to suggest that such an attempt would meet the expectations of an ethical society and, therefore, the approach would be sufficient. Individual companies may want to go beyond "sufficient" in their behavior, and when they do, their behavior should be applauded. However, the approach suggested here seems to satisfy the basic requirements for an ethical company.

Trust-building is not the only approach for becoming an ethical company. It seems possible for companies to satisfy the demands of an ethical society without committing to trust-building. However, trust-building provides an efficient and effective method for synergistically achieving the dual goals of ethics and profits.

Trust-Building and Profits

A decline in trustworthiness at the individual and organizational levels imposes a type of tax on economic activity in society. This tax is paid to formal contract writers and lawyers. Economic efficiency is also impaired in this environment due to the time and energy required to complete a transaction. Thus, conditions of low trust at the individual and organizational levels harm a society's economic system. A society's legal system can never replace trust in lower-level interactions, and when the law becomes the primary basis for trust, the result is generally harmful to business transactions.

When companies do not treat stakeholders fairly and with respect, the legal system of society is the stakeholders' primary recourse. At the beginning of the twentieth century in the United States, very little legislation directing or constraining business activities existed. At the close of the twentieth century, legislation protecting society from monopolistic activities, protecting the environment, protecting consumers, protecting employees, and protecting other stakeholders is substantial. Legislation exists because companies broke trust with their stakeholder groups, and the legislation adds costs and reduces profits for all businesses—even those that behave ethically. Much of this legislation would not be necessary if all companies treated their stakeholders respectfully and fairly.

The positive benefits to society from establishing trust links are also apparent. Established trust links create social capital because the conduct of business costs less when trust exists (Fukuyama 1995). Nobel laureate Kenneth Arrow (1974, 23) noted, "Trust is an important lubricant of a social system. It is extremely efficient; it saves a lot of trouble to have a fair degree of reliance on other people's word. . . . Trust and similar values, loyalty and truth-telling, have real, practical, economic value; they increase the efficiency of the system." For that reason alone, an ethical society would expect its organizations to work on trust-building. Additionally, though, efficient societal economic systems provide the opportunity for greater company profitability.

Profit Implications of Building Trust Links with Individual Stakeholders

The two most important individual stakeholders are customers and employees. Both are vulnerable because they often lack information potentially important to them. This vulnerability places the company in a position of power, and these stakeholders must trust the company not to abuse that power. There are often opportunities for short-term company gains at the expense of individual stakeholders.

Customers

As was mentioned earlier, there is usually a significant knowledge gap between a company and its customers about things potentially important to customers. Customers usually fill that gap by trusting the company. Specifically, customers trust the company to treat them fairly and with respect, and not to abuse the company's knowledge advantage. To honor the trust placed in them, the company should use its knowledge advantage as if it or a manager's family was the customer. Another approach is to ask top management if it would feel comfortable with its actions if those actions were reported in the news media. Both of these approaches fit the "reasonable and rational stakeholder" test.

It is often possible for a company to take advantage of the knowledge gap for short-term gain. Further, it is sometimes possible for the company to extend its financial advantage for fairly long periods of time, because some products and services are difficult to evaluate, even after the purchase. For example, buyers may have a difficult time evaluating the safety or expected life of an automobile, even after using it for several years. Is an automobile unreasonably dangerous? No automobile is perfectly safe, nor do customers expect them to be. But, as in the case of the Ford Pinto, neither do customers expect the company to forgo repairing a potentially deadly flaw when the cost is minimal.

Other companies have also abused the knowledge gap. For example, the Sears Auto Centers case has become a classic. Customers who brought their cars in for service or repair trusted the expertise of the company about necessary service and legitimate preventive maintenance. Sears Auto Centers abused this customer trust by recommending that unnecessary work be done. When the abuse was discovered, the direct cost of the resulting court settlement was estimated to be $60 million (Paine 1994, 108). However, the long-term harm to Sears's reputation may have been even more damaging. Customers whose trust was abused are likely to have long memories.

Are there examples of companies that have taken advantage of the knowledge gap and were never discovered? Undoubtedly, there are. Unfortunately, these examples never find their way to print and thus cannot be cited here. The author's view of companies that use their power of the knowledge gap to take advantage of their customers' trust can be illustrated with an analogy.

The company is playing a game like Russian roulette. The odds of a bullet appearing in the chamber could even be changed to, say, 50 to 1. But even at those odds, what gains would make the game worthwhile? In technical terms, the expected cost to a company that gets caught will usually far outweigh the expected gain from exploiting customers.

On the positive side, customers look for companies they can trust. Companies that are fair and show respect for their customers can successfully compete, even in markets where competitors are larger or where their products or services are no better than those of competitors.

Employees

When employees do not trust the company to show respect and be fair, several negatives occur. There is a reduction in the sense of community on the job, and employees feel they must protect themselves and their jobs. Loyalty to the company is reduced; fear reduces the willingness of employees to take risks; group effectiveness is reduced; and the possibility for meaningful employee empowerment is essentially eliminated. On the company's side, the span of management is smaller (fewer employees per manager), and more policies, procedures, and rules and hence more bureaucracy are necessary. And of course, poorer relations exist with unions and employees.

Farnham (1989) believed that the company-employee trust gap is large, and in a follow-up article, Stewart (1996, 138) agreed: "That gap is worse than ever." Farnham suggested that several negative effects result from the trust gap, including employee cynicism about whether management understands or cares about employees or their opinions. He also concluded that there is really very little common ground between the average worker and top management, a situation that tends to produce a disconnect and cynicism between the two. The result is that top management is isolated and does not hear what it needs to hear "about markets, competitors, problems, and opportunities" (Farnham 1989, 62). Moreover, "If management seems arrogant and does not treat employees fairly, employees start placing themselves ahead of the company, and some may go to extremes 'to balance the books'—even sabotage" (66).

Farnham also provided examples in which applying the tenets of trust, fairness, and a basic respect for the individual has worked to the advantage of companies. His examples included the acknowledgments of Preston Trucking and Southwest Airlines that practicing fairness and respect led to company loyalty, which produced employee behavior above and beyond the norm. Thus, without trust, costs typically go up and efficiency often goes down; but with trust, costs are likely to go down and efficiency usually goes up.

Results comparing the trust-based, people-oriented approach with the still popular "strategy-structure-systems" approach are presented in Bartlett and Ghoshal (1995). Two companies, Norton and 3M, were used as examples of how the two approaches compare in effectiveness. After World War II, Norton and 3M were approximately the same size, but "by the mid-1980's, 3M was reporting sales eight times those of its old competitor" (Bartlett and Ghoshal 1995, 133).

Norton was an early adopter of strategies such as profit impact of market strategies (PIMS) and the Boston Consulting Group's growth/share matrix. It also used traditional planning and control techniques. However, with all of these state-of-the-art management approaches, diversification efforts and profits were not very good. Alternatively, 3M adopted a people-centered, entrepreneurial model, and it was considerably later than Norton in adopting a strategic planning system. 3M's diversification and profitability efforts were very successful over the same period, and it continues to be a strong, well-respected company. Norton, on the other hand, was absorbed by the French company Compagnie de Saint-Gobain in 1990. 3M's philosophy is described thus: "Senior management's primary role is to create an internal environment in which people understand and value our way of operating. . . . Our job is . . . supporting individual initiative while breaking down bureaucracy and cynicism. It all depends on developing a *personal trust relationship* between those at the top and those at lower levels" (Bartlett and Ghoshal 1995, 133, emphasis added).

The message seems clear. Building trust with stakeholders can help profitability as well as facilitate ethical behavior. Using trust links in business may not be the only approach for making profits, but it certainly has the potential for achieving that objective.

Conclusion

Businesses must follow the capitalistic model and do everything they can to be tough, efficient competitors in an open market. However, businesses must simultaneously attempt to satisfy the goals of an ethical society. This chapter offers an approach for melding the mission of ethics and the mission of capitalism and provides new directions for business ethics theory, practice, and research. By following the guidelines set forth in the chapter, a business can be more successful and more competitive by being ethical than by any other approach.

12

Denial and Leadership in Business Ethics Education

Diane L. Swanson and William C. Frederick

Corporate reputations are under siege, especially in the United States, where public outrage over the proliferation of Enron-like scandals has turned into a general distrust of business. The cynicism involves a growing awareness that business schools are at least partly to blame for the precipitous decline in corporate goodwill. The realization is that business schools are falling short of educating future managers in their legal and ethical responsibilities to society (Hindo 2002; Swanson and Frederick 2003b). Business education is truly at a crossroads (Waddock 2003). Yet the nation's business school deans as a group have had little to say about the crisis in public confidence. In fact, the silence has been deafening.

To help fill this void, we launched Campaign AACSB as a large-scale, collective effort to upgrade and strengthen ethics accreditation standards in U.S. business schools (Moline 2002). As part of this endeavor, large numbers of professors who teach business ethics, management practitioners, and corporate ethics officers endorsed an open letter to the Association to Advance Collegiate Schools of Business (AACSB), the agency that accredits business degree programs, written by Professor Duane Windsor of Rice University. Professor Windsor's letter called for at least one ethics course to be required as a condition for AACSB accreditation (Windsor 2002). The flood of petitions hit the agency in fall 2002 when the earthquakes of corporate scandals still shook America. Amid the aftershocks, AACSB officials were quietly drafting new standards that would influence management education for decades to come. These officials had a unique opportunity to upgrade ethics education at a critical juncture in history. Unfortunately, they failed to

222

do so. Like many business school deans, AACSB officials have resisted recognizing the importance of ethics education (Benner 2002).

This denial is firmly rooted in a long-standing tradition of sidestepping ethics in business school curricula. Fortunately, the situation is not totally grim, as some schools have moved ahead of the pack with ethics coverage that surpasses weak accrediting standards. We will argue that constituents of business education need to support these efforts and encourage lagging schools to catch up. Otherwise, the nation's future managers will continue to get mixed messages about the significance of ethics in practice. As things stand now, the paucity of ethics in business school curricula speaks the loudest.

Denying Ethics in Curricula

A common misunderstanding fuels the denial of business ethics education. Those who oppose teaching ethics to business students usually have a narrow definition of ethics in mind, believing it to be impractical and difficult to apply on the job. To them, ethics refers to a strictly philosophical approach, where one discusses rights, justice, and fairness in an abstract way, without relating them to any one context such as a business firm. But those who advocate ethics education have a more generic definition in mind, reasoning that business ethics involves any right or wrong actions taken by corporations. It follows that students need to be made aware of the many times they will face such situations when they become managers. Indeed, experienced managers know that these right-wrong factors, or normative issues, are always present, especially in a post-Enron environment.

So ethics in this broader, contextual, practical sense covers such areas as business law (especially the new Sarbanes-Oxley Act), public policy (new Securities and Exchange Commission guidelines), organizational ethics (e.g., corporate governance), environmentalism (sustainable business practices), and corporate social responsibility (obligations to community and stakeholders) (Swanson and Frederick 2003a, b). Many professors are trained to teach ethics from this perspective and scores of textbooks are available. Moreover, several professional associations promote this approach, including the Society for Business Ethics, the International Association of Business and Society, and two divisions of the Academy of Management: the Social Issues in Management division and the Organizations and Natural Environment division.

Instead of taking advantage of this wealth of available expertise by mandating that business schools require at least one such ethics course as a condition for accreditation, AACSB deans voted in April 2003 to maintain a doctrine of curriculum flexibility. This means that each business school is allowed to set its own ethics requirements in accordance with each school's mission statement. While this policy may sound good in theory, it effectively absolves schools from requiring any courses in ethics. Deans can claim that ethics is incorporated into the overall curriculum, meaning that professors in such disciplines as marketing, finance, operations management, accounting, and strategic management can be tasked to include ethics in mainstream courses. However, these professors may find it burdensome to integrate well-developed variants of ethics across a curriculum, particularly given their understandable desire to teach their own areas of expertise first and foremost.

As long as AACSB does not stipulate a required course in ethics, business school deans facing curriculum battles can point to this position as an excuse to cater to faculty vying for other coursework. When this happens—and it happens a lot, given faculty skirmishes over a crowded curriculum—then students may not take even one ethics course before graduating from undergraduate business and master of business administration (MBA) programs. The result is a scattershot approach to ethics, which only a stand-alone, mandated course can bring back into focus. Whether titled Business Ethics, Business, Government, Society, Corporate Citizenship, or The Social Environment of Business, such coursework lays out ethical issues cohesively. Schools not requiring this kind of course risk woefully inadequate coverage of the subject.

Many have chosen just that. After all, the costs have not been high, since the accrediting agency will rubber-stamp the weaker approach. This absence of ethics courses has been one of the best-kept secrets in business schools to date. But lately some editors and reporters have discovered interesting facts. In an article aptly titled "It's a Heckuva Time to Be Dropping Business Ethics Courses," Kelly identified several schools that have participated in the well-recognized pastime of downsizing ethics courses, even in the wake of corporate scandals (Kelly 2002). The *Virginian-Pilot* weighed in by reporting that half of Virginia's eighteen MBA programs do not require students to take an ethics course (Walzer 2003). A study by the Aspen/ World Institute indicates similar ambivalence nationally in that only 45 percent of the schools polled had requisite courses in areas of ethics, corporate social responsibility, or environmental sustainability (Schneider 2003). A narrower survey of the top thirteen U.S. business schools reveals that only 23 percent require a course in ethics, whereas 30 percent stipulate a course in which ethics is combined with another subject. The clincher is that nearly half (46 percent) of these top schools offer only an ethics elective, which equates to no requirement at all (Mac Lean and Litzky 2003). AACSB reports that only one-third of accredited programs offer an ethics course (Derocher 2004). Given this state of affairs, schools with strong coverage deserve special applause. After all, they could get AACSB's coveted stamp of approval by doing far less.

To be fair, AACSB officials have included ethics in a list of content areas for schools seeking accreditation. They have also added some ethics material to AACSB's Web site, but only after the flood of previously mentioned petitions prompted media coverage and heated debate on scholarly discussion lists. But the professors and business practitioners who wrote to AACSB wanted more than mere Web site window dressing. And many were less than thrilled with the boilerplate responses they received from AACSB, which indicated that accrediting officials were closing ranks around the doctrine of flexibility. Deciphered, this means that AACSB can give its stamp of approval to the most superficial coverage of ethics in MBA and undergraduate degree programs, such as the promise that ethics will be mentioned in a few courses or condensed into a two-week noncredit seminar for new students. When asked if ethics can be adequately covered this way, Ray Hilgert, emeritus professor of management and industrial relations at Washington University's Olin School of Business, said: "If you believe it's integrated in all the courses, then I'm willing to offer you the Brooklyn Bridge" (Nicklaus 2002).

What is the bottom line? Some students will get an ethics course but many will not. AACSB president John Fernandes, who presided over the decision in 2003 to approve weak ethics standards, defended this outcome: "We still believe that schools should have the ability to determine whether they want to have a single course or to integrate ethics throughout the curriculum" (Mangan 2003). Incoming AACSB president Carolyn Woo echoed this sentiment, declaring that dedicating a course to ethics would be equivalent to letting it become a ghetto (Nicklaus 2002). Her statement of allegiance to AACSB policy is particularly puzzling, given that business ethics courses are required at the Mendoza School of Business at Notre Dame University, where Woo is dean. We doubt seriously that these courses, which include Conceptual Foundations in Business Ethics, have ghetto status under Woo's administration. This rather contradictory representation by a top-ranked AACSB official demonstrates how ethics gets mired in a netherworld between denial and leadership. Instead of clarifying the issue, AACSB officials neatly sidestepped it, refusing to meet even informally with Campaign AACSB representatives at the AACSB annual meeting in April 2003 (Swanson and Frederick 2003a). If they had agreed to such a meeting, Campaign AACSB endorsers would have reiterated, yet again, that ethics education is not an either-or proposition. Integration of ethics into other courses is highly desirable but only if it complements foundational coursework like that required at the Mendoza School. In short, ethics needs to be delivered holistically, not piecemeal.

Trapped in denial, the nation's official accreditor, AACSB, put the cart before the horse fixating on flexibility while framing the issue as a false dichotomy. All the while, accrediting officials ignored reports from experienced professors that the experimental (flexible) approach to ethics had been a huge failure. These knowledgeable academics wrote en masse to AACSB officials, attesting that there is no substitute for a stand-alone course delivered by faculty trained in applying ethics to areas of management, including stakeholder relations, crisis management, environmental stewardship, leadership, corporate culture, law, government regulation, and public policy. The message was that this kind of course adds up to something for students.

In the end, member deans voted privately and without the benefit of public discourse to continue inadequate standards for ethics education. By doing so, they did our nation a great disservice and left a vacuum that other constituents will need to fill if business education is to be reclaimed for social purposes. We will return to this point after examining the culture that perpetuates the denial of ethics education in business schools.

Perpetuating Denial in Business Schools

In the months following the outbreak of corporate scandals, many press agents contacted us about business ethics education and Campaign AACSB. During these conversations, which included radio talk shows, many people were surprised to hear that ethics courses even existed. Many mused, "Isn't business ethics an oxymoron?" This response was revealing, given that the subject at hand was corporate misconduct and criminality. It seems that the public recognizes a lack of business ethics readily enough but not the need for educational efforts aimed at promoting more responsible corporate behavior. This imbalance can be traced to years of management education that has maintained a general confusion about the role of business in society by keeping ethics at bay instead of making it the cornerstone of degree programs.

On the one hand, people are all too aware of the devastation wrought by unethical corporate conduct. On the other, they have not heard decisive support for ethics education from business school corridors. Hence, it is all too easy for them to conclude that business ethics must be a contradiction in terms. Several mutually reinforcing dynamics perpetuate this confusion as well as the vacuum in business school leadership.

Dynamic #1: Business school curricula have historically reflected the value-free approach of standard economics.

The idea that business ethics is an oxymoron stems from the artificial fact-value dichotomy customary to the neoclassical economics that pervades business education. In schizophrenic fashion, this dichotomy separates descriptive and normative realms so that "what is" and "what should be" are viewed as different domains of human experience. The corollary, that managers' decisions are value-free, pervades the ideological foundation of business schools, especially in finance and strategy courses, essentially offshoots of economic theory. One has only to consider the widespread impacts of management decisions on stakeholder communities and the natural environment to grasp that this foundation is built on sand (Waddock 2003). Even so, management education continues to convey the illusion of value-free decision making and ignores its far-reaching dysfunctional consequences (Klein 1998; Orlitzky and Swanson 2002). Of these consequences, the commingling of amoral economics with narrowly functional coursework has fragmented knowledge and fostered an inability and unwillingness to comprehend system-wide consequences of decisions and actions (Waddock 2003).

AACSB could have ameliorated this dangerously myopic education by mandating ethics as a required course. Instead, the association, demonstrating that it is part of the problem, openly excluded ethics from the list of "traditional business subjects" in its new accrediting document (Association to Advance Collegiate Schools of Business 2003):

> For the purpose of determining inclusion in AACSB accreditation, the following will be considered "traditional business subjects": Accounting, Business Law, Decision Sciences, Finance (including Insurance, Real Estate and Banking), Human Resources, Management, Management Information Systems, Management Science, Marketing, Operations Management, Organizational Behavior, Organizational Development, Strategic Management, Supply Chain Management (including Transportation and Logistics), and Technology Management.

That a course on business, government and society or related course coverage is omitted from this litany of "traditional business subjects" can only be deemed a deliberate oversight, since Campaign AACSB endorsers specifically pointed to such as course as a logical vehicle for conveying the ethical dimensions of business as a social institution. AACSB's response of exclusion is meant to reinforce the prerogative of value-free coursework immunized from ethics. The inoculation extends the life of a dogma that should have expired long ago. Meanwhile, ethics education risks extinction in many quarters.

Dynamic #2: Absent countervailing pressure from AACSB, ethics education across business schools is uneven, inconsistent, and tenuous.

As Duane Windsor noted in his open letter to AACSB, the fragility of
ethics coursework was somewhat ameliorated by the accreditation standards of the early 1970s, which plainly pointed business schools in the
direction of some kind of required course in business and society. As a
result, business and society coursework started to flourish, spurred by the
release of an influential position paper prepared by the Governance Committee of the Social Issues in Management (SIM) Division of the Academy
of Management, which provided the criteria for such coverage (Frederick
1977). But the gains were not to last. In the early 1990s, AACSB switched
to mission-driven, more flexible standards, and ethics coursework started
to dwindle (Swanson and Frederick 2003b). Interestingly enough, another
policy change occurred around the same time. The U.S. Department of
Higher Education stopped recognizing AACSB as an accrediting agency.
Although we have talked with public policy makers about this issue, it is
not clear to us why AACSB lost government recognition (or even what that
recognition meant to begin with). But the trend to "flexify" ethics shortly
thereafter deserves further investigation.

Dynamic #3: The trend to flexify ethics education translates into less de-
              mand for qualified ethics professors, decreased supply, and
              less voice in curriculum decisions.

When business schools downsize ethics education, they cut back on ethics professors. Subsequently, the availability of trained ethicists declines, as
doctoral students pursue more employable degrees. This tendency exacerbates the already marginal status of ethics and prevents ethics professors
from gaining enough political influence to turn the situation around. In spite
of this dynamic, many colleges and universities, particularly those with a
religious affiliation, have maintained strong ethics coverage. Moreover, new
ethics initiatives have cropped up recently, even as other programs have been
cut back (Kelly 2002). Unfortunately, the net effect is inadequate ethics education, especially since newer initiatives might not survive. A little-known
fact is that ethics is often a casualty of attrition. When founding deans and
other senior professors leave schools, ethics often gets sacrificed to faculty
jockeying for other coursework. This is what happened at the Katz Graduate
School of Business at the University of Pittsburgh in August 2002, even as
the public reeled from the news of corporate scandals (Kelly 2002; Thomas
2002). The newly approved AACSB standards will not prevent this sorry
history from repeating itself. Indeed, the standards could make matters even
worse, given the recent signal from AACSB that anyone can teach ethics,
regardless of training.

Dynamic #4: The signal from AACSB that professors do not have to be trained
in ethics to teach it further trivializes business ethics education.

The newly approved accrediting standards suggest that ethics can be
handled haphazardly and delivered by professors who have plenty to do
without trying to learn practical applications of ethics in business. According to the *Chronicle of Higher Education,* critics are skeptical whether professors in other disciplines will devote more than just a cursory nod toward
ethics (Mangan 2003). But the problem goes deeper than that. Given the
grip of value-free economics on business school cultures, many professors
have inculcated a markedly hostile attitude toward ethics. In their hands,
ethics could be distorted, diluted, or trivialized past recognition. In cold
language, the Assurance of Learning Standards section of the AACSB eligibility document (Association to Advance Collegiate Schools of Business
2003) absolves the AACSB, stating that "[t]he standard requires use of a
systematic process for curriculum management but does not require any
specific courses in the curriculum."

The document goes on to include a list of "normal learning experiences"
for undergraduate and graduate business degree programs, including ethical
understanding and reasoning and ethical and legal responsibilities in organizations and society. Yet because the equivalent of a course on business and
society is not required by the standards, the message is that ethics can be
tacked on to other courses. This flexibility amounts to a loophole through
which ethics can be slipped out. In many cases, the politics of accreditation
almost guarantees that it will be slipped out, especially since effective oversight is lacking. AACSB representatives who visit schools to assess accreditation status find it difficult if not impossible to assess the quality of ethics
across curricula. We know of one such case, when an accrediting team pored
over a school's course offerings for an entire day, looking as if through mag-
nifying glasses for just enough ethics content to "pass" the school. The mere
listing of ethics on various syllabi does not qualify as satisfying any particular standard.

Dynamic #5: In terms of learning outcomes, AACSB's policy that ethics
can be incorporated across a curriculum invites assessment
errors favoring inadequate and inappropriate coverage.

Two such assessment errors are inevitable. The first is that ethics coverage will be assessed as sufficient when it is woefully inadequate. The second
assessment error is that ethics can be marginalized yet still pass inspection.

A bias for the second error can be found in yet another section of AACSB standards (Association to Advance Collegiate Schools of Business 2003) as an example of how ethics performance can be measured in a capstone business-strategy course:

> A school with learning goals that require students to integrate knowledge across business functional areas or to incorporate ethical considerations into decision-making may embed the measurement of accomplishment of those goals into a capstone business-strategy course. In addition to the information provided for course assessment by the projects that measure learning on these topics, the assessments provide the school with the assurance measures needed to ascertain whether the school's learning goals are being met.

If AACSB had wanted to promote ethics as a learning goal, it would have made far more sense to recommend a capstone business and society course for assessing ethical performance, not a strategy course. Despite the so-called neutral language of a "systematically flexible curriculum," AACSB continues to convey certain prejudices, such as the assumption that a capstone business strategy course is normally required, while an equivalent business and society course is not. By advocating the former as a vehicle for assessing ethics, AACSB exhibits yet another telling blind spot. As many knowledgeable and classroom-experienced professors conveyed in their letters to AACSB, strategy is typically one of the worst venues for teaching or assessing ethics. An offshoot of industrial economics, conventional strategy coursework is still marred by the myth that business decisions are value-free. Suggesting this particular course as a vehicle for assessing the efficacy of ethics strewn across a curriculum is symptomatic of more denial. In a letter to AACSB, Professor Jeff Gale of Loyola Marymount University warned of this very dilemma (Swanson and Frederick 2003a, 158–159):

> As I currently teach in the Strategic Management area, I can affirmatively say that this course is NOT the appropriate primary venue for inclusion of ethical, legal or societal concerns. I find it increasingly distressing that students coming through our business programs have so little idea of the influence of government, corporate governance, and legal standards upon what they do. While micro-economics may provide theoretical arguments as to how an ideal world "should" work, there is a dimension of how it does work in practice that only the inclusion of business and society material can provide.

This message, if read, was not taken to heart. Instead, AACSB officials thanked some of the 200 petitioners for their letters supporting a stand-alone course and then proceeded to vote their original loyalty to flexibility.

Dynamic #6: Students get the message that ethics does not matter, which translates into denying their future social responsibilities as managers.

Because AACSB has defaulted to a laissez-faire, value-free ethics posture, ethics will continue to be ignored across curricula while students get the message that it does not count. Students who imbibe this sentiment will graduate with weak moral compasses. Many will not be able to recognize ethical dilemmas in the workplace, much less reconcile or prevent them. Detractors shrug off this problem, claiming that ethics cannot be taught. But this retort begs the question, Why teach any subject? Why expose students to organizational behavior, leadership, human resource management, and other behaviorally based management skills? The answer is obvious. Students should enter their professions armed with useful knowledge and examples of sound reasoning. Detractors miss another point as well. While social and behavioral skills are partly determined early in life, there is growing evidence that they can be learned and improved on through exposure to educational programs that blend theoretical principles and practice (Rest, Narvaez, Bebeau, and Thoma 1999; Rynes et al. 2003). This would seem particularly true for business ethics, as Professor Donald Schepers of Baruch College conveyed in his letter to AACSB (Swanson and Frederick 2003a, 162):

> There is an underlying sentiment, I believe, that is dangerous. There is a sense that ethics is what we learn at our parents' knees. While there is truth to that, such truth is only partial. The ethical education I received at my parents' knees had little to do with the complexities of sweatshop issues, global outsourcing, or special-purpose entity accounting, for example. These are the critical discussions we must have in the business school environment if we are to be true to the purpose of the university environment, i.e., education of the whole person. Failing that, we become mere technical schools. Laudable as that might be, it is not the purpose of [the] university.

Given the purpose of the university, the proposal that business students take one ethics course is not asking much.

Dynamic #7: Since business schools are self-accredited, there is little impetus to break the habit of denying ethics in a curriculum.

The wall of resistance from AACSB stems not only from fealty to value-free economics, but involves a clandestine circularity as well. That is, AACSB membership is made up of deans who craft rules that they then apply to their cohorts and themselves. The deans essentially police themselves. There is no government oversight and hardly any external pressure on this private deans' club. By all appearances, member deans are crafting standards flexible enough to give them room to wriggle out of recurring curriculum battles. In faculty political maneuvers, ethics easily gets sacrificed to courses that are sacred cows or fads or fashions in management.

We have now come full circle in a gridlock of denial. To compound issues of accountability and transparency in curricular standards, some member deans of AACSB accrediting teams have long-standing professional relationships or personal friendships with the deans of the schools they visit, calling into question the arm's-length relationship expected of accreditation judgments. One might as well ask Arthur Andersen to audit Enron, where cronyism reigned. In drawing this parallel, we do not question the sincerity of deans or AACSB. Nor do we cast aspersions on most practicing managers. To do so would be to avoid the real issue, which is that large-scale organizations are chain-of-command structures that encourage policies and behaviors that narrowly serve the status quo or, in this case, amoral business education. In such a system, true leadership is rare.

Admitting the Public Danger of Business School Graduates

The amoral cultures of business schools have backfired, especially since some programs now have the dubious distinction of counting infamous corporate crooks among their graduates. Getting beyond denial means admitting that an unknown number of these graduates, as products of amoral, myopic education, are primed to act out deviant behavior sooner or later. Not surprisingly, evidence suggests that their moral myopia gets worse after taking traditional finance and economics coursework (Orlitzky and Swanson 2002). Another reflection of this value-free coursework is that MBA students tend to shift from a consumer orientation to a stockholder affiliation after only two years of study (Aspen Initiative for Social Innovation through Business 2002). Not even stockholders are served by this narrow view, as demonstrated by the disastrous financial meltdown accompanying the eruption of corporate scandals.

That students can graduate from business schools with a narrower perspective than they had going in is not lost on the students themselves. Only 22 percent of MBA students polled said that business schools are doing a lot to prepare them ethically, most adding that they would rather change firms than fight for their own values (Aspen Initiative 2002). This bracketing of personal values, a behavioral artifact of value-free education, stifles potential ethical leadership. As one business professor observed (7):

There is a flaw in business education if students say they will leave a company when faced with a values conflict. Business schools are supposed to be in the business of training leaders. They should be teaching them to raise the issues—not bail out. That is the only way we are going to see change happen—if people actually ask the tough questions within their organizations.

Bear in mind that business school graduates, especially MBAs, are sent out into society to occupy key positions of great significance and influence within corporations. Their decisions affect the quality of life for millions or even billions of people around the globe. Their professional and fiduciary responsibilities parallel those of doctors, lawyers, teachers, engineers, and others. They are not the raisins in the cake but the cake itself, comprising the very substance of corporate life.

Most likely, they are self-selected to enter business careers after years of subtle ideological conditioning that prepares them for what they believe is a value-free profession. Many become little more than managerial mechanics who oil the corporate machinery as loyal soldiers, believing all the while that they and their companies are standing firm for individual freedom and initiative. Not until it is too late do they discover how very easy it is to accept internal corporate corruption. Consider former Arthur Andersen ethics manager Barbara Toffler, who found herself caught up in the glories and rewards of overcharging clients (Toffler and Reingold 2003). From such a perspective one can appreciate the potential threat to both business and society that lies hidden in business school graduates.

The dubious quality of business education programs is hardly news. As far back as 1959, the Carnegie and Ford reports chastised business education for its minimal respectability in academe, the Carnegie report making it clear that AACSB would not be able to provide the kind of leadership it would take to turn things around (Klein 1998). In the early 1970s, the Committee for Economic Development (1971), a group of leading corporate executives, echoed the call for well-rounded management education. That same decade, the SIM Governance Committee took up the challenge, providing AACSB with the rationale and criteria for a threshold course on the social environment of business (Frederick 1977).

Now, when these courses are needed the most, they are either not being offered or, if offered, diluted or trivialized with the tacit (and sometimes conscious) approval of AACSB. Consequently, many business students will graduate without understanding the new public and private initiatives that are changing the landscape against which business curricula will be judged. Their failure to comprehend sweeping reforms in corporate governance, financial market regulations, sentencing guidelines for organizations, and rules for prosecuting corporate criminals almost guarantees another wave of corporate malfeasance in the future. Although these reforms are living proof that ethical issues and factual analysis go hand in hand, many business schools will continue to deliver value-free education that rationalizes the behavioral excesses now prosecuted as corporate criminality. Given the magnitude of denial, it is not surprising that most business majors claim that they will not fight for their own personally held values, much less community well-being. Although one ethics course will not solve all ills, it could be the only opportunity some students have to grasp a saner view. It might also keep some of them out of jail.

By the summer of 2002, public faith in business had dropped to disastrous lows. CEOs and stockbrokers were trusted by only 23 percent of the public, just a few points above used car dealers at 15 percent. During that time, the Gallup Organization found that the net positive rating for accountants had plummeted to zero (Derocher 2003). In late June 2002, President George W. Bush told the nation, "We must have rules and laws that restore faith in the integrity of American business" (White House Press Release 2002a). Two weeks later, he spoke directly to Wall Street financial leaders, saying, "We need men and women of character, who know the difference between ambition and destructive greed, between justified risk and irresponsibility, between enterprise and fraud. Our schools of business must be principled teachers of right and wrong, and not surrender to moral confusion and relativism" (White House Press Release 2002b).

When President Bush called for a new ethic of responsibility, he obviously was applying his call to the nation's business schools as well as to corporations (White House Press Release 2003). AACSB officials could have risen to the occasion by mandating that new accrediting standards include one ethics course. Yet they shied away, much like business students who strive to avoid normative issues in the workplace. This inbred reflex suggests that AACSB is incapable of self-improvement where ethics is concerned. Instead, schools breaking ranks with weak accrediting standards are leading the way.

Recognizing Schools with Ethics Coverage

According to the most recent report by the Aspen/World Resources Institute, most MBAs still graduate without an anchor in social and environmental management. Of the 188 schools surveyed, only six were identified as cutting-edge in areas of ethics, corporate social responsibility, and environmental sustainability (Schneider 2003). Clearly the hope for reform lies in the schools with robust ethics requirements, not the majority lagging behind. Given the scope of institutional denial, it is important to recognize those schools that do not take the easy way out by scattering ethics across their curricula. They are benchmarks against which other programs can be measured. For example, the A.J. Palumbo School of Business Administration at Duquesne University revamped its curriculum after the faculty deemed the scattershot approach to ethics a failure (Thomas 2002). According to Professor James Weber, director of Duquesne's Beard Center for Leadership in Ethics, the school now requires a stand-alone ethics course in both undergraduate and MBA programs. The faculty also approved an MBA concentration in business ethics and a master of science in leadership and business ethics. Complementing these efforts, students and faculty in consultation with the Beard Center developed a code of ethical conduct. As part of this initiative, "ethical advocates" were appointed by the dean to serve as confidential resources on ethical questions. Finally, the Beard Center offers a semiannual distinguished ethics speaker program and liaisons with the local community to support service projects.

Another program promising leadership in ethics education is emerging at the University of Colorado at Boulder (UCB). According to Professor Bob Kolb, assistant dean for business and society at UCB's Leeds School of Business, all undergraduate business and MBA students are required to take business and society coursework. As part of the school's new business and society initiatives, students are encouraged to attend a full-day seminar in business and professional ethics and to participate in an established national case competition hosted by the Leeds School. Business and society projects on the near horizon include a national annual symposium, a campus-wide speaker series, faculty workshops, a study abroad program, and two corporate social responsibility awards programs.

These efforts at Duquesne and UCB represent both exemplary leadership and a holistic approach to ethics. Other programs can follow their example, on the learning curve, as the formula for this benchmark standard is quite straightforward; it consists of three components:

- A required foundational ethics course is essential.
- Efforts to integrate ethics across the curriculum should be a goal.
- Other initiatives, such as hosting guest speakers, offering service learning projects, and establishing endowed chairs in ethics, are highly desirable.

Other innovative efforts under way include new MBA programs in sustainable management at Presidio College in San Francisco and environmental entrepreneurship at the New College of California in Santa Rosa (*Business Ethics* 2003). These "green MBAs" deserve special attention, especially given reports that the vast majority of MBA students get little or no environmental coursework (e.g., Schneider 2003). These programs also bear watching because they might be able to innovate in ethics more nimbly than some larger schools stifled by bureaucracy and perhaps closer affiliation with AACSB.

Reforming Ethics Education

Many groups, including corporate officers, have direct stakes in sustaining leadership in ethics education as a basis for widespread reforms. The main power players on campus include business school deans, their faculties, university presidents, and provosts. Off campus they include corporate leaders, MBA recruiters, the media that publish business school rankings, and private and public agencies that fund business school research. Leverage can be exerted by each of these groups.

We have already described the failure of the nation's business school deans (AACSB) to bring their collective influence to bear in meaningful ways. Nor is action likely to be forthcoming from entrenched faculty groups opposed to mandating ethics courses. One must look elsewhere—and largely off campus —for the desired leadership.

Corporate Officers Should Demand Changes

Corporate officers should recognize that most business school graduates are no bargains. Their handicaps include narrow mental maps, readily malleable personal values, and an uncertain sense of community responsibility. Recruiters cannot assume that these graduates bring even rudimentary ethics reasoning skills to the table. The costs of rectifying their lack of proper education are threefold. First, corporations striving for integrity will have to put these risky graduates through in-house ethics training, which amounts to a direct cost. Second, the opportunity costs of these corporate training programs are the time and money that could be spent elsewhere. Third, if in-house ethics training does not take hold, some graduates will become saboteurs who continually undermine the firm's integrity and goodwill. Some will go to jail. Corporate officers should not allow their firms to continue to be dumping grounds for products of an educational system with a long history of downplaying ethics and prizing selfishness over organizational and community needs.

We do not mean to suggest that all corporate misconduct can be laid at the feet of business school degree programs. Nor will the requirement of one ethics course solve all problems. Nevertheless, corporate leaders have the right to expect that business schools will do their part to salvage corporate reputations and public confidence in business. Corporate officers should tell university presidents, provosts, and deans to stop heaping unnecessary costs on their firms. Corporate recruiters have already told college placement officials that they want not only functional expertise but also breadth in general management and behavioral skills (Rynes et al. 2003). Recruiters need to raise the bar by demanding that students be able to demonstrate basic ethical reasoning skills. Otherwise, corporations should hang out a sign that says "MBAs need not apply." It would not take long for academic administrators, especially business school deans, to get the message.

University Administrators Should Apply Pressure

Universities can ill afford to be seen as falling behind on this issue. Those that do will be judged as second-rate to the cadre of schools gaining national reputations for robust ethics education. According to the president of Texas A&M, Dr. Robert Gates, the university's responsibility in a post-Enron world is obvious: "All of these liars and cheats and thieves are graduates of our universities. The university community cannot avert its eyes and proclaim that this is not our problem, that there is nothing we can do, or that these behaviors are an aberration from the norm" (Gates 2002).

As Gates suggests, the problem could be quickly resolved if top university administrators, especially provosts, vice presidents of academic affairs, and presidents took appropriate action. The average business school dean, a cohort in a peer-reviewed system, will not resolve the problem unless encouraged to do so by higher authority. AACSB provides the protective cover for such recalcitrance, buffering deans from conflict with incumbent faculty with vested interests in other coursework. The easy and misguided way out is for deans to add a two-week noncredit seminar in ethics for incoming freshman and/or ask faculty members to address ethics across their curricula. That some schools have gone as far as to cut ethics courses in the wake of the corporate scandals demonstrates that the issue is too vulnerable to be left to internal politics. Upper-level university officers should cut through the quagmire of resistance with budgetary pressure, seeking donor contributions when needed and earmarking funds for required coursework in ethics. Deans would follow suit quickly.

AACSB Should Provide "Postmortem Oversight"

As a body for ethics standards, AACSB shows signs of rigor mortis. Even so, it could still breathe some life into accrediting policy. We suggest "postmortem oversight" aimed at minimizing errors of inadequate and inappropriate ethics coverage. Such policy, if adopted, would mean that professors tasked with incorporating ethics into coursework would have to demonstrate proper training. For instance, a finance professor who lists ethics on a syllabus should have to prove sufficient doctoral or postdoctoral training in ethics. After all, accrediting officials would want similar evidence if finance topics got tossed around in a curriculum. In such a case they would ask informed questions: Where are tools of working capital management taught? Where are liquidity, profitability, debt, and activity ratios covered? Does the Capital Asset Pricing Model get quick mention in a strategy course or in-depth coverage by a professor trained in the theory of efficient markets? Do students actually apply financial principles or merely hear about them in a two-week non-credit seminar for new students? In reality, AACSB would not accept anything less than stand-alone courses in areas considered "traditional business subjects," such as marketing, finance, and strategy. That same assessment should hold for business ethics.

Essentially, a postmortem strategy would mean that accrediting teams put ethics coverage on the defensive whenever they visit schools. This would include comparing students' knowledge of ethics before and after completing coursework. As part of this process, schools would have to demonstrate that their methods of generating and measuring such data were sound. Members of accrediting teams would be tasked with examining the merits of these data carefully instead of searching disingenuously for key words in course titles and syllabi. If the data do not support the outcome of enhanced ethics reasoning skills, then AACSB should decline to accredit schools. In short, a postmortem strategy would rule out ethics window dressing. However, such oversight would not rule out attempts to integrate ethics throughout a curriculum. Nor would it preclude the flexibility called for by the plurality of AACSB constituents, since it would not dictate the design or placement of individual courses in a curriculum. The issue is scope. As the SIM Governance Committee proposed in 1977, one required threshold course in ethics need not dampen other curricular initiatives (Frederick 1977). Potentially everyone gains by keeping the material on ethics intact as a required threshold course. By design, this approach encourages cross-fertilization of ideas within other business courses. It is an eminently "flexible" base from which schools can infuse greater ethical awareness into their students.

We doubt that AACSB is capable of postmortem oversight, given the evidence at hand. For example, on hearing that AACSB had formulated an Ethics Education Task Force (EETF) in lieu of mandating a required course, we asked about its purpose. AACSB president Carolyn Woo responded, "The EETF is created to provide a resource document that will assist business schools in implementing their ethics curricula and also to inform AACSB peer teams in their assessment of a school's effort. The EETF is set up to collect resources from diverse perspectives and groups."[1]

We are not impressed. If "diverse perspectives" are merely loaded as ammunition into a scattershot approach, then more confusion and assessment errors are inevitable, especially since the code words "assist" and "inform" signal no real enforcement. Worse, the plan for EETF to function as an in-house library overlooks the abundant ethics resources available for decades in the public domain. The pressing need is for this material to be delivered cohesively by trained faculty, not sampled randomly with the approval of a post hoc library committee. If AACSB continues down this path, its irrelevance to business ethics education is undoubtedly assured (and may be tacitly intended).

Public Policy Initiatives Could Make a Difference

An AACSB official points out that seeking accreditation is voluntary and that no one forces schools to accept AACSB standards.[2] But this response begs the question for schools bearing AACSB's seal of approval. An association that accredits professional degree programs should take the high road on ethics standards, especially after the crisis in confidence caused by the epidemic of corporate misconduct. Certainly it is disheartening to hear the rhetoric of "free to choose" from AACSB, given that this same refrain has been a long-standing chorus of free market pundits who argue vociferously that corporate managers should not try consciously to fulfill moral obligations to society. Such invocation of freedom is misguided when it functions as a cover for the right to act selfishly and irresponsibly in business or for an educational approach that denies students a sense of their ethical and moral responsibilities to society. It is a classic failure of self-regulation.

When self-regulation fails, government oversight is often the next step. At this point, certain state-level efforts bear watching. For instance, the California legislature has established a task force on business ethics in educational curricula and the Golden State Business and Social Responsibility Award to reward students who show socially responsible leadership. To qualify for the award, graduate students in business must complete a minimum of two ethics courses and at least fifty hours of community service. The qualifying student would have the seal of the state senate, the state assembly, or the governor affixed on his or her diploma or transcript (Coggins forthcoming). Other state-level initiatives include continuing education. The Texas Real Estate Commission (2003) has recommended mandating coursework in law and ethics, similar to requirements in New Mexico, where complaints against practitioners have steadily declined since such courses were established. Similarly, several states now require continuing education hours in ethics for certified public accountants; for example, in New York, licensees must complete at least four contact hours in professional ethics each year in order to qualify for renewed registration (New York State Society of CPAs 2003).

Ironically, while academics continue to fiddle over the merits of business ethics, some public policy makers and professional organizations are using common sense to design and implement programs aimed at enhancing professional integrity. Such efforts constitute an important, refreshing source of influence.

The Media Should Intensify Coverage

According to research on public policy issues, raising public awareness is often the first step in gaining momentum toward policy resolution (Cobb and Elder 1972; Mahon and Waddock 1992). Instead of reemphasizing the need for ethics education with each outbreak of corporate misconduct, the media should continually air the issue. If business schools are constantly held up to the limelight, their policy of delivering amoral education while downsizing ethics courses will become increasingly difficult to defend. The public will not buy it. Advocates of ethics education should keep the issue alive by issuing press releases. Along these lines, corporate officials should issue position statements through their offices of public affairs calling for better business ethics education. University administrators can demonstrate their concern by working with campus media to keep the public apprised of ethics initiatives in their business schools.

Toward Leading Ethics Education

Requiring ethics coursework will not cure all ills, but it is a necessary step in addressing the nation's crisis in business. Some campus initiatives are leading the way, yet they could prove fragile, given the bulwark of resistance from business schools reinforced by weak accrediting standards. All whose hands rest on the levers of power—corporate leaders, university presidents, public policy officials, the media, funding organizations—need to exert pressure that tips the balance toward stronger ethics education for tomorrow's business leaders. There is no time to lose, as most business schools continue to function as breeding grounds for corporate malfeasants poised to wreak large-scale damage on the business system and society at large.

Notes

1. Personal communications with Carolyn Woo, Dean of the Mendoza School of Business, University of Notre Dame, and President of the Association to Advance Collegiate Schools of Business, October 13 and 16, 2003.
2. Personal communication with Milton Blood, Chief Accreditation Officer, Association to Advance Collegiate Schools of Business, October 16, 2003.

13

Reflections

Robert A. Peterson

Given that the intent of this volume is to provide business schools and corporations with new insights for their organizational ethics initiatives, it is fitting to conclude with a few reflections on the state of ethics in business and the state of business ethics. Most knowledgeable individuals, especially after reading this volume or being exposed to the nightly television news or virtually any newspaper or news magazine, would probably agree that the state of ethics in business is not good. The recent, widely publicized spate of corporate scandals, including ethical misconduct and illegal behaviors, has galvanized the public and resulted in numerous new government regulations and laws, changes in corporate governance, and countless civil and criminal lawsuits.

Ethics in Business

Simultaneously, though, individuals with any semblance of perspective and memory recognize that the current corporate scandals are not necessarily unique in number or nature. They may simply be more visible because they coincidentally happened to be widespread, involved large sums of money and well-known companies and executives, and received extensive media coverage. As Chapter 8 points out, corporate scandals of various magnitudes and ilks have occurred throughout history, and indeed, there may be cyclicality to their nature and duration. Moreover, what is deemed to constitute a "corporate scandal" or, for that matter, ethical or unethical behavior, probably changes over time.

Unlike some well-publicized business scandals, however, such as the savings and loan scandal, the present scandals produced wholesale changes in government regulations and laws. These changes no doubt reflected a wide-spread feeling that the economic and business infrastructures of the country were at risk due to a significant deterioration in public trust. The most prominent new federal law enacted in response to the latest scandals, commonly referred to as the Sarbanes-Oxley Act, has received an enormous amount of publicity. Although it was initially greeted with considerable enthusiasm, especially from the general populace, there appears to be increasing skepticism that the act delivers less than meets the eye. Critical business and academic observers have pointed to several perceived limitations of the act, including its failure to address the root causes of corporate malfeasance and its creation of unnecessary resource burdens on all businesses, regardless of their size and present and prior ethical behavior.

One of the consequences of the act and the scandals appears to be that companies are more cognizant of ethical issues and the impact of these issues on company behaviors generally and decisions specifically. For example, companies seem to be making at least temporary attempts to increase their organizational transparency and to develop and showcase their ethics programs. Interestingly enough, as Brenner (1992) observed, every organization has an ethics program, regardless of whether it knows that it has one.

Moreover, as Brenner (1992, 393) aptly noted, a corporate ethics program consists of both explicit and implicit components. The explicit component in turn consists of "codes of ethics, policy manuals, employee training materials, employee orientation programs, ethics seminars, management speeches, management ethics decisions, board of director decisions and committee activities, internal control systems, and ethics staff activities." The implicit component consists of the "corporate culture, incentive systems, valued behaviors, promotion policies, performance measurement systems, and management behavior." As Ferrell (in Chapter 1 of this volume) points out, the complex, obtuse, and multifaceted nature of corporate ethics programs suggests the need for formal, structured ethics audits, similar to financial audits, management audits, and marketing audits, to sort out and investigate the explicit and implicit components and their elements. Unless the interrelationships and relative importance of the respective component elements are understood and appropriately managed, no corporate ethics program or ethics initiatives will be successful.

Among the implications of Brenner's observation is that an organization must be cognizant of, and manage, all of those factors that determine the ethical behavior of employees and managers, regardless of whether the factors have previously been recognized as influencing behavior. Thus, simply hiring the right employees, holding ethics seminars and training sessions, and so forth will not guarantee ethical organizational behavior. This conclusion was repeatedly reached throughout this volume in various ways by several contributors. Even so, it warrants reiteration. For ethical behavior to be the norm in an organization, there must be ethical leadership. Until there is ethical leadership, the state of ethics in business will remain clouded. Unfortunately, there is no known panacea for identifying, developing, or maintaining ethical leadership at this time.

Business Ethics

Whereas the state of ethics in business is clouded because of behavioral lapses and leadership lacunae, the state of business ethics is clouded due to a lack of understanding of what constitutes "business ethics." DeGeorge (1987) argued that "business ethics" should be treated as an academic field, thus formally distinguishing it from "ethics in business," which loosely refers to contextual attitudes and behavior. He believed that for business ethics to ultimately have any impact as a respected academic field, "the quality and quantity of research done in it" (206) must be the equivalent of research done in relevant business disciplines such as accounting, finance, management, and marketing. In other words, DeGeorge argued that research in business ethics must be rigorous for the field to have any credibility. He further argued that business ethics must be treated as an interdisciplinary field and recommended that research teams composed of business professors and philosophers conduct integrated studies on important topics of mutual interest. Extending DeGeorge's arguments, once business ethics gains academic respect and a knowledge base is produced that is actually useful to managers, the knowledge base can be transported to classrooms and boardrooms. Until then, business ethicists will languish in a world without respect and have little influence on business practice or business education.

Despite the intuitive appeal of a formal academic field of business ethics and the emerging interest in a theory of business ethics, several questions remain. For example, where should academics who theorize and conduct research in such a field be located? Should they be located in a philosophy department, a liberal arts college, a business school, or some combination of these organizational units? Does it matter where they are located? Relatedly, how should theory and research in such a field be integrated with theory and research on individual ethics? Are not business ethics and individual ethics related, both conceptually and practically?

To date, most business ethicists have been not only ignored, but perceived negatively by business people and business educators. Stark, for example, unleashed a broadside at business ethicists in a *Harvard Business Review* article:

> I suspect that the field of business ethics is largely irrelevant for most managers. It's not that they are hostile to the *idea* of business ethics. . . . The problem is that the discipline of business ethics has yet to provide much concrete help to managers . . . and even business ethicists sense it.
>
> Far too many business ethicists have occupied a rarified moral high ground, removed from the real concerns and real-world problems of the vast majority of managers. They have been too preoccupied with absolutist notions of what it means for managers to be ethical, with overly general criticisms of capitalism as an economic system, with dense and abstract theorizing, and with prescriptions that apply only remotely to managerial practice. (1993, 38)

However, even though he was negatively disposed toward business ethicists, Stark proceeded to argue for rapprochement between business ethicists and business managers with the goal of providing managers with practical, useful ethics guidance. It is suggested here that, among other things, such guidance take the form of a model to qualitatively and quantitatively, descriptively and normatively, assess the "ethical maturity" of an organization along a variety of dimensions. (See Wong and Beckman [1992] for an attempt to develop a framework for quantifying the ethical worth of a business decision.)

In addition to rigorous research, an academic field needs one or more theoretical bases to truly legitimize itself. Unfortunately, until now there have been few attempts to develop theories of business ethics. Instead, the focus in business ethics studies generally seems to have been on applying, adapting, or testing theories developed for different purposes or in different contexts. However, the theory proffered by Hunt and Vitell (in Chapter 2 in this volume) appears to have some promise in that it was developed specifically for business ethics. Hopefully the Hunt-Vitell theory will stimulate both theoretical and empirical research on business ethics and serve as a foundation for the field. (See Chapter 3 for a related discussion of the issues considered by Hunt and Vitell.)

Business Ethics Education

The immediate challenge for business ethics education is to develop a definition and a conceptualization of business ethics that can be universally understood and meaningfully communicated to a variety of audiences. As Aristotle (1952, 152) observed many centuries ago, "For as long as it is not clear in how many senses a term is used, it is possible that the answerer and the questioner are not directing their minds upon the same thing." In formal terms, any meaningful definition or conceptualization of "business ethics" must state its essential attributes, not be circular, be neither too broad nor too narrow, and not employ ambiguous or obscure language (cf. Copi and Cohen 1994; Kahane 1982).

Further, for business ethics to be viable as an academic field, it must have an agreed-upon nexus (centerpiece) and domain (scope). Although no formal nexus is offered here, the suggestion of Robin (in Chapter 11 of this volume) that trust serve as business ethics' raison d'être deserves serious consideration and has great intuitive appeal, both theoretically and practically. Indeed, one of the sponsors of the symposium that made this volume possible, Cutco/Vector Marketing Corporation, offers a practical example of Robin's suggestion. The company has consciously and deliberately focused its corporate culture on the notion of trust; its corporate "framework of trust" encompasses customers, employees, suppliers, and community.

Moreover, the domain (scope) of business ethics must be formally and explicitly delineated if for no other reason than that doing so allows cutting-edge research, corporate best practices, business education best practices, and the current state of theoretical knowledge to be integrated into business education curricula at both the graduate and undergraduate levels.

Although it is often convenient to think about business ethics in the context of good versus bad or right versus wrong, such thinking is too superficial. This is especially so in business decision making, which frequently consists of fuzzy decision alternatives with ambiguous outcomes and multiple groups of differentially impacted stakeholders possessing conflicting ethics paradigms.

Similarly, there seems to be little agreement among business educators as to the importance of business ethics in a curriculum, what the focus of business ethics education should be—individual and/or organizational and/or societal—or how business ethics concepts should be delivered in the curriculum, if at all. In other words, there appears to be little agreement as to what exactly is to be accomplished by incorporating business ethics into business education. Integrating business ethics in a meaningful way into business education will continue to be hindered by this lack of agreement about the conceptualization, importance, focus, and delivery of business ethics in business school curricula. Despite such hindrances, business ethics must be integrated into business school curricula. Note that five out of six undergraduate business students surveyed by Peterson and Albaum (see Chapter 7) believed that all business students should take a formal course in business ethics.

As an interesting aside, Pfeffer (2003) has argued that even if business ethics was universally conceptualized and its importance, focus, and educational delivery agreed upon, unless business schools enforce their own codes of ethics, their students' ethical development will not occur. He opined that business schools and instructors must harshly penalize students who cheat on examinations, plagiarize, or commit other unethical academically related acts. Failure to punish such acts sends a powerful message that the school or instructor is not really serious about ethics, even though students may be required to take formal business ethics coursework. Pfeffer's argument brings to mind Brenner's observation that every organization has an ethics program, regardless of whether it is formally acknowledged, and the old saw that actions speak louder than words.

Ethics Leadership

A common thread running through this volume, and one touched on earlier in this chapter, is the notion of ethics leadership. Many of the contributors to the volume (see Chapters 4, 5, 6, 9, 10, and 12 in particular) explicitly addressed and embraced the importance of ethics leadership, albeit from different perspectives. Leadership clearly is a critically important construct with respect to both ethics in business and business ethics. Even so, because the construct of leadership, per se, is so amorphous, value-laden, and poorly understood, a concerted effort is required to fully comprehend the extent of its implications in the present context.

Awareness of ethics in business and business ethics is at an all-time high. There is presently momentum to improve ethics in business and to elevate the importance of business ethics in business education curricula. Consequently, it is imperative to leverage this awareness and ensure there is no diminution in momentum, if for no other reason than that the effectiveness and efficiency of the economic system are literally at risk.

References

Ackoff, Russell L. 1999. "On Learning and the Systems That Facilitate It." *Reflections* 1 (Fall): 14–24.

Across the Board. 2002. "In Plain Sight, In Plain English." Vol. 39 (November–December): 24–27.

Adler, Paul S. 2002. "Corporate Scandals: It's Time for Reflection in Business Schools." *Academy of Management Executive* 16 (August): 148–149.

Ajzen, Icek. 1985. "From Intentions to Actions: A Theory of Planned Behavior." In *Action Control: From Cognition to Behavior*, ed. Julius Kuhl and Jurgen Beckman. Berlin: Springer-Verlag, 11–39.

Alchian, Armen A., and William R. Allen. 1977. *Exchange and Production: Competition, Coordination, and Control.* 2nd ed. Belmont, CA: Wadsworth.

Allport, Gordon W., and J. Michael Ross. 1967. "Personal Religious Orientation and Prejudice." *Journal of Personality and Social Psychology* 5 (October): 432–443.

Alsop, Ronald. 2003. "Right and Wrong: Can Business Schools Teach Students to Be Virtuous?" *Wall Street Journal*, September 17, R9.

Ameen, Elsie C., Daryl M. Guffey, and Jeffrey J. McMillan. 1996. "Gender Differences in Determining the Ethical Sensitivity of Future Accounting Professionals." *Journal of Business Ethics* 15 (May): 591–597.

American Institute of Certified Public Accountants. 1978. *Code of Professional Ethics.*

———. 1992. *Code of Professional Conduct.*

Anderson, Mark. 1999. "W.R. Grace Settles Shareholder Suit Led by CalPERS." *Sacramento Business Journal* 22 (October 29): 12.

Anderson, Sarah, John Cavanagh, Ralph Estes, Chuck Collins, and Chris Hartman. 1999. *A Decade of Executive Excess: The 1990s Sixth Annual Executive Compensation Survey.* Boston: United for a Fair Economy.

Aristotle. 1952. *The Works of Aristotle. The Great Books of the Western World*, Vol. 8. Chicago: Encyclopaedia Britannica.

Arlow, Peter. 1991. "Personal Characteristics in College Students' Evaluations of Business Ethics and Corporate Social Responsibility." *Journal of Business Ethics* 10 (January): 63–69.

Arrow, Kenneth J. 1974. *The Limits of Organization.* New York: Norton.

Aspen Initiative for Social Innovation through Business. 2002. *Where Will They Lead? MBA Student Attitudes about Business and Society.* New York: Aspen ISIB.

Association to Advance Collegiate Schools of Business. 1996. "A Report of the AACSB Faculty Leadership Task Force." www.aacsb.edu/index.html.

————. 2003. "AACSB Eligibility Procedures and Standards for Business Accreditation." www.aacsb.edu/accreditation/standards.asp.

Azzi, Corry, and Ronald Ehrenberg. 1975. "Household Allocation of Time and Church Attendance." *Journal of Political Economy* 83 (February): 27–56.

Backover, Andrew. 2002. "Report Cites 'Widely Enthusiastic' Analyst Reports." *USA Today*, November 5, 1B, 6B.

Bacon, Kenneth H., and Kevin G. Salwen. 1991. "Summer of Financial Scandals Raises Questions about the Ability of Regulators to Control Markets." *Wall Street Journal*, August 28, A10.

Balzar, John. 2002. "Hope Corporate Cronies Can't Regain Trust So Easily." *Milwaukee Journal Sentinel*, August 24, 15A.

Barr, Andrew. 1959. "The Independent Accountant and the SEC." *Journal of Accountancy* 108 (October): 32–37.

Bartels, Robert. 1967. "A Model for Ethics in Marketing." *Journal of Marketing* 31 (January): 20–26.

Bartlett, Christopher A., and Sumantra Ghoshal. 1995. "Changing the Role of Top Management: Beyond Systems to People." *Harvard Business Review* 73 (May–June): 132–134.

Bartley, Robert L. 2002. "Andersen: A Pyrrhic Victory?" *Wall Street Journal*, June 24, A17.

Bartolome, Fernando. 1989. "Nobody Trusts the Boss Completely—Now What?" *Harvard Business Review* 67 (March–April): 135–142.

Bartunek, Jean M. 2002. "The Proper Place of Organizational Scholarship: A Comment on Hinings and Greenwood." *Administrative Science Quarterly* 47 (September): 422–427.

Bass, Bernard M. 1998. *Transformational Leadership: Industrial, Military, and Educational Impact.* Mahwah, NJ: Lawrence Erlbaum.

Bauder, Don. 2002. "Study Blames Excessive Pay on Stock Options." *Copley News Service* (August 26).

Bazerman, Max H., George Loewenstein, and Don A. Moore. 2002. "Why Do Accountants Do Bad Things?" *Harvard Business Review.* 80 (November): 96–102.

Beauchamp, Tom L. 1991. *Philosophical Ethics: An Introduction to Moral Philosophy.* 2nd ed. New York: McGraw-Hill.

Bebeau, Muriel J., James R. Rest, and Catherine M. Yamoor. 1985. "Measuring Dental Students' Ethical Sensitivity." *Journal of Dental Education* 49 (August): 225–235.

Bellizzi, Joseph A., and Ronald W. Hasty. 2003. "Supervising Unethical Sales Force Behavior: How Strong Is the Tendency to Treat Top Sales Performers Leniently?" *Journal of Business Ethics* 43 (April): 337–351.

Beltramini, Richard F., Robert A. Peterson, and George Kozmetsky. 1984. "Concerns of College Students Regarding Business Ethics." *Journal of Business Ethics* 3 (Summer): 195–200.

Benner, Jeffrey. 2002. "MBA Accreditation Body Resists Professors' Call for Required Ethics Course." *AFX Global Ethics Monitor Online* (November 14), www.globalethicsmonitor.com/afx-eth/homepage_summary.html.

Bennis, Warren. 1989. *Why Leaders Can't Lead.* San Francisco: Jossey-Bass.

Bennis, Warren, and Burt Nanus. 1985. *Leaders.* New York: HarperCollins.

————. 1997. *Leaders: The Strategies for Taking Charge.* New York: HarperBusiness.

Bentham, Jeremy. 1789. *Introduction to the Principles of Morals and Legislation.* Oxford, UK: Oxford University Press.

Berle, Adolf A. 1963. *The American Economic Republic.* New York: Harcourt, Brace & World.

Bernstein, Aaron. 2000. "How Business Rates: By the Numbers." *BusinessWeek*, September 11, 148–149.

Betz, Michael, Lenahan O'Connell, and Jon M. Shepard. 1989. "Gender Differences in Proclivity for Unethical Behavior," *Journal of Business Ethics* 8 (May): 321–324.

Bhide, Amar, and Howard H. Stevenson. 1990. "Why Be Honest If Honesty Doesn't Pay?" *Harvard Business Review* 68 (September–October): 121–129.

Billington, Jim. 1997. "A Few Things Every Manager Ought to Know about Risk." *Harvard Management Update* 2 (March): 10–11.

Borkowski, Susan C. and Yusuf J. Ugras. 1992. "The Ethical Attitudes of Students as a Function of Age, Sex and Experience." *Journal of Business Ethics* 11 (December): 961–979.

———. 1998. "Business Students and Ethics: A Meta-Analysis." *Journal of Business Ethics* 17 (August): 1117–1127.

Boulding, Kenneth E. 1981. A Preface to *Grant's Economics: The Economy of Love and Fear.* New York: Praeger.

Bowie, Norman. 1996. *Business Ethics: A Kantian Perspective.* Oxford, UK: Blackwell.

Brass, Daniel J., Kenneth D. Butterfield, and Bruce C. Skaggs. 1998. "Relationship and Unethical Behavior: A Social Network Perspective." *Academy of Management Review* 23 (January): 14–31.

Brenner, Steven N. 1992. "Ethics Programs and Their Dimensions." *Journal of Business Ethics* 11 (May): 391–399.

Brewer, Lynn, and Matthew Scott Hanson. 2002. *House of Cards: Confessions of an Enron Executive.* College Station, TX: Virtualbookworm.com Publishing.

Bromiley, Philip, and Larry L. Cummings. 1996. "Transaction Costs in Organizations with Trust," in *Research on Negotiations in Organizations*, vol. 5, ed. Robert Bies, Roy Lewicki, and Blair Shepard. Greenwich, CT: JAI Press, 219–247.

Brooks, Geraldine. 1994. "Slick Alliance: Shell's Nigerian Fields Produce Few Benefits for Region's Villagers . . . Despite Huge Oil Revenues." *Wall Street Journal*, May 6, 1.

Brown, Ken. 2003. "Vanguard Gives Corporate Chiefs a Report Card." *Wall Street Journal*, November 10, C1, C3.

Browning, Edgar K., and Jacqueline M. Browning. 1983. *Microeconomic Theory and Applications.* Boston: Little, Brown.

Burns, James MacGregor. 1978. *Leadership.* New York: Harper & Row.

———. 1985. *Leadership.* 2nd ed. New York: Harper & Row.

Burns, Jane O., and Pamela Kiecker. 1995. "Tax Practitioner Ethics: An Empirical Investigation of Organizational Consequences." *Journal of the American Taxation Association* 17 (April): 20–49.

Burr, Barry. 2002. "Shareholder Activism Hot in Poor Business Climate." *Pensions & Investments* 4 (July 8): 32.

Business Ethics. 2003. "Trend Watch." Summer, 8.

BusinessWeek. 2002. "What We Learned in 2002." (December 30): 170.

BusinessWeek. 2004. "The Mutual-Fund Scandals." (January 12): 82–83.

Butler, John K., and R. Stephen Cantrell. 1984. "A Behavioral Decision Theory Approach to Modeling Dyadic Trust in Superiors and Subordinates." *Psychological Reports* 55 (August): 19–28.

Byrne, John A. 2002a. "Commentary: No Excuses for Enron's Board." *Business Week Online*, July 29.

———. 2002b. "Joe Bernardino's Fall from Grace." *BusinessWeek*, August 12, 50–56.

———. 2003. "This Corporate Reform Lacks Spine." *BusinessWeek Online*, January 13.

Byrnes, Nanette, Mike France, Susan Zegel, Paula Dwyer, and Lorraine Woellert. 2003. "Angling for the Really Big Fish." *BusinessWeek*, September 15, 42–43.

Byrnes, Nanette, Mike McNamee, Diane Brady, Louis Lavelle, and Christopher Palmeri. 2002. "Accounting in Crisis: What Needs to be Done." *BusinessWeek*, January 28, 44–49.

Calabro, Lori. 2003. "Above Board." *CFO* 19 (April): 43.

Calton, Jerry M., and Steven L. Payne. 2003. "Coping With Paradox: Multistakeholder Learning Dialogue as a Pluralist Sensemaking Process for Addressing Messy Problems." *Business & Society* 42 (March): 7–42.

Cameroon Environmental Defense. 2002. *The Chad-Cameroon Oil and Pipeline Project: A Call for Accountability*. New York: Association Tchadienen pour la Promotion et la Défense des Droits de l'Homme, Chad, Centre pour l'Environnement et le Developpement.

Carey, John L. 1940. "Independence of Auditors." *Journal of Accountancy* 80 (April): 250.

———. 1945. "Independence of Accountants." *Journal of Accountancy* 85 (February): 93.

———. 1965. *The CPA Plans for the Future*. New York: AICPA.

———. 1985. "The Independence Concept Revisited." *Ohio CPA Journal* 44 (Spring): 5–8.

Carver, John. 2002. "Is There a Fundamental Difference between Governance and Management?" *Board Leadership* 62 (July): 6.

Cavanagh, John, et al. 2002. *Alternatives to Economic Globalization*. San Francisco: Berrett-Koehler.

Cifrino, David A., and Garrison R. Smith. 2002. "NYSE and NASDAQ Propose to Review Corporate Governance Listing Standards." *Corporate Governance Advisor* 10 (November–December): 18–25.

Clegg, Stewart R. 2002. "Lives in the Balance: A Comment on Hinings and Greenwood's 'Disconnects and Consequences in Organization Theory,'" *Administrative Science Quarterly* 47 (September): 428–441.

Clinard, Marshall B., and Peter C. Yeager. 1980. *Corporate Crime*. New York: Free Press.

Cobb, Roger W., and Charles D. Elder. 1972. *Participation in American Politics: The Dynamics of Agenda Building*. Baltimore, MD: Johns Hopkins University Press.

Coggins, Brian L. Forthcoming. "California's Response to the Lack of Business Ethics." *McGeorge Law Review*.

Cole, Barbara C., and Dennie L. Smith. 1996. "Perceptions of Business Ethics: Students vs. Business People." *Journal of Business Ethics* 15 (August): 889–896.

Cole, Dennis, M. Joseph Sirgy, and Monroe Murphy Bird. 2000. "How Do Managers Make Teleological Evaluations in Ethical Dilemmas? Testing Part of the Hunt-Vitell Model." *Journal of Business Ethics* 26 (August): 259–269.

Collins, James C., and Jerry I. Porras. 1994. *Built to Last: Successful Habits of Visionary Companies*. New York: HarperCollins.

———. 1996. "Building Your Company's Vision." *Harvard Business Review* 74 (September–October): 65–77.

Committe, Bruce Edward. 1989. "Independence of Accountants and Legislative Intent." *Administrative Law Review* 41 (Winter): 33, 53.

Committee for Economic Development. 1971. *Social Responsibilities of Business Corporations.* New York: Committee for Economic Development.

Conference Board. 2003. "Top Ethics Officers Say They Don't Train Their Board in Ethics." Benchmark Questions, Survey/Conference Board Business Ethics Conference, www.conference-board.org.

Conference Board Commission on Public Trust and Private Enterprise. 2002. *Findings and Recommendations, Part 1: Executive Compensation,* www.conference-board.org/pdf_free/756.pdf.

Cooperrider, David L., Peter F. Sorensen, Jr., Therese F. Yaeger, and Diana Whitney. 2001. *Appreciative Inquiry: An Emerging Direction for Organization Development.* Champaign, IL: Stipes.

Copi, Irving M., and Carl Cohen. 1994. *Introduction to Logic.* 9th ed. Englewood Cliffs, NJ: Prentice Hall.

Corporate Reputation Watch. 2003. "2003 Corporate Reputation Watch Survey," www.corporatereputationwatch.com.

Covey, Stephen R. 1990. *Principle-Centered Leadership.* New York: Fireside.

———. 2002. "Where Do We Go from Here?" *USA Today,* October 21, 7B.

Daily, Catherine M., Dan R. Dalton, and Albert A. Cannella Jr. 2003. "Corporate Governance: A Decade of Dialogue and Data." *Academy of Management Review* 28 (July): 371–382.

DeGeorge, Richard T. 1987. "The Stature of Business Ethics: Past and Future." *Journal of Business Ethics* 6 (April): 201–211.

———. 1993. *Competing With Integrity in International Business.* New York: Oxford University Press.

Demb, Ada, and F. Friedrich Neubauer. 1992. *The Corporate Board: Confronting the Paradoxes.* Oxford, UK: Oxford University Press.

Derocher, Robert. J. 2003. "Time Heals All Wounds," *Insight Magazine Online* (November/December): www.insight-mag.com/insight/03/11–12/feat-1–pt-1–TimeHealsAllWounds.asp.

———. 2004. "Knowing Right from Wrong: Today's Young Accountants Need to Be Prepared to Toe a Tougher Ethics Line." *Insight Magazine Online* (January/February): www.insight-mag.com/insight.

Donaldson, Thomas. 1989. *The Ethics of International Business.* New York: Oxford University Press.

———. 1996. "Values in Tension: Ethics Away from Home." *Harvard Business Review* 74 (September–October): 1–12.

———. 2000. "Adding Corporate Ethics to the Bottom Line." *Financial Times,* November 13, 6.

Donaldson, Thomas, and Thomas W. Dunfee. 1994. "Toward a Unified Conception of Business Ethics: Integrative Social Contracts Theory." *Academy of Management Review* 19 (April): 252–284.

Donaldson, Thomas, and Lee E. Preston. 1994. "The Stakeholder Theory of the Corporation: Concepts, Evidence and Implications." *Academy of Management Review* 20 (January): 65–81.

Donaldson, Thomas, and Patricia H. Werhane. 2001. *Ethical Issues in Business.* 7th ed. Upper Saddle River, NJ: Prentice Hall.

Duska, Ronald. 2003. "The Effects of Business Schools on Ethical Behavior in Business." Paper presented at Society for Business Ethics Annual Meeting, Seattle, WA.

Dutton, Jane E., and Emily D. Heaphy. 2003. "The Power of High-Quality Connections." In *Positive Organizational Scholarship: Foundations of a New Discipline*, ed. Kim S. Cameron, Jane E. Dutton, and Robert E. Quinn. San Francisco: Berrett-Koehler, 259–262.

Economist, The. 2002. "Special Report: Corporate America's Woes, Continued—Enron, One Year On." November 30, 59–61.

Economist, The. 2003. "The Way We Govern Now—Corporate Boards." January 11, 59–61.

Eisenberg, Melvin A. 1997. "Corporate Governance: The Board of Directors and Internal Control." *Cardozo Law Review* 19 (September–November): 237.

Elkington, John. 1997. *Cannibals with Forks: The Triple Bottom Line of 21st Century Business*. New York: John Wiley.

Elson, Charles. 2003. "What's Wrong with Executive Compensation?" *Harvard Business Review* 81 (January): 5–12.

Engel, James F., Roger D. Blackwell, and David T. Kollat. 1978. *Consumer Behavior*. 3rd ed. Hinsdale, IL: Dryden.

Equality Project. 2003. "How Shareholder Proposals Work," www.equalityproject.org/how.htm#do.

Estes, Ralph. 1996. *Tyranny of the Bottom Line: Why Corporations Make Good People Do Bad Things*. San Francisco: Berrett-Koehler.

Etzioni, Amitai. 1988. *The Moral Dimension: Toward a New Economics*. New York: Free Press.

———. 2002. "When It Comes to Ethics, B-Schools Get an F." *Washington Post*, August 4, B4.

Fabrickant, Geraldine. 2002. "GE Provides Platinum Parachute for Welsh." *Milwaukee Journal Sentinel*, September 6, 1D, 3D.

Farnham, Alan. 1989. "The Trust Gap." *Fortune*, December 4, 56–78.

Farrell, Greg. 2002. "Business Leaders Fault Excessive CEO Pay." *USA Today*, September 18, 5B.

Fass, Allison. 2003. "One Year Later, The Impact of Sarbanes-Oxley," www.forbes.com/2003/07/22/CZ_af_0722sarbanes.html.

Ferrell, O.C., and Larry G. Gresham. 1985. "A Contingency Framework for Understanding Ethical Decision Making in Marketing." *Journal of Marketing* 49 (Summer): 87–96.

Ferrell, O.C., Larry G. Gresham, and John P. Fraedrich. 1989. "A Synthesis of Ethical Decision Models for Marketing." *Journal of Macromarketing* 9 (Fall): 55–64.

Ferrell, O.C., Debbie Thorne, and Linda Ferrell. 1998. "The Federal Sentencing Guidelines: A Framework for Ethical Compliance." *Journal of Business Ethics* 17 (March): 353–363.

Fishbein, Martin, and Icek Ajzen. 1975. *Belief, Attitude, Intention and Behavior: An Introduction to Theory and Research*. Reading, MA: Addison.

Fisher, Daniel. 2003. "ExxonMobil's Kazakhstan Quagmire." *Forbes*, April 28, 84–92.

Flesher, Dale L., and Tonya K. Flesher. 1986. "Ivar Kreuger's Contribution to U.S. Financial Reporting." *Accounting Review* 61 (July): 421–434.

Flesher, Dale L., Gary J. Previts, and William D. Samson. 2000. "Riding the Rails: An English Auditor's 1850s Trip on the Illinois Central Railroad." Paper presented at Midwest Regional Meeting of the American Accounting Association, Indianapolis, IN.

Fraedrich, John P., and O.C. Ferrell. 1992. "Cognitive Consistency of Marketing Managers in Ethical Situations." *Journal of the Academy of Marketing Science* 20 (Summer): 245–252.

Frankena, William. 1963. *Ethics*. Englewood Cliffs, NJ: Prentice Hall.

Frederick, William C. 1977. "Business and Society Curriculum: Suggested Guidelines for Accreditation." *AACSB Bulletin* 13 (Spring): 1–5.

———. 1995. *Values, Nature, and Culture in the American Corporation*. New York: Oxford University Press.

Freeman, R. Edward. 1984. *Strategic Management: A Stakeholder Approach*. Boston: Pitman.

———. 1994. "The Politics of Stakeholder Theory." *Business Ethics Quarterly* 4 (October): 409–421.

———. 2003. "Value Creation and Trade: A Stakeholder Approach." Working paper, University of Virginia.

Freeman, R. Edward, and Daniel R. Gilbert Jr. 1988. *Corporate Strategy and the Search for Ethics*. Englewood Cliffs, NJ: Prentice Hall.

Freer, Jim. 2002. "Accounting Firms Looking at Impact of Sarbanes-Oxley." *Orlando Business Journal*, October 21, 7–8.

Friedman, Milton. 1953. "The Methodology of Positive Economics." In *Essays in Positive Economics*, ed. Milton Friedman. Chicago: University of Chicago Press, 3–43.

Fukuyama, Francis. 1992. *The End of History and the Last Man*. New York: Free Press.

———. 1995. *Trust: The Social Virtues and the Creation of Prosperity*. New York: Free Press.

Gabor, Andrea. 1990. *The Man Who Discovered Quality*. New York: Penguin.

Galbraith, Sharon, and Harriet Buckman Stephenson. 1993. "Decision Rules Used by Male and Female Business Students in Making Ethical Value Judgments: Another Look." *Journal of Business Ethics* 12 (March): 227–233.

Gardiner, Chris. 2002. "Balanced Scorecard Ethics." *Business & Professional Ethics Journal* 21 (Fall/Winter): 129–150.

Gardner, John William. 1990. *On Leadership*. New York: Free Press.

Garten, Jeffrey E. 2002. *The Politics of Fortune*. Boston, MA: Harvard University Press.

Gates, Robert M. 2002. Convocation address, www.tamu.edu/president/speeches/021003cov.html.

Gellerman, Saul W. 1986. "Why 'Good' Managers Make Bad Ethical Choices." *Harvard Business Review* 64 (July–August): 85–90.

George, Bill. 2003. *Authentic Leadership: Rediscovering the Secrets to Creating Lasting Value*. San Francisco: Jossey-Bass.

Ghoshal, Sumantra. 2003. "Business Schools Share the Blame for Enron." *Financial Times*, July 18, 11.

Gioia, Dennis A. 1992. "Pinto Fires and Personal Ethics: A Script Analysis of Missed Opportunities." *Journal of Business Ethics* 11 (May): 379–389.

———. 2002. "Business Education's Role in the Crisis of Corporate Confidence." *Academy of Management Executive* 16 (August): 142–144.

Goleman, Daniel. 1998. "What Makes a Leader?" *Harvard Business Review* 76 (November–December): 93–102.

Goolsby, Jerry R., and Shelby D. Hunt. 1992. "Cognitive Moral Development and Marketing." *Journal of Marketing* 56 (January): 55–68.

Gores, Paul. 2002. "Short Course on Avoiding Scandal." *Milwaukee Journal Sentinel*, September 5, 1D, 6D.

Granovetter, Mark. 1985. "Economic Action and Social Structure: The Problem of Embeddedness." *American Journal of Sociology* 91 (November): 481–510.

Grant, Alison. 2002. "Companies Now under Suspicion Paid Well; CEOs Got 70 Percent More than Average." *Cleveland Plain Dealer*, August 26, E1.

Grant, Eugene W., Jr., and Lowell S. Broom. 1988. "Attitudes toward Ethics: A View of the College Student." *Journal of Business Ethics* 7 (August): 617–619.

Greenwood, Royston, Roy Suddaby, and C. Robert Hinings. 2002. "Theorizing Change: The Role of Professional Associations in the Transformation of Institutionalized Fields." *Academy of Management Journal* 45 (January): 58–80.

Grover, Ronald. 2002. "Adelphia's Fall Will Bruise a Crowd." *BusinessWeek*, July 8, 44.

Hahn, Avital Louria. 2002. "The Jailed, the Probed, the Embarrassed: A New Who's Who of the Afflicted in the Business and Street Worlds." *Investment Dealers' Digest*, September 16, 4.

Handy, Charles. 1995. "Trust and the Virtual Organization." *Harvard Business Review* 73 (May–June): 40–50.

———. 2002. "What's a Business For?" *Harvard Business Review* 80 (December): 49–55.

Harris, Jared, and Philip Bromiley. 2003. "Incentives to Cheat: Executive Compensation and Corporate Malfeasance." Paper presented at Society for Business Ethics Annual Meeting, Seattle, WA.

Harvard Management Update. 1999. "Three Skills for Today's Leaders." Vol. 4 (November): 11.

Hayes, Robert H., and William J. Abernathy. 1980. "Managing Our Way to Economic Decline." *Harvard Business Review* 58 (July–August): 67–77.

Hayes, Troy. 2002. "The New Bottom Line for Business Executives." *Journal of Business Strategy* 23 (November–December): 34–36.

Hegarty, W. Harvey, and Henry P. Sims. 1978. "Some Determinants of Unethical Behavior: An Experiment." *Journal of Applied Psychology* 63 (August): 451–457.

Hersey, Paul, and Kenneth H. Blanchard. 1988. *Management of Organizational Behavior: Utilizing Human Resources.* Englewood Cliffs, NJ: Prentice Hall.

Higgins, Thomas G. 1962. "Professional Ethics: A Time for Reappraisal." *Journal of Accountancy* 113 (March): 29–35.

Hindo, Brian. 2002. "Where Can Execs Learn Ethics?" *BusinessWeek Online*, June 13.

Hinings, Charles R., and Royston Greenwood. 2002. "Disconnects and Consequences in Organization Theory." *Administrative Science Quarterly* 47 (September): 411–421.

Hirshleifer, Jack. 1980. *Price Theory and Applications.* 2nd ed. Englewood Cliffs, NJ: Prentice Hall.

Hobbes, Thomas. 1651/1991. *Leviathan.* ed. Richard Tuck. Cambridge, UK: Cambridge University Press.

Hoke, Kathy. 1999. "Eyes Wide Open." *Business First—Columbus*, August 27, 27–28.

Horovitz, Bruce. 2002. "Scandals Grow out of CEO's Warped Mind-Set." *USA Today*, October 11, B1–2.

Hosmer, Larue Tone. 1995. "Trust: The Connecting Link between Organizational Theory and Philosophical Ethics." *Academy of Management Review* 20 (April): 379–403.

———. 2000. "It's Time for Empirical Research in Business Ethics." *Business Ethics Quarterly* 10 (January): 233–242.

Howard, John A., and Jagdish N. Sheth. 1969. *The Theory of Buyer Behavior.* New York: John Wiley.

Howard, Philip K. 1994. *The Death of Common Sense: How Law Is Suffocating America.* New York: Random House.

Huber, Peter. 2000. "Old Regulations Stifle the New Economy." *Wall Street Journal*, June 5, A32.

Hunt, Shelby D. 1990. "Commentary on an Empirical Investigation of a General Theory of Marketing Ethics." *Journal of the Academy of Marketing Science* 18 (Spring): 173–177.

———. 2000. *A General Theory of Competition: Resources, Competences, Productivity, Economic Growth.* Thousand Oaks, CA: Sage.

———. 2003. *Controversy in Marketing Theory.* Armonk, NY: M.E. Sharpe.

Hunt, Shelby D., and Lawrence B. Chonko. 1984. "Marketing and Machiavellianism." *Journal of Marketing* 48 (Summer): 30–42.

Hunt, Shelby D., and Arturo Vasquez-Parraga. 1993. "Organizational Consequences, Marketing Ethics and Salesforce Supervision." *Journal of Marketing Research* 30 (February): 78–90.

Hunt, Shelby D., and Scott J. Vitell. 1986. "A General Theory of Marketing Ethics." *Journal of Macromarketing* 6 (Spring): 5–15.

———. 1993. "The General Theory of Marketing Ethics: A Retrospective and Revision." In *Ethics in Marketing*, ed. N. Craig Smith and John A. Quelch. Homewood, IL: Richard D. Irwin, 775–784.

Hunt, Shelby D., Van R. Wood, and Lawrence B. Chonko. 1989. "Corporate Ethical Values and Organizational Commitment in Marketing." *Journal of Marketing* 53 (July): 79–90.

Hymowitz, Carol. 2003. "Corporate Governance: How to Fix a Broken System." *Wall Street Journal*, February 24, R1–R3.

Internal Auditor. 2002. "Internal Auditors: Integral to Good Corporate Governance." 59 (August): 44–49.

Jackall, Robert. 1983. "Moral Mazes: Bureaucracy and Managerial Work." *Harvard Business Review* 61 (September–October): 118–130.

Jackson, Stanley. 1983. *J.P. Morgan: A Biography.* New York: Stein and Day.

Jennings, Marianne M. 2000. "Ford Firestone Lesson: Heed the Moment of Truth." *Wall Street Journal*, September 11, A4.

Jones, Del. 2003. "Sarbanes-Oxley: Dragon or White Knight?" *USA Today,* October 20, B1–2.

Jones, Del and Barbara Hansen. 2003. "Chairmen Still Doing Do-Si-Do." *USA Today*, November 5, 3B.

Jones, Del, and Matt Krantz. 2002. "Andersen Flap Puts Focus on Companies' Ties to Auditor." *USA Today*, January 15, 3B.

Jones, Thomas M. 1991. "Ethical Decision Making by Individuals in Organizations:

An Issue-Contingent Model." *Academy of Management Review* 16 (February): 366–395.

———. 1995. "Instrumental Stakeholder Theory: A Synthesis of Ethics and Economics." *Academy of Management Review* 20 (April): 404–437.

Jones, Thomas M., and Frederick H. Gautschi III. 1988. "Will the Ethics of Business Change? A Survey of Future Executives." *Journal of Business Ethics* 7 (April): 231–248.

Jones, William A., Jr. 1990. "Student Views of 'Ethical' Issues: A Situational Analysis." *Journal of Business Ethics* 9 (March): 201–205.

Joyner, Tammy. 2003. "Departing Executives Are Getting Some Lovely Parting Gifts." *Milwaukee Journal Sentinel,* March 2, 11D.

Kabat-Zinn, Jon. 1995. *Wherever You Go There You Are: Mindfulness Meditation in Everyday Life.* New York: Hyperion.

———. 2002. "Meditation is about Paying Attention." *Reflections* 3 (Spring); 68–71.

Kahane, Howard. 1982. *Logic and Philosophy: A Modern Introduction.* 4th ed. Belmont, CA: Wadsworth.

Kant, Immanuel. 1785/1964. *Groundwork for the Metaphysics of Morals.* New York: Harper & Row.

Kanungo, Rabindra. 2001. "Ethical Values of Transactional and Transformational Leaders." *Canadian Journal of Administrative Sciences* 18 (December): 257–265.

Kaplan, Robert S., and David P. Norton. 1996. "Using the Balanced Scorecard as a Strategic Management System." *Harvard Business Review* 74 (January–February): 18–27.

Kelly, Marjorie. 2001. *The Divine Right of Capital: Dethroning the Corporate Aristocracy.* San Francisco: Berrett-Koehler.

———. 2002. "It's a Heckuva Time to Be Dropping Business Ethics Courses." *Business Ethics* 16 (September/October/November/December): 17–18.

Kennedy, Ellen J., and Leigh Lawton. 1998. "Religiousness and Business Ethics." *Journal of Business Ethics* 17 (January): 163–175.

Kennedy, Joseph P. 1934/1998. "Securities and Exchange Commission." (A 1934 Address to the National Press Club), *Research in Accounting Regulation*, Vol. 12. Stamford, CT: JAI Press, 320–322.

Kinder, Peter D., Steven D. Lyndenberg, and Amy L. Domini. 1992. *The Social Investment Almanac.* New York: Holt.

Klein, Walter H. 1998. "Recollections on Implementing the Ideas of *Conceptual Foundations.*" In *Education, Leadership and Business Ethics: Essays on the Work of Clarence Walton*, ed. Ronald F. Duska. Dordrecht, Netherlands: Kluwer Academic Publishers, 91–109.

Knight, James A. 2002. "Pay for Performance." *Journal of Business Strategy* 22 (July–August): 24–27.

Kochan, Thomas A. 2002. "Addressing the Crisis in Confidence in Corporations: Root Causes, Victims, and Strategies for Reform." *Academy of Management Executive* 16 (August): 139–141.

Koehn, Daryl. 2003. "Business Instruction: Post-Enron." Presidential Address, Society for Business Ethics Annual Meeting, Seattle, WA.

Kohlberg, Lawrence. 1969. "Stage and Sequence: The Cognitive-Developmental Approach to Socialization," in *Handbook of Socialization Theory and Research*, ed. David A. Goslin. Chicago: Rand McNally, 347–480.

———. 1976. "Moral Stages and Moralization: The Cognitive-Developmental Approach to Socialization." In *Moral Development and Behavior: Theory, Research, and Social Issues*, ed. Thomas Lickona. New York: Holt, Rinehart and Winston, 31–53.

———. 1984. *Essays on Moral Development: The Psychology of Moral Development.* New York: Harper & Row.

Kouzes, James M., and Barry Z. Posner. 1993. *Credibility: How Leaders Gain and Lose It, Why People Demand It.* San Francisco: Jossey-Bass.

———. 1995. *The Leadership Challenge.* San Francisco: Jossey-Bass.

Krugman, Paul. 2002. "Greed Is Bad," *New York Times*, June 4, 19.

Laczniak, Gene R. 1983. "Business Ethics: A Manager's Primer." *Business* 33 (January–March): 23–29.

———. 1998. "Distributive Justice, Catholic Social Teaching and the Morality of Marketers." *Journal of Public Policy Marketing* 18 (Fall): 125–129.

Laczniak, Gene R., and Patrick E. Murphy. 1985. *Marketing Ethics.* Lexington, MA: Lexington/Heath.

———. 1993. *Ethical Marketing Decisions: The Higher Road.* Needham Heights, MA: Allyn and Bacon.

Landis, James M. 1959. "The Legislative History of the Securities Act. "*George Washington Law Review* 28 (October): 29–49.

Langtry, Bruce. 2002. "The Ethics of Shareholding." *Journal of Business Ethics* 37 (May): 175–185.

Lavelle, Louis. 2002. "The Best and Worst Boards." *BusinessWeek*, October 7, 104.

Leaf, Clifton. 2002. "Temptation Is All around Us." *Fortune*, November 18, 112.

LeClair, Debbie Thorne, O.C. Ferrell, and John P. Fraedrich. 1998. *Integrity Management.* Tampa: University of Tampa Press.

Leonard, Devin, Ann Harrington, Doris Burke, Michael Rigas, Tim Rigas, and Oren Cohen. 2002. "The Adelphia Story." *Fortune*, August 12, 136–143.

Lewis, J. David, and Andrew Weigert. 1985. "Trust as a Social Reality." *Social Forces* 63 (June): 967–985.

Liedtka, Jeanne. 1998. "Constructing an Ethic for Business Practice: Competing Effectively and Doing Good." *Business & Society* 37 (September): 254–280.

———. 1999. "Linking Competitive Advantage with Communities of Practice." *Journal of Management Inquiry* 8 (March): 5–16.

Lipsey, Richard G., and Peter Steiner. 1975. *Economics*, 4th ed. New York: Harper & Row.

Little, Ian M.D. 1957. A *Critique of Welfare Economics.* Oxford, UK: Clarendon Press.

Lozano, Josep M. 2000. *Ethics and Organizations.* London: Kluwer Academic Publishers.

Lublin, Joann S. 2002a. "Executive Pay Keeps Rising Despite Outcry." *Wall Street Journal*, October 3, B1.

——— 2002b. "Splitting Posts of Chairman, CEO Catches On." *Wall Street Journal*, November 11, B1, B3.

Luke, Robert. 2002. "Role of Directors Being Put under Spotlight." *Atlanta Journal Constitution*, http://nl.newsbank.com/nl-search/we/Archives?p_action=list&p_topdoc=21.

Mac Lean, Tammy, and Barrie Litzky. 2003. "Task Force on Integrating Ethics and Business in Society in the U.S. Management Curriculum." Paper presented at the

International Association for Business and Society conference, Rotterdam, The Netherlands.

Maher, Maria, and Thomas Anderson. 1999. *Corporate Governance: Effects on Firm Performance and Economic Growth.* Paris: Organization for Economic Cooperation and Development.

Mahon, John F., and Sandra A. Waddock. 1992. "Strategic Issues in Management: An Integration of Life Cycle Perspectives." *Business & Society* 31 (Spring): 19–32.

Malinowski, Carl, and Karen A. Berger. 1996. "Undergraduate Student Attitudes about Hypothetical Marketing Dilemmas." *Journal of Business Ethics* 15 (May): 525–535.

Mangan, Katherine S. 2002a. "MBAs Would Rather Quit than Fight for Values." *The Chronicle of Higher Education*, September 20: 15.

———. 2002b. "The Ethics of Business Schools." *The Chronicle of Higher Education*, September 20, A14–A16.

———. 2003. "Accrediting Board Endorses Stronger Focus on Ethics in Business-school Curriculums." *The Chronicle of Higher Education Online*, January 8, www.chronicle.com/daily/2003/01/2003010805n.htm.

Mankiw, N. Gregory. 1998. *Principles of Economics.* New York: Dryden.

Maremont, Mark, and Laurie P. Cohen. 2002. "How Tyco's CEO Enriched Himself." *Wall Street Journal*, August 7, A1, A6.

Margolis, Howard. 1982. *Selfishness, Altruism and Rationality: A Theory of Social Choice.* Cambridge, UK: Cambridge University Press.

Martin, Roger L. 2002. "Taking Stock." *Harvard Business Review* 81 (January): 19.

Marwell, Gerald, and Ruth E. Ames. 1981. "Economists Free Ride: Does Anyone Else?" *Journal of Public Economics* 15 (June): 295–310.

Mautz, Robert K., and Hussein A. Sharaf. 1961. *The Philosophy of Auditing.* Evanston, IL: American Accounting Association.

May, Jeff. 2003. "Reforms Haven't Erased All Funny Business." *Seattle Times*, July 27, E1.

Mayer, Raymond R. 1970. "Management's Responsibility for Purchasing Ethics." *Journal of Purchasing* 6 (November): 13–20.

Mayo, Michael A., and Lawrence J. Marks. 1990. "An Empirical Investigation of a General Theory of Marketing Ethics." *Journal of the Academy of Marketing Science* 18 (Spring): 163–172.

McAlister, Debbie Thorne. 2003. "Governance Theory and Practice for Non-Profit Organizations." Working paper, Texas State University–San Marcos.

McAlister, Debbie Thorne, O.C. Ferrell, and Linda Ferrell. Forthcoming. *Business and Society.* Boston: Houghton Mifflin.

McCoy, Kevin. 2003. "Decorator: Kozlowski Billed Millions to Firm." *USA Today*, December 16, 3B.

McCoy, Kevin, and Gary Strauss. 2002. "Kozlowski, Others Accused of Using Tyco as 'Piggybank.'" *USA Today*, September 13, 1B–2B.

McCraw, Thomas K. 1984. *Prophets of Regulation.* Cambridge, MA: Belknap Press.

McCuddy, Michael K., and Barbara L. Peery. 1996. "Selected Individual Differences and Collegians' Ethical Beliefs." *Journal of Business Ethics* 15 (March): 261–272.

McNeel, Steven P. 1994. "College Teaching and Student Moral Development." In *Moral Development in the Professions: Psychology and Applied Ethics*, eds. James Rest and Darcia Narvaez. Hillsdale, NJ: Erlbaum, 27–49.

McRitchie, James. 1999. "Ending the Wall Street Walk: Why Corporate Governance Now?" www.corpgov.net/forums/commentary/ending.html.

Mead, Emily, Andrew C. Wicks, and Patricia H. Werhane. 2003. "ExxonMobil in Chad and Cameroon." Darden School Case Bibliography No. UVA-E-0262.

Mednick, Robert, and Gary John Previts. 1987. "The Scope of CPA Services: A View from the Future." *Journal of Accountancy* 163 (May): 220–238.

Menguc, Bulent. 1997. "Organizational Consequences, Marketing Ethics, and Salesforce Supervision: Further Empirical Evidence." *Journal of Business Ethics* 16 (March): 1–20.

Merritt, Jennifer. 2003. "Why Ethics is Also B-school Business." *BusinessWeek*, January 27, 105.

Mill, John Stuart. 1859/1956. *On Liberty*. Ed. Currin V. Shields. New York: Bobbs-Merrill.

Miller, Mary. 2002. "Warning Signs." *Business Ethics* 11 (January–February): 8.

Mitroff, Ian I. 1983. *Stakeholders of the Organizational Mind*. San Francisco: Jossey-Bass.

Mitroff, Ian I., and Murat C. Alpaslan. 2003. "Preparing for Evil." *Harvard Business Review* 81 (April): 109–115.

Mitroff, Ian I., and Harold Linstone. 1993. *The Unbounded Mind*. New York: Oxford University Press.

Moline, Matt. 2002. "Professors to Focus on Ethics." *Topeka Capital Journal Online*, (September 30), www.cjonline.com/stories/093002/kan_ethics.shtml.

Monks, Robert A.G. 1996. *Corporate Governance in the Twenty-First Century: A Preliminary Outline*. Portland, ME: LENS.

Morgenson, Gretchen. 2002. "Fat Options at the Top are Bad for Business, Study Suggests." *Milwaukee Journal Sentinel*, November 10, 11D.

Murphy, Patrick E. 1989. "Creating Ethical Corporate Structures." *Sloan Management Review* 30 (Winter): 81–87.

———. 1998. *Eighty Exemplary Ethics Statements*. Notre Dame, IN: University of Notre Dame Press.

Neese, William T., O.C. Ferrell, and Linda Ferrell. Forthcoming. "An Analysis of Mail and Wire Fraud Cases Related to Marketing." *Journal of Business Research*.

Nelson, Emily, and Laurie P. Cohen. 2002. "Why Jack Grubman Was So Keen to Get His Twins into the YMCA." *Wall Street Journal*, November 15, A1.

Newberry, William E., and Thomas N. Gladwin. 2002. "Shell and Nigerian Oil." In *Ethical Issues in Business*. 7th ed. Ed. Thomas Donaldson, Margaret Cording, and Patricia Werhane, Upper Saddle River, NJ: Prentice Hall, 522–540.

Newstrom, John W., and William A. Ruch. 1975. "The Ethics of Management and the Management of Ethics." *MSU Business Topics* 23 (Winter): 29–37.

New York State Bar Association. 2000. *Preserving the Core Values of the American Legal Profession—The Place of Multidisciplinary Practice in the Law Governing Lawyers*. New York: Special Committee on Law Governing Firm Structure and Operation.

New York State Society of CPAs. 2003. "Changes Affecting NY CPE Regulations," www.nysscpa.org/faeorg/courseguidelines.

Nicklaus, David. 2002. "Is a Bigger Dose of Ethics Needed in Business Schools?" *St. Louis Post Dispatch*, December 18, C10, www.stltoday.com/stltoday/business/stories.nsf/Business/1862491875CBAE9F8 62.

Nielsen, Richard, and Jennifer Leigh. 2003. "Implications for Business Ethics of the Recent U.S. Corporate Scandals." Paper presented at Society for Business Ethics Annual Meeting, Seattle, WA.

Novak, Michael. 1996. *Business as a Calling*. New York: Free Press.

Nucci, Larry, and Ernest Pascarella. 1987. "The Influence of College on Moral Development." In *Higher Education: Handbook of Theory and Research*, ed. John C. Smart. New York: Agathon Press, 271–326.

Nussbaum, Bruce. 2002. "Can You Trust Anybody Anymore?" *BusinessWeek Online*, January 28.

O'Reilly, Brian. 1994. "J & J Is on a Roll." *Fortune*, December 26, 180, 186.

O'Reilly, Brian, and John Wyatt. 1994. "What Companies and Employees Owe One Another." *Fortune*, June 13, 44–52.

Organization for Economic Cooperation and Development. 1999. *The OECD Principles of Corporate Governance*. Paris: Organization for Economic Cooperation and Development.

Orlitzky, Marc, and Diane L. Swanson. 2002. "Exploring Individual Differences in Normative Myopia: Executives' Personality Factors, Pay Preferences, and Ethics of Care." Paper presented at Academy of Management Conference, Denver, CO.

Ottoson, Gerald E. 1982. "Essentials of an Ethical Corporate Climate." In *Doing Ethics in Business: New Ventures in Management Development*, ed. Donald G. Jones. Cambridge, MA: Oelgoschlager, Gann & Hain, 155–163.

Owen, Harrison. 1997a. *Expanding Our Now: The Story of Open Space Technology*. San Francisco: Berrett-Koehler.

———. 1997b. *Open Space Technology: A User's Guide*. 2nd ed. San Francisco: Berrett-Koehler.

Oxford English Dictionary. 2003. dictionary.oed.com/cgi/entry/00025695/00025695se52?query_type=word& queryword=bottom+line&edition=2e&first=1&max_to_show=10&sort_type=alp ha&result_place=1&search_id=CzRM-124mF4–4283&hilite=00025695se52.

Pagano, Barbara, and Elizabeth Pagano. 2003. *The Transparency Edge: How Credibility Can Make or Break You in Business*. New York: McGraw-Hill.

Paine, Lynn Sharp. 1994. "Managing for Organizational Integrity." *Harvard Business Review* 72 (March–April): 106–117.

———. 1997. *Leadership, Ethics and Organizational Integrity*. Chicago: Richard D. Irwin.

———. 2003. *Value Shift*. New York: McGraw-Hill.

Peterson, Robert A., Richard F. Beltramini, and George Kozmetsky. 1991. "Concerns of College Students Regarding Business Ethics: A Replication." *Journal of Business Ethics* 10 (October): 733–738.

Petty, Richard E., and John T. Cacioppo. 1986. *Communication and Persuasion: Central and Peripheral Routes to Persuasion*. New York: Springer-Verlag.

Pfeffer, Jeffrey. 2003. "Teaching the Wrong Lesson." *Business 2.0* (November): 60.

Pfeffer, Jeffrey, and John F. Veiga. 1999. "Putting People First for Organizational Success." *Academy of Management Executive* 13 (May): 37–48.

Pinkerton, Stewart. 2003. "How Deep Is the Ethics Crisis?" Forbes.com (July 24).

Porter, Lyman W., and Lawrence E. McKibbin. 1988. *Management Education and Development: Drift or Thrust into the 21st Century?* New York: McGraw-Hill.

Previts, Gary John. 1985. *The Scope of CPA Services*. New York: John Wiley.

———. 2002. "Global Multi Disciplinary Practice: A Word on 'The Future.'" *Case Western Reserve Law Review* 52 (Summer): 947–959.

Previts, Gary John, and Barbara D. Merino. 1998a. *A History of Accountancy in the United States*. Columbus: Ohio State University Press.

————. 1998b. "Auditor Independence: A Perspective on Its Origins and Orientations." *Research in Accounting Regulation*, vol. 12. Stamford, CT: JAI Press, 299–317.

————. 2003. "The 'Information Right' and the CPA Profession." *Research in Accounting Regulation*, vol. 16. Amsterdam: Elsevier Science, 275–277.

Pullman, Susan. 2003. "A Staffer Ordered to Commit Fraud Balked, Then Caved." *Wall Street Journal*, June 23, A1.

Rallapalli, Kumar C., Scott J. Vitell, Frank A. Wiebe, and James H. Barnes. 1994. "Consumer Ethical Beliefs and Personality Traits: An Exploratory Analysis." *Journal of Business Ethics* 13 (July): 487–495.

Randall, Donna M., and Annetta M. Gibson. 1990. "Methodology in Business Ethics Research: A Review and Critical Assessment." *Journal of Business Ethics* 9 (June): 457–471.

Rawls, John. 1971. *A Theory of Justice.* Cambridge, MA: Harvard University Press.

Reingold, Jennifer. 1999. "Dot.Com Boards Are Flouting the Rules." *BusinessWeek*, December 20, 130–134.

Rest, James R. 1986. *Moral Development: Advances in Research and Theory.* New York: Praeger.

Rest, James R., Darcia Narvaez, Muriel J. Bebeau, and Stephen. J. Thoma. 1999. *Postconventional Moral Thinking: A Neo-Kohlbergian Approach.* Mahwah, NJ: Lawrence Erlbaum.

Robin, Donald P. 2000. *Questions and Answers about Business Ethics: Running an Ethical and Successful Business.* Cincinnati: Dame/Thomson Learning.

Robin, Donald P., Michael Giallourakis, Fred R. David, and Thomas E. Moritz. 1989. "A Different Look at Codes of Ethics." *Business Horizons* 32 (January–February): 66–73.

Robin, Donald P., R. Eric Reidenbach, and Barry Babin. 1997. "The Nature, Measurement, and Stability of Ethical Judgments in the Workplace." *Psychological Reports* 80 (April): 563–580.

Robin, Donald P., R. Eric Reidenbach, and P.J. Forrest. 1996. "The Perceived Importance of an Ethical Issue as an Influence on the Ethical Decision Making of Ad Managers." *Journal of Business Research* 35 (January): 17–28.

Robin, Donald P., and Charles W. Sawyer. 1998. "The Ethics of Antidumping Petitions." *Journal of World Business* 33 (Fall), 315–328.

Rosenstein, Bruce. 2002. "Scandals Nothing New to Business Guru." *USA Today*, July 15, 8B.

Rotter, Julian B. 1966. "Generalized Expectancies for Internal versus External Control of Reinforcement." *Psychological Monographs* 80 (January): 1–28.

Ruegger, Durwood, and Ernest W. King. 1992. "A Study of the Effect of Age and Gender upon Student Business Ethics." *Journal of Business Ethics* 11 (March): 179–186.

Russ, Gail. 2003. "Corporate Governance and Ethics." *The Ambassador* 3 (Spring): 4.

Russ, Robert, and Edward Coffman. 2002. "A Review of the Financial Reports of the Chesapeake and Ohio Canal Company: Some Preliminary Findings." Working paper, Virginia Commonwealth University.

Rynes, Sara L., Christine Q. Trank, Anne M. Lawson, and Remus Ilies. 2003. "Behavioral Coursework in Business Education: Growing Evidence of a Legitimacy Crisis." *Academy of Management Learning and Education* 2 (September): 269–283.

Samson, William D., Gary J. Previts, and Dale Flesher. 2003. "The Early Nineteenth Century Development of Auditing in the U.S.: The Past Does Speak to the Present Crises." Unpublished manuscript.

Samuelson, Judith. 2002. "Back to Business Ethics." *Biz Ed* (September–October): 4–5.

Samuelson, Paul A. 1947/1983. *Foundations of Economic Analysis.* Cambridge, MA: MIT Press.

Samuelson, Paul A., and William. D. Nordhaus. 1995. *Economics.* 15th ed. Englewood Cliffs, NJ: Prentice Hall.

Schepp, David. 2002. "U.S. Urged to Lift Investor Confidence." *BBC News Online*, September 27, news.bbc.co.uk/2/hi/business/2285847.stm.

Scherreik, Susan. 2002. "Following Your Conscience Is Just a Few Clicks Away." *BusinessWeek*, May 13, 116–118.

Schmalensee, Richard L. 2003. "The 'Thou Shalt' School of Business." *Wall Street Journal*, December 30, A4.

Schneider, Mica. 2003. "B-Schools with a Broader Bottom Line." *BusinessWeek Online*, October 3, www.businessweek.com/bschools/content/oct2003/bs2003103_8409_bs001.htm.

Schroeder, Michael. 2003. "Cleaner Living, No Easy Riches." *Wall Street Journal*, July 22, C1, C3, C7.

Schwartz, Peter. 1991. *The Art of the Long View: The Path to Strategic Insights for Yourself and Your Company.* New York: Doubleday.

Securities and Exchange Commission. 1938. "Independence of Accountants—Relationships to Registrant." *Accounting Series Release No. 2.*

Sells, Bill. 1994. "What Asbestos Taught Me about Managing Risk." *Harvard Business Review* 72 (March–April): 76–90.

Senge, Peter M. 1990. *The Fifth Discipline: The Art and Practice of the Learning Organization.* New York: Doubleday.

Shaub Michael K. 1989. "An Empirical Examination of the Determinants of Auditors' Ethical Sensitivity." Ph.D. diss., Texas Tech University.

Shepard, Jon M., and Linda S. Hartenian. 1990. "Egoistic and Ethical Orientations of University Students toward Work-related Decisions." *Journal of Business Ethics* 10 (April): 303–310.

Shmukler, Evelina. 2003. "Back to School." *Wall Street Journal*, February 24, R6.

Sikula, Andrew, Sr., and Adelmiro D. Costa. 1994. "Are Women More Ethical than Men?" *Journal of Business Ethics* 13 (November): 859–871.

Sims, Ronald R., and Jonannes Brinkmann. 2002. "Leaders and Moral Role Models: The Case of John Gutfreund at Salomon Brothers." *Journal of Business Ethics*, 35 (February): 327–339.

Singer, Paul. 2002. "Proper Ethics," *Marketing News,* September 16, 16.

Singhapakdi, Anusorn, and Scott J. Vitell. 1990. "Marketing Ethics: Factors Influencing Perceptions of Ethical Problems and Alternatives." *Journal of Macromarketing* 10 (Spring): 4–18.

———. 1991. "Research Note: Selected Factors Influencing Marketers' Deontological Norms." *Journal of the Academy of Marketing Science* 19 (Winter): 37–42.

Smith, Adam. 1776/1937. *Wealth of Nations.* New York: Random House.

Smith, Elliot Blair. 2003. "Probe: Former Kmart CEO 'Grossly Derelict.'" *USA Today*, January 27, B1.

Smith, N. Craig. 2003. "Corporate Social Responsibility: Whether or How." *California Management Review* 45 (Summer): 52–76.

SocialFunds.com. 2003. "Investor Survey on Corporate Responsibility," www.socialfunds.com/page.cgi/fool_results.html.

Spain, Judith W., Peggy Brewer, Virgil Brewer, and S.J. Garner. 2002. "Ethics and Geography: Impact of Geographical Cultural Differences on Students' Ethical Decisions." *Journal of Business Ethics* 41 (November): 187–194.

Sparks, John R., and Shelby D. Hunt. 1998. "Marketing Researcher Ethical Sensitivity: Conceptualization, Measurement, and Exploratory Investigation." *Journal of Marketing* 62 (February): 92–109.

Stanga, Keith G., and Richard A. Turpen. 1991. "Ethical Judgments on Selected Accounting Issues: An Empirical Study." *Journal of Business Ethics* 10 (October): 739–747.

Stark, Andrew. 1993. "What's the Matter with Business Ethics?" *Harvard Business Review* 71 (May–June): 38–40, 43–46, 48.

Steiner, George A., and John F. Steiner. 1988. *Business, Government, and Society.* 5th ed. New York: Random House.

Stevens, Robert E., O. Jeff Harris, and Stan Williamson. 1993. "A Comparison of Ethical Evaluations of Business School Faculty and Students: A Pilot Study." *Journal of Business Ethics* 12 (August): 611–619.

Stewart, Karen, Linda Felicetti, and Scott Kuehn. 1996. "The Attitudes of Business Majors toward the Teaching of Business Ethics." *Journal of Business Ethics* 15 (August): 913–918.

Stewart, Thomas A. 1996. "Why Value Statements Don't Work." *Fortune*, June 10, 138.

Stigler, George J. 1966. *The Theory of Price.* 3rd ed. New York: Macmillan.

Stoller, Gary. 2002. "Funny Numbers." *USA Today*, October 21, 3B.

Strauss, Gary 2002a. "Scandal Further Decimates Investor Confidence." *USA Today*, June 27, 1B.

———. 2002b. "Tyco Events Put Spotlight on Directors' Role." *USA Today*, September 16, 3B.

———. 2003. "Despite Reforms, CEOs Still Rake in Generous Bonuses." *USA Today*, August 24, 1B.

Summerour, Jenny. 2000. "Bribery Game." *Progressive Grocer* 79 (January): 43–44.

Svendsen, Ann. 1998. *The Stakeholder Strategy: Profiting from Collaborative Business Relationships.* San Francisco: Berrett-Koehler.

Swanson, Diane L., and William C. Frederick. 2003a. "Campaign AACSB: Are Business Schools Complicit in Corporate Corruption?" *Journal of Individual Employment Rights* 10 (November): 151–165.

———. 2003b. "Are Business Schools Silent Partners in Corporate Crime?" *Journal of Corporate Citizenship* 9 (Spring): 24–27.

Swartz, Mimi, with Sherron Watkins. 2003. *Power Failure.* New York: Doubleday.

Taylor, Bernard. 2003. "Board Leadership: Balancing Entrepreneurship and Strategy with Accountability and Control." *Corporate Governance: The International Journal of Effective Board Performance* 3 (May): 3–5.

Texas Real Estate Commission. 2003. "Final Report of Education Task Force," www.trec.state.tx.us/pdf/education/EducationTaskForce_FinalReport.pdf.

Thomas, Clarke. 2002. "Ethics Are Good Business." *Pittsburgh Post-Gazette Online*, December 4, www.post-gazette.com/forum/comm/20021204edclar04p.1asp.

Thomas, Landon, and Floyd Norris. 2002. "Board Was in the Dark about Grasso Contracts," *Milwaukee Journal Sentinel*, September 11, 1D–2D.

Thoreau, Henry David. 1854/1990. *Walden*. Philadelphia: Running Press.

Tichy, Noel, and Ram Charan. 1989. "Speed, Simplicity, Self-Confidence: An Interview with Jack Welch." *Harvard Business Review* 67 (September–October): 112–120.

Toffler, Barbara L., and Jennifer Reingold. 2003. *Final Accounting: Ambition, Greed and the Fall of Arthur Andersen*. New York: Broadway Books.

Torbert, Bill. 1991. *The Power of Balance: Transforming Self, Society, and Scientific Inquiry.* Newbury Park, CA: Sage.

———. 2004. *Action Inquiry: The Secret of Timely and Transforming Leadership.* San Francisco: Berrett-Koehler.

Trank, Christine Quinn, and Sara L. Rynes. 2003. "Who Moved Our Cheese? Reclaiming Professionalism in Business Education." *Academy of Management Learning and Education* 2 (June): 189–205.

Trevino, Linda Klebe. 1986. "Ethical Decision-Making in Organizations: A Person-Situation Interactionist Model." *Academy of Management Review* 11 (July): 601–617.

Trevino, Linda Klebe, Michael Brown, and Linda Pincus Hartman. 2003. "A Qualitative Investigation of Perceived Executive Ethical Leadership: Perceptions From Inside and Outside the Executive Suite." *Human Relations* 56 (January): 5–37.

Trevino, Linda Klebe, Gary R. Weaver, David G. Gibson, and Barbara Ley Toffler. 1999. "Managing Ethics and Legal Compliance: What Works and What Hurts." *California Management Review* 41 (Winter): 131–151.

Tsalikis, John, and Marta Ortiz-Buonafina. 1990. "Ethical Belief Differences of Males and Females." *Journal of Business Ethics* 9 (June): 509–517.

Tubbs, Mark E., and Steven E. Ekeberg. 1991. "The Role of Intentions in Work Motivation: Implications for Goal-Setting Theory and Research." *Academy of Management Review* 16 (January): 180–199.

Turley, James S. 2002. "How Accounting Can Get Back Its Good Name." *Wall Street Journal*, February 4, A16.

United States Congress. 1933. "Senate Committee on Banking and Currency Hearings on Senate Bill 875," April 1, 1933, p. 58 {15 US Section 78 D-1}.

United States Senate. 1976. *The Accounting Establishment.* A Staff Study prepared by the Subcommittee on Reports, Accounting and Management, Washington, DC: Government Printing Office.

United States Senate Committee on Governmental Affairs. 2002. *The Role of the Board of Directors in Enron's Collapse*, www.senate.gov/~gov_affairs/070702enronreport.pdf.

United States Sentencing Commission. 2003. "Report of the Ad Hoc Advisory Group on the Organizational Sentencing Guidelines," www.ussc.gov/corp/advgrprpt/advgrprpt.htm.

USA Today. 2002a. "Accounting Firms Would Rather Settle Than Reform." March 7, 11A.

USA Today. 2002b. "CEO Greed Targeted." September 17, 14A.

Useem, Jerry. 2002. "Exxon's African Adventure." *Fortune*, April 15, 102–114.

van Gelder, Sarah. 1995. "The Next Reformation." *In Context* 41 (Summer): 17–22.

Vitell, Scott J., and Shelby D. Hunt. 1990. "The General Theory of Marketing Ethics: A Partial Test of the Model." In *Research in Marketing*, vol. 10, ed. Jagdish N. Sheth. Stamford, CT: JAI Press, 237–265.

Vitell, Scott J., and Joseph G.P. Paolillo. 2003. "The Perceived Role of Ethics and

Social Responsibility: A Cross-Cultural Study of Marketing Professionals." Working paper University of Mississippi.

Vogel, David. 2002. "Recycling Corporate Responsibility." *Wall Street Journal*, August 20, B2.

Volker, John M. 1979. "Moral Reasoning and College Experience." Unpublished manuscript, University of Minnesota.

Waddock, Sandra. 2001. "Integrity and Mindfulness: Foundations of Corporate Citizenship." *Journal of Corporate Citizenship* 1 (Spring): 25–37.

———. 2002. *Leading Corporate Citizens: Vision, Values, Value Added.* New York: McGraw-Hill.

———. 2003. "A Radical Agenda for Business in Society Education." Paper presented at the Academy of Management Conference, Social Issues in Management Division, Seattle, WA.

Wall Street Journal. 2003. "WorldCom Chief Outlines Initial Turnaround Strategy." (January 14): http://online.wsj.com.

Walzer, Philip. 2003. "Virginia MBA Programs Split on Question of Ethics." *Virginian-Pilot Online*, August 25, D1.

Warnock, Geoffrey James. 1971. *The Object of Morality.* London: Methuen.

Watkins, Sherron S. 2003. "Ethical Conflicts at Enron: Moral Responsibility in Corporate Capitalism." *California Management Review* 45 (Summer): 8–9.

Weaver, Gary, and Linda Trevino. 1999. "Compliance and Values Oriented Ethics Programs: Influences on Employees' Attitudes and Behavior." *Business Ethics Quarterly* 9 (April): 315–335.

Weick, Karl E. 1999. "Educating for the Unknowable: The Infamous Real World." Paper presented at Academy of Management Annual Meeting, Chicago, IL.

Weil, Jonathan. 2003. "PricewaterhouseCoopers Partners Criticized Travel Billing." *Wall Street Journal*, September 30, C1, C9.

Weintraub, Arlene, Ronald Grover, and Pallavi Gogoi. 2002. "Look Who's Still at the Trough." *BusinessWeek*, September 9, 58.

Weisbord, Marvin R., and Sandra Janoff. 1995. *Future Search: An Action Guide to Finding Common Ground in Organizations and Communities*, San Francisco: Berrett-Koehler.

Werhane, Patricia H. 1999. *Moral Imagination and Management Decision-Making.* New York: Oxford University Press.

———. 2002. "Moral Imagination and Systems Thinking." *Journal of Business Ethics* 38 (June): 33–42.

Wessel, David. 2002. "The Criticism Coming From Inside Corporations." *Wall Street Journal*, June 27, A2.

Wetzel, Kara. 2003. "SEC Files Complaint Against ClearOne." *Wall Street Journal Online* January 15, www.online.wsj.com/article0,BT_CO_20030115_00691000.htm.

White House Press Release. 2002a. "Radio Address by the President to the Nation." June 29.

White House Press Release. 2002b. "President Announces Tough New Enforcement Initiatives for Reform." July 9.

White House Press Release. 2003. "President Bush Signs Corporate Corruption Bill." July 30.

Whyte, William H. 1956. *The Organization Man.* New York: Simon & Schuster.

Wilber, Ken. 1995. *Sex, Ecology, Spirituality: The Spirit of Evolution.* Boston: Shambala.

————. 1996. *A Brief History of Everything.* Boston: Shambala.

————. 1998. *The Eye of Spirit: An Integral Vision for a World Gone Slightly Mad.* Boston: Shambala.

————. Forthcoming. Foreword to *The Spirit of Conscious Business* by Fred Kofman. Boston: Shambala.

Wilkes, Robert E., John J. Burnett, and Roy D. Howell. 1986. "On the Meaning and Measurement of Religiosity in Consumer Research." *Journal of the Academy of Marketing Science* 14 (Spring): 47–56.

Williams, Oliver F., and Patrick E. Murphy. 1990. "The Ethics of Virtue: A Moral Theory for Marketing." *Journal of Macromarketing* 10 (Spring): 19–29.

Williamson, Oliver E. 1975. *Markets and Hierarchies: Analysis and Anti-trust Implications.* New York: Free Press.

————. 1979. "Transaction-cost Economics: The Governance of Contractual Relations." *Journal of Law and Economics* 22 October: 233–261.

————. 1981. "The Modern Corporation: Origins, Evolution, Attributes." *Journal of Economic Literature* 19 (December): 1537–1568.

————. 1994. "Transaction Cost Economics and Organization Theory." In *The Handbook of Economic Sociology*, ed. Neil J. Smelser and Richard Swedberg. Princeton, NJ: Princeton University Press, 77–107.

————. 1996. *The Mechanisms of Governance.* Oxford, UK: Oxford University Press.

Windsor, Duane. 2002. "An Open Letter on Business School Responsibility." Addressed to the Association to Advance Collegiate Schools of Business Blue Ribbon Committee on Accreditation.

Wolff, Edward N. 2000. "What Has Happened to Stock Ownership in the United States?" Unpublished manuscript, New York University.

Wong, Alan, and Eugene Beckman. 1992. "An Applied Ethical Analysis System in Business." *Journal of Business Ethics* 11 (March): 173–178.

World Bank Group. 2003a. "About Corporate Governance," www.worldbank.org/html/fpd/privatesector/cg/.

World Bank Group. 2003b. "The Chad-Cammeroon Petroleum Development and Pipeline Project," www.worldbank.org/afr/ccproj/project/pro_overview.htm.

World Resources Institute and The Aspen Institute's Business and Society Program. 2001. "Beyond Grey Pinstripes: Preparing MBAs for Social and Environmental Stewardship," www.beyondgreypinstripes.org/results/past_reports/bgps2001.cfm.

Worthington, Beresford. 1895. *Professional Accountants.* London: Gee & Co.

Zand, Dale E. 1997. *The Leadership Triad: Knowledge, Trust, and Power.* Oxford, UK: Oxford University Press.

Zey-Ferrell, Mary, K. Mark Weaver, and O.C. Ferrell. 1979. "Predicting Unethical Behavior among Marketing Practitioners." *Human Relations* 32 (July): 557–569.

About the Editors and Contributors

Gerald Albaum is research professor at the Robert O. Anderson Schools of Management at the University of New Mexico and professor emeritus of marketing at the University of Oregon. He is the author of eight books and more than seventy-five articles dealing with marketing and international business.

O.C. Ferrell is chair of the Department of Marketing and codirector of the Center for Business Ethics and Social Issues at Colorado State University. He is the author of seventeen books and more than seventy journal articles; his introductory marketing and business ethics textbooks are the best-selling volumes in their respective fields. He is currently serving as the marketing ethics and values section editor for the *Journal of Macromarketing*.

William C. Frederick is emeritus professor of business administration in the Katz Graduate School of Business at the University of Pittsburgh. His areas of interest include corporate social responsibility, business ethics and values, socioeconomics, and natural science links to economics and business. He is one of the founders of the Business and Society field of management.

R. Edward Freeman is director of the Olsson Center for Applied Ethics and the Elis and Signe Olsson Professor of Business Administration in the Darden School at the University of Virginia. He is also the academic director of the newly established Business Roundtable Institute for Corporate Ethics. He has authored numerous articles and written or edited ten books on business ethics, environmental management, and strategic management.

Shelby D. Hunt is the Jerry S. Rawls and P.W. Horn Professor of Marketing at Texas Tech University. A past editor of the *Journal of Marketing*, he is one of the 250 most frequently cited researchers in economics and business. He has authored numerous books and award-winning articles on competitive theory, macromarketing, ethics, channels of distribution, philosophy of science, and marketing theory.

Marjorie Kelly is the cofounder and editor of *Business Ethics*, a national publication on corporate social responsibility. She is the author of *The Divine Right of Capital: Dethroning the Corporate Aristocracy*, which has been widely disseminated and presently is being translated into Chinese, German, and Korean.

Gene R. Laczniak is the Wayne R. and Kathleen E. Sanders Professor of Business at Marquette University. Until recently he served as associate vice president for academic affairs at Marquette. His research and teaching focus on the societal influences of marketing strategy as well as business ethics.

Debbie Thorne McAlister is chair of the Department of Marketing and an associate professor at Texas State University–San Marcos. She is the recipient of awards for excellence in both teaching and research. Among her publications are *Integrity Management* and *Business and Society: A Strategic Approach to Social Responsibility*.

Patrick E. Murphy is the C.R. Smith Codirector of the Institute for Ethical Business Worldwide and professor of marketing at the University of Notre Dame. His research focuses on business and marketing ethics. He has served as editor of the *Journal of Public Policy & Marketing* and is currently marketing ethics section editor for *Business Ethics Quarterly*.

Robert A. Peterson is associate dean for research and holds the John T. Stuart III Centennial Chair in Business Administration in the McCombs School of Business; he also holds the Charles Hurwitz Fellowship at the IC² Institute at The University of Texas at Austin. A former editor of the *Journal of Marketing Research* and *Journal of the Academy of Marketing Science*, he has authored more than 150 articles and books.

Gary John Previts is associate dean for undergraduate and integrated study programs and professor of accountancy at the Weatherhead School, Case Western Reserve University. An active researcher in corporate reporting, accounting regulation, and accounting history, he currently serves as a member of the General Accounting Office's Accountability Council and as an adviser to the Comptroller General of the United States.

Donald P. Robin is the J. Tylee Wilson Professor of Business Ethics in the Wayne Calloway School of Business and Accountancy at Wake Forest University. He has published widely in business and ethics-related journals and has authored several books; he currently serves on the editorial boards of two business ethics journals.

Diane L. Swanson is the von Waaden Professor of Business Administration and chair of the Business Ethics Education Initiative at Kansas State University. She has received numerous awards for teaching and research and has held governing positions in several academic associations.

Scott J. Vitell is the Phil B. Hardin Professor of Marketing at the University of Mississippi. His publications have appeared in a wide variety of marketing and business journals. Presently he is the marketing section editor for the *Journal of Business Ethics*.

Sandra Waddock is a professor of management in the Carroll School of Management and senior research fellow in the Center for Corporate Citizenship at Boston College. She is the editor of the *Journal of Corporate Citizenship* and has written on corporate citizenship, corporate responsibility, and school-business collaboration.

Patricia H. Werhane is the Wicklander Chair of Business Ethics and director of the Institute for Business and Professional Ethics at DePaul University, and the Peter and Adeline Ruffin Professor of Business Ethics and senior fellow at the Olsson Center for Applied Ethics in the Darden School at the University of Virginia. She is the founder and former editor of *Business Ethics Quarterly*. Included among her numerous publications are *Ethical Issues in Business* and *Moral Imagination and Managerial Decision-Making*.

Index